AF413159

SONG
OF THE HERO

A Book for Men to
Develop Redemptive and
Heroic Relationship Skills

Ed Nissen

INSTITUTE
ofPURPOSE

To my father, who gave me the freedom to judge him, which afforded me the confidence to choose my own path.

Table of Contents

FOREWORD

There is no shortage of books written specifically for men to improve their relationships. Virtually all of them have been written based on subjective, anecdotal frameworks that lack the much-desired exhaustive approach that is necessarily supported by evidence-based science and well-researched theories.

It is not often that the combination of personal and professional experience creates a symbiotic relationship that leads to a changing of the world, one person at a time. The serendipity of a difficult life well lived by two people, who were once strangers, is the foundation of the concepts and theories outlined in this book. It is a survival handbook for meaning and purpose, a gift to the world.

Song of the Hero is an exploratory analysis of how men in long-term relationships have stalled in their growth and relationships, what they can do to correct themselves, and how to transcend a diminished version of themselves through the challenges presented by their feminine partner. The concepts and theories explored in the book are viewed through the lenses of analytical, evolutionary, and personality psychology, biology, neuroscience, and behavioral economics, with an undertone of mythology. As Ed's wife, it has been personally meaningful to me to see his evolution through writing this book.

As a wife, mother, scientist, and executive leader, I am profoundly grateful to have the articulation of his transformative journey into the dungeon of chaos, only to emerge back into the world as my hero, expressed gracefully within the pages of this book.

May he always be relentless in establishing order in my chaos. I will love him more on our last day than I do on this day. And that is an exceptional feat!

Nikki Nissen, MSN, RN

PREFACE

My friends, I did not want to write this book. While my personal and professional endeavors have led me to experience some of the incredible splendor of the human story, it has also led to some of the most terrifying aspects of my soul. Being a husband is one of my most cherished roles, and I have always been good-natured and well-meaning. Nevertheless, I found myself in need of a rather profound transformation as a man in a marriage. I was not living up to my potential as a husband, which was taking a toll on my marriage. Thus, I embarked on a moral undertaking that would bring a surprising transformation of my soul. It would be a painstaking and grueling process. It still is.

This book came to be through an evolution of sorts. What began as a transformation as a man in a marriage broadened into my professional work as a psychotherapist. After spending some time undergoing a personal transformation, I noticed many of the male clients I saw experienced similar issues. In my personal life, I was experiencing success with managing the issues and challenges in my marriage. And it wasn't always easy. In fact, it was usually difficult, and I often considered new ways of managing such difficulties only in hindsight.

After I had gained some degree of mastery, I was compelled to guide some of my male clients through their marital issues. The trouble was that my path was a bit unconventional, which consisted of books, online forums, podcasts, etc., whose content was almost always by people with little to no credibility in the sciences. As a psychotherapist, I must operate within the bounds of so-called "evidence-based practice." Therefore, I could not simply recommend the material I had utilized to my clients without potentially risking ethical violations. Hence, I began exploring research that led me an adequate support for the strategies and skills I needed to teach my male clients. And it worked!

Most, if not all, of these men began to experience success in their own right. As these cases multiplied, I decided to write down some things that were working for these men to synthesize what I thought was a relatively simple approach. A few pages turned into 30 pages. My thoughts then shifted to creating a treatment enhancement model that I could support with a series of case studies and various clinical measurement tools, which I had already been conducting. One of the areas of focus that emerged with these male clients was assertiveness. This would foreshadow the crux of the approach I would later develop.

Other areas also emerged, such as confidence, sense of character, and a concept of frame control (skills to achieve outcomes). 30 pages turned into 80, and by then, it occurred to me that I was writing a book. On the one hand, I thought this would be a somewhat quick process. On the other hand, I saw it as daunting, for I knew I was not well-suited to do it the justice it deserved. The next few years would be painstaking and trying. There were numerous times that I wanted to delete the whole project, to throw it in the digital trash can. With some encouragement, primarily from my wife, I persevered and completed the project. Although, I'm not convinced I've done it the justice it deserves. Nonetheless, it is done, and the rest of its journey will be determined by you, my friends.

It is difficult to comprehend the immensity of the meaning of writing this book. It didn't start as a book; instead, I was merely writing down some things that seemed to be working. Then it was a sort of "treatment manual." Only when I felt the immense sense of duty and responsibility with it did I realize I have to honor this feeling, and one way of doing so was by putting it in book form. It emerged as a result of seeing things as I (and likely many others) had never seen before. I saw beyond the facade of most modern men's problems with development and marriage, and I felt compelled to revive an ancient element all but lost in our society.

I am thus aware of how writing this book has catapulted my experiences as a man into the stratosphere. The resulting psychological development I have undergone is worth every second of the journey. In a sense, this project was akin to a dissertation for a Ph.D. I had an idea of what I wanted to write about, but there was an incredible amount of research to be reviewed and conducted. The vast majority of its contents were unknown to me when I began this endeavor. I knew very little about the subject, and this book taught me more than I could have imagined. And for that, I am grateful. I am also fortunate that several men (and even a few women) have benefited from this book. And for that, I am hopeful.

It is my hope that my personal suffering can be a beacon of hope and a guide for others to transform themselves. I strive to be competent in my work; with that, there is a baseline tendency to believe I am not competent enough. Thus, it is with humility that I express to you, my friends, the depth of my attempt to contribute something of this nature to the world. I have experienced many great losses in life. Many of my male friends have gone through painful and even traumatic divorces. My own parents divorced when I was 19. My friend, Jeremy, committed suicide, in part, I believe, because he couldn't comprehend the dynamics of the masculine and feminine natures. I have several other friends who I believe committed suicide in part for the same reason. I've witnessed and been affected by so many people's suffering around such things.

The most impactful of these experiences is my father's attempted suicide (which resulted in a terrible and debilitating stroke). I'm convinced that this was primarily because he did not know how to be a man in a marriage. His failure to do so created a traumatic experience for the whole family that still endures. In a large sense, I lost my dad because he could not handle the challenges of marriage and the masculine/feminine dynamics that drive them.

In spite of—no, because of— all those tragedies, I have found meaning in this life, much of which has been brought about by offering hope and experience to other men who share similar struggles as I have. To overcome suffering in such a way is to experience something sacred, and, if I may say, to be exalted in the glory of God. So, I leave you with a passage from the book that started it all for me. My Dad gave it to me when I was sixteen, and it awakened the depths of my soul. Only I would not understand that until I was well into my thirties. Nonetheless, I am here, and my existence is indebted to my father, and all those whose grace was extended to me, encouraging me to be the most magnificent man I can be. This passage sums up the meaning behind writing this book:

"Therefore I begin to think, my Lord, you purposely allow us to be brought into contact with the bad and evil things that you want changed. Perhaps that is the very reason that we are here in this world, where sin and sorrow and suffering and evil abound, so that we may let you teach us so to react to them, that out of them we can create lovely qualities to live forever. That is the only really satisfactory way of dealing with evil, not simply binding it so that it cannot work harm, but whenever possible overcoming it with good."

— *Hinds' Feet on High Places by Hannah Hurnard*

An important note about this book

There is a fictional story of a couple I have interwoven into this rather technical book. The names are Rodion and Regina. They met at a point in life where people begin longing for the companionship of marriage. Like most of us, they considered themselves quite compatible early on, only to inevitably encounter a series of obstacles that exposed the truth—that they are, in fact, less compatible than they thought.

Naturally, they fail to recognize this core issue. Thus, Rodion and Regina begin to succumb to the same notion any of us would—that they are growing apart. What transpires then is a quest for Rodion to take a searching and courageous descent into his own shortcomings, values, and his own darkness—his Shadow. The aim, unbeknownst to him, is to develop his masculine spirit by successfully navigating the gauntlet of Regina's bewildering challenges. If he succeeds, he rescues her feminine spirit from the belly of the dragon, so to speak. If he fails, then the dragon devours him. And that is not good!

Rodion and Regina are us. They are an amalgamation of the many clients I've worked with in my clinical practice. My case studies of them revealed a number of themes common across the broad range of personalities of those clients. These themes exist in their story, which focuses on Rodion as the protagonist. At the same time, Regina is the antagonist, the necessary opposition to all that is not true in Rodion. This fictional current serves to bring the often-complex concepts of this book into the light of understanding in a relatable manner.

With this, I aim to make the technical content more accessible to you so that you may find at least some of the knowledge in this book valuable. And now I give you the hard-won gift of my heroic redemption, the elements of which I have attempted to capture in detail. May it find you longing for a much-needed adventure.

EXORDIUM

The feminine dragon of chaos, no longer asleep, stirs in her dungeon. For ages, she has silently and passively refrained from asserting herself into her rightful place in this world. Restless, she begins to look around for her ancient counterpart, her lover, the ancient masculine. He is nowhere to be found, and she grows more impatient. Angrily, desperately, she moves about, searching for him. Realizing he is not present, she ventures from the dungeon, emerging into the modern world, unfamiliar to her, and bringing with her, chaos.

In this new world, this creature is a myth that started in ancient times, thought to have been debunked long ago. Even the myths of the Middle Ages portray her as something quite different from the ancient myths. All the more, her obscurity was too great to capture in a way that could be interpreted in a later era. Therefore, the ancient feminine's emergence in the modern world is so misunderstood that she is completely unrecognizable. She is viewed as a strange and inadmissible aberration, a foreigner, and nothing more. Confused, the feminine dragon of chaos violently demands attention and to have her ancient masculine lover brought to her at once.

However, no one understands her, for her language is an ancient, unknown, and forgotten language. Her cries and demands for her hero fall on deaf ears. She waxes and wanes between sorrow and violence. Still, no one understands this, for what they see is obscured by the subdued persona of a woman, a persona shaped and manipulated by lesser men throughout the ages. Rather than seeing her true value, today's man thinks she is irrational and aggressive, and he detests her, fears her; at the very least, he finds her to be an annoying distraction. That is until the feminine dragon of chaos unleashes her fury in one final attempt to awaken the ancient masculine within her man.

If this ancient story plays out accordingly, today's man braves the chaotic world of the feminine by going down into the dungeon of the dragon of chaos and emerging as a transcended version of himself—a magnificent version. He emerges with a gift: his ancient feminine partner, whole and intact. Today's man does this by honoring his masculinity through embracing today's woman. This embrace will transform him into the hero.

Part 1

Who Am I?

Chapter One

In the Beginning...

Life itself is unmanageable. As prepared as we try to make ourselves for what's to come over the horizon—the unknown—there will be some new situation, some further uncertainty, in which we must determine how to respond. We do our best to evaluate the situation and decide what skills are appropriate for solving the problem. As we master a particular issue, we meet a new problem. We search our medicine bag for the best possible antidote for this new problem, starting the process anew. While some issues are simple to resolve, others are complex and require a higher degree of conscientiousness and creativity. Sometimes, we pull off the occasional streak of solving problems quite efficiently.

However, this is not a common experience for the majority of people. We observe the relative ease with which some people solve their problems, see the value in their approach, and attempt to emulate them. Nevertheless, many of our approaches to managing obstacles are often faulty by nature. Some of these flaws have been a part of us since childhood and are quite profound.

As children, we often learned through hard-won experiences how to perceive and navigate the more complicated obstacles that seemed to threaten the achievability of our goals. Individually, we had distinct ways of dealing with such barriers. These were our unique methods of coping with adversity and progressing forward—somewhat shaped by our temperament, which contributed to the development of our personality. Collectively, we shared some universal skills regarding these challenging obstacles by observing how others mastered obstacles then mimicked what worked for them. Due to various factors, we also established support systems to give us an advantage in solving problems.

These support systems included family, friends, and people in the community, particularly those whose life skills appealed to our personality. The added benefit of developing these support systems was that we didn't have to go it alone. If we were fortunate enough to have adequate support systems, we developed a decent set of life skills for navigating the world—both known and unknown.

Even so, some were not as fortunate as others and had a more troublesome time establishing adequate life skills. However, over time, we generally developed enough skills to address the obstacles in our path, at least at a basic level. The entirety of this process shaped our understanding of the world, positively or negatively. These perceptions would hold firm for years to come.

Starting around the age of 12, children undergo a process of development that gives rise to abstract thinking. They begin to think beyond the present, forming ideas about everything, particularly about that which has not yet come to pass.[1]

Adolescence begins at around this time and can last until around 25. Adolescence has less to do with age and more with brain development. Adolescence is the last developmental stage of the brain—the frontal lobes. The frontal lobe's primary function lies in impulse control and complex decision-making, where we weigh choices and consequences. Even as adolescents begin to think more abstractly and contemplate the effects of their actions, the degree to which they can utilize this quality in the present moment is contingent on how far along they are in their development. It is often only in hindsight that they contemplate their actions and consequences, and usually only when they are negative.

As our adolescent development progressed, the obstacles in our lives became more obscure and complicated to us. The obscurity and complexity of such obstacles are due, in part, to an instinctual drive for adolescents to break from conformity—particularly with parents—to establish their identity and individuality. Not only did we have to learn how to manage obstacles effectively, but we also had to establish a more defined sense of self. This was made especially difficult because the adversity that comes with establishing an identity in adolescence exacerbated the preadolescent obstacles we were already facing. Perhaps we had to push the limits of our creativity and search every corner of our limited realm of experiences to find more adequate resources and new tools.

These novel complexities forced us to develop some of our core coping skills, many of which we still use today. More precisely, they made our personality traits more pronounced and our overall personality narrow. Some of us learned to laugh at obstacles, cry about them, or get angry at them. Some of us learned to strengthen our stance or even get aggressive with them. Some of us learned to avoid them or make ourselves small so as not to be detected by them. Some of us learned to deal with the obstacles in our path by framing our circumstances as though we didn't want to go that way anyway, shifting our direction altogether.

These behaviors—or problem-solving methodologies—were reinforced as we continued to face difficult and complicated challenges. For better or worse, these behaviors served a purpose for us because they got us what we wanted—or at least kept us safe. We engaged in whatever particular experiences fed our interests and sense of self.

The experiences we wanted were driven mainly by our drive to grow and evolve, by the need to form a sense of identity. Yet, our inability to anticipate who we could become limited us from playing the long game, and these limitations would inevitably catch up to us. In those days, we focused on the kinds of things we wanted, and we used every resource we could find to help us get those things, based on our personality for the most part. We were relatively proficient with this in our own youthful way.

The problem is that what we wanted would eventually evolve. Our inability to abstract our future self from the uncertainty of the world made us naive to the ever-changing obstacles of life. As a result, the problems became more challenging. Over time, our behaviors became avoidance-based instead of addressing our issues—sometimes overtly, although most often subtly. A more well-rounded approach would have been more sustainable and would have better equipped us for adulthood and the relationships that were to come.

As most adolescents do, we adapted. Our resiliency and identity-seeking attitudes eventually propelled us into adulthood. We went to college, got jobs, made friends, had fun, and experienced more struggles. We began learning who we were and started forming more defined ideas of who we wanted to be. We arranged aspects of our lives to fit what we believed were right for us. We wanted control of our own lives, and our attempts to gain such power were a way to ensure our happiness. We began creating an experience for ourselves, and we were well on our way to living the dream. We were driven by our desires to enjoy life and to be free, doing what we believed was necessary to enjoy that life. Sooner or later, we got into a long-term relationship. Things were going our way. This forward momentum was good for us!

Once we made it out of the gauntlet of adolescent development, we had settled into an idea of ourselves and set life on cruise control. Then, something happened. Life became familiar. We started to get comfortable with what we had created for ourselves. Perhaps, we got a little too relaxed, at least with some aspects of our lives, such as relationships, and we unknowingly began to regress in our qualities.

Life is not motionless; we are either progressing or regressing. Our regression was often most evident with the quality of how we handled conflict in relationships, particularly within intimate relationships. Although there may have been the occasional argument or fight, we started experiencing more and more relational conflict. We often found ourselves frustrated about such disputes because their increased frequency seemed to make ideal resolutions unattainable—what once worked for us was no longer working. We were not prepared for this degree of difficulty. No matter what we tried, we could not manage our relationship as well as we used to. We began to form ill-conceived ideas about the constant conflict. We often arrived at false conclusions, such as *our relationship is holding me back*, or *this relationship is too far gone*. This type of thinking was our first flaw: thinking the relationship itself is the root of our relationship problems.

Rodion & Regina I

Rodion, a man relatively early in his long-term relationship, overcoming his own emerging personal struggles, is growing frustrated with his partner's emotional distress as the weight of his own needs makes it difficult to tend to hers. Rodion's partner, Regina, has been expressing to him that she feels he has been pulling away from her, how he doesn't spend enough time with her because he is spending so much time with his friends. She tells him that he's been short with her and is stressing her because he seems so irritable.

Driven by his underlying frustration, Rodion deflects her statements by defending himself. With his arms folded—and through a frustrated tone—he tells her that he is doing his best and that she seems ungrateful for what he does for her.

With a subtle but fierce squinting of her eyes, Regina responds with a slightly angry tone, saying to Rodion, "How dare you say I'm ungrateful after all that I do to show my gratitude!"

Feeling her rapidly growing distress, Rodion assumes a stance of inferiority, withdrawing from the aggression and backing down from her contempt. Although he frames it as *keeping peace* and *not rocking the boat*, Rodion walks away frustrated, having gotten nowhere.

Rodion is unaware of what the root of this growing tension is. He does not know to identify it as tension; therefore, he is not aware that there is a deeper issue at play. His unmet needs reside in the unconscious part of his psyche. So, for now, Rodion can only comprehend what's happening on a superficial level at this point in life and his relationship.

What is at play here is that Rodion has encountered a novel situation for which his previous experiences in life have not equipped him. It has not dawned on him that there is an emerging sense of inferiority regarding his inability to manage both his and Regina's needs.

This is the beginning of Rodion's transcendence, yet he does not know it. In time, he will begin to see that it is the ancient feminine within his partner who is attempting to communicate with him. Rodion represents today's man who thus far has failed to awaken his ancient masculine.

Masculinity

Relationship problems are, in a sense, a manifestation of incorrectly assessing the meaning of the information presented, coupled with an ill-equipped set of skills for relationship success.

Childhood coping skills shape our perspectives for adolescent relationships. However, we often fail to handle more complex relationships as we enter adulthood. The failure to learn how to manage relational conflict and sort through differential values between partners limits the likelihood of successful relationships. The process of relationship growth comes from a deeper, enriched understanding of our Self (capitalized to denote the totality of ourselves rather than just the conscious part of our psyche).

As men, this foundation is the very place where masculinity is at its most pivotal developmental stage. A deeper understanding of our masculinity, and our Self, allows us to expand our capacity to manage the complex problems of life and relationships. Masculinity demands the best from us. Masculinity exposes our shortcomings. When we fall short of our potential to respond appropriately to conflict, we display an inability to manage our relationships. We are dishonoring our masculinity, and our value as a man diminishes.

As our responses to conflict and differential values in our relationship worsen, we no longer feel in control of our emotions as much as we used to. We lose control of ourselves. We no longer feel in control of our happiness and do not know how to regain that power. Even if we believe we are having the experience of being in control of our happiness, we are often blind to the negative emotional experiences of our partner. Worse yet, we attribute this chaos to external factors rather than our defects of character.

More precisely, we see the chaos as only containing threats to our happiness, failing to see the true meaning within it. Rather than understanding how the faulty aspects of our personality cause us problems, we blame others. We blame society, her friends, her parents, our parents, her coworkers, her political views, or the fact that she is a woman.

Perhaps you see your woman as irrational and aggressive—or simply an annoying distraction. This is the view and meaning of men who are not integrated, who do not understand the ancient feminine language his partner speaks, who fail to see the ancient feminine within his partner. This is the man who will henceforth be called today's man.

Blaming is counterproductive and detrimental to the intimate connections in our lives. Blaming makes us emotionally unreliable. Becoming emotionally unreliable hinders our attempts to respond to life very well. Our emotional unreliability is a poor response in and of itself. Poor responses translate to poor relationships. This book is for today's man who needs to look within himself and exercise his choice to respond to the suffering he endures. It is for the man who struggles in his relationship and is ready to brave the chaotic world of the feminine, to be transformed. Viktor Frankl stated, in his book, *Man's Search for Meaning*, "When we are no longer able to change a situation, we are challenged to change ourselves." He went on to explain, "Between stimulus and response, there is a space. In that space is our power to choose our response. In our response lies our growth and our freedom."

We have a choice as to what we respond to in life, but the nature of our responses is the most crucial aspect of a man's body of work. There are many factors that can improve the nature of our responses. First, assuming responsibility for our actions—and everything in our lives—gives us the most optimal chance of achieving the highest outcomes and the satisfaction of moving toward our most magnificent self. If we neglect to adopt the principle of responsibility, we will fail.

We once set out full of hope and with a determination to thrive in a life we were creating for ourselves, yet we declined into substandard behaviors, and our drive weakened. We got lazy, complacent, arrogant, and even resentful. We failed to educate ourselves with enough meaningful knowledge and stopped developing pro-social skills. We settled for boundaries that cost us ours, slowly sacrificing our self-respect. Homeostasis then took hold, and we seemed stuck.

Suppose you are in a problematic relationship and could use some strategies to pull yourself together; you wish to regain the intimate connection you once built. In that case, some rude awakening brought you here. You have struggled, fought, argued, been hurt, hurt your partner, declined in your work performance, or even lost friends. You may have had a critical event that led you here. Yet, if this is not you, and you believe you can benefit from such strategies, consider yourself fortunate—it is a gift that most men missed out on. For whatever reason you have arrived here, strive to respond well. Respond well to adversity. Respond well to becoming an adult. Respond well to your job. Respond well to your choices. Respond well to your woman. Respond well to the call of your masculinity.

The concepts offered here can be challenging to grasp. Yet, as you practice them, they become exponentially easier to learn and apply. Deciding to improve yourself as a man is a good idea, but you must have an aim and develop a path to get there. Observing what you do allows you to recognize the changes needed on the surface.

Changing things on the surface can bring immediate gains when improving yourself as a man, yet it is not the most effective long-term approach. Observing how you do what you do requires looking deeper into your behaviors and reactions, especially your responses to your partner's behavior. This kind of observation provides more insight into practical ways of changing. However, the pragmatic approach is to look at why things function the way they do and why you need a particular change. This exploration of the function of behaviors provides a comprehensive insight into your experiences, particularly with your partner. The "why" should be what guides you.

There are essential tools and skills you must utilize as guiding principles. These principles will reveal which direction is best for you, or at least which way is worst. Many of these principles serve as tools to remove distractions. Distractions blur, obscure, and hide your purpose and self-worth from you. The integrated man is a man who has mastered these principles and practices the core concepts of masculinity in the context of his marriage—or any long-term relationship. They will guide your fundamental behaviors regarding your direction and what options are vital to your relationship. Beyond that is where the real celebration of masculinity begins and where we cultivate harmonious connections. Men grow through challenges and overcoming them is one of the most meaningful experiences they can have. Once you have mastered assertiveness, character, frame (the mental structure that enables us to overcome obstacles of achieving an outcome), and confidence, your focus can shift to intimacy, harmonious connections, responsible leadership, and being a magnificent man. These aspects of masculinity open the door for you to discover a more profound sense of purpose and genuinely start reaching your maximized potential. This deliberate movement is how you will reach self-actualization, especially in the context of your relationship.

Self-actualization is the drive to understand your most significant potential and demonstrate your creativity to become the most authentic version of yourself. In relationships, becoming your most authentic self comes with its own set of challenges. As a man, the process of navigating relationships calls for a particular set of skills, especially regarding the challenges of connecting with the feminine within your partner.

Coming to understand masculinity is the essence of this process. This book explores the procedural process of the underlying masculine and feminine dynamics that steer relationships. The feminine nature holds an element of duality in the sense that she is both destructive and creative. As a man engages her, he falls victim or emerges as a more magnificent version of himself. There are answers in this book, or, at the least, there is a spark that is intended to contribute to a fire that burns off the false narratives that suppress both the masculine and feminine aspects of us all. For some, these answers are what they have been looking for. For others, they are answers to problems they are not yet aware of. This book aims to provide insights into becoming your own hero and equips you with knowledge that has served many men who have revolutionized their relationships. Improving masculinity is about unlearning detrimental beliefs, narratives, and biases that hinder progress. In turn, it is about learning effective means to create more positive experiences for ourselves, allowing those around us to be the beneficiaries of our gifts. This book illuminates concepts that help today's man integrate all his masculine aspects into a healthy and wholesome existence.

Gaining an understanding of masculinity exposes things about a man he can improve, use to his advantage, and make the world a better place. Addressing masculinity in the context of relationships and compatibility reveals our most deeply rooted flaws and most consequential mistakes as men. It can also refine the skills that elevate our ideas and behaviors as men. As we will see, it is through the feminine challenge from a man's partner that he can optimally cultivate his masculine aspects. The key is to cultivate them to mature levels rather than to allow them to develop in the dark and shadowy corners of his insecurities or indifference.

Masculinity can be a platform for men to make the world a better place. This is not to say that femininity cannot make the world better. Femininity has an equally profound impact, and we should never diminish the feminine nature. This book will show you how to support femininity as a masculine man. Understanding masculinity can challenge today's man in ways that broaden his personality and stretch his capacity to withstand suffering. When taken responsibly, masculinity can cultivate harmony in the world. It is not easy. Its ways are jagged and steep. Masculinity will often make you question your personal growth in ways that challenge you to maximize your potential. Masculinity can be a powerful part of a man; how he chooses to use it is paramount.

This book is not for the weak and cowardly. This book is for today's man, courageous and bold enough to search within himself and realize that there is more to him than just his fear, anger, and avoidance. It is for he who intends to transcend his misery. This change requires him to assess negative opinions about himself and his inaccurate perceptions of how well he responds to life. If you believe you are strong enough for such a change, welcome. If you believe you cannot rise above your suffering, choose to embark upon this journey anyway; you might surprise yourself.

Defining Masculine and Feminine

Masculine and feminine are commonly used but problematically defined terms. It can be said that those terms have been used since antiquity to describe numerous phenomena, such as traits, qualities, characteristics, and features to stories, gods, mythologies, psychological processes (both conscious and unconscious), behaviors, and ideologies. All the major religions of the world, as well as those less known ancient religions, incorporate the attribution of masculine and feminine aspects in their stories. These terms have also been the subjects of a wide variety of interpretations that have, in some cases, watered down their true essence have downright skewed their true meaning. For context, the ancient Chinese concept of Yin and Yang establishes a useful basis for understanding the terms masculine and feminine as they are used in this book.

Yang represents order, masculinity, and the known world. Yin represents chaos, femininity, and the unknown world. These attributes are inherently neither bad nor good. Our interpretations of them are subjective, and when our experiences of them are negative, it is usually because we have not differentiated them. There is more than what meets the eye with these attributes. When we have aversive experiences of them, it is due, in part, to a failure to see the virtues in them. Masculine and feminine hold the potential for both good and bad.

Masculine and feminine are not easily definable terms. Hence, they are also problematic to deal with. As with many challenging aspects of life, people tend to avoid the difficult task of thinking about how to contend with them. This is because in order to contend with challenges we must understand them. The more abstract a problem is, the less inclined we are to explore it. The consequence of such avoidance is that we then tend to attribute those challenging aspects of life as either good or bad. This leads to ideological thinking, which can be dangerous because it leaves us with an incomplete understanding with what we are contending, often erroneously declaring that there is nothing good to be found in any thoughts outside our own. As a result, we miss out on the gifts that lie beyond our realm of understanding, diminishing the meaning of our lives and relationships. Courage and curiosity are paramount, for they yield more promise than if we merely succumb to the fear so often induced by events that challenge our cherished beliefs.

In the context of this book, masculine will be associated with words such as order, consciousness, logic, rationale, sense, known world, container, inflexible, static, overt, disagreeable, stoic, oak, strength, endurance, and nobility.

The masculine is described in two types of men, two archetypes, so to speak. They are today's man and the integrated man. Today's man is a man who does not project his masculine nature in a healthy, beneficial way, or he may even repress it to the point of sabotaging not only himself but those closest to him. Today's man is either willfully naive to his masculine nature or willfully refuses to develop it, ignorant of the consequences of this—especially long-term. The integrated man is a man who projects his masculinity magnificently and gloriously and even inspires those around him to elevate themselves, too—particularly those closest to him. The integrated man is conscious of his masculinity yet is also committed to understanding the unrealized potential that lies in his unconscious. Through coming to understand the feminine nature in his partner, he integrates his own inner feminine—the anima—into a more complete sense of self.

On the other hand, feminine will be associated with words such as chaos, the unconscious, intuition, motion, nonsense, unknown world, creativity, fluid, dynamic, covert, agreeable, skeptical, regenerative, testing, distressed, wise.

It is difficult to move past the negative connotations of the word "chaos" when it is associated with the feminine. We must realize that chaos holds the potential for the creative and regenerative aspects of life. It is the life-giving element. The feminine is described in one type of woman: today's woman. Yet, she will be described in two archetypes: the ancient feminine and the dragon of chaos.

Today's woman is a woman who projects a distorted feminine nature watered-down by the failure of lesser men who gained power in the world without understanding the value and purpose of the feminine. Today's woman is unaware of her true feminine nature. She subscribes to many arbitrary narratives perpetuated by a society that has forgotten the true value of the complete feminine. She is distrustful of men who invite her to join together on a single path. Today's woman impatiently waits to be brought to her creative potential, to be awakened from her slumber and reconnect with her ancient masculine counterpart. Unconsciously, she knows that if today's man can provide the necessary container, she can project her feminine nature in a life-giving creation. Until then, however, she will be skeptical and fierce. Worst case, and most tragically, she will lose hope and fade into meaninglessness.

Chapter Two

The Path of Relationships

This book is designed to help men discover a sense of direction best suited for them. It does so by exploring his path in relation to his partner's love and challenges, creating an elaborate and functional road map to his deepest purpose.

Relationships present men with opportunities for personal growth and meaningful connections with people. Navigating the dynamics of intimate relationships provides experiences that can build character, broaden your sense of self, and provide a deepened sense of purpose. The interactions with your partner can reveal much about your character. This is especially true because of the complex, vast array of emotional nuances she brings to the relationship. Even if your personality leans toward the nurturing end of the spectrum, women tend to bring a more feminine element. The feminine is primarily driven by emotional experience, not for the sake of reaching the completion of an experience—as the masculine strives for—but for the sake of fulfilling the experience in and of itself. Women are molded by emotional experience, not just well-versed in it. Experiencing his partner's complex, emotional nuances pose an elaborate array of challenges for today's man. Ideally, such challenges help develop assertiveness, responsible leadership, a strong, positive frame of mind, and confidence. As a result, he begins to master the complexities of his partner's relationship tests and seductive, covert communication style in the sense of recognizing her magnificence and providing the space for it to manifest. He will come to embrace her femininity while mastering his own sense of self. Ultimately, he will begin to honor his masculinity by embracing today's woman.

The concepts in this book serve as a guide to developing a personal road map to becoming a more enriched version of yourself and doing so within the context of your relationship. Conceptually, this road map can improve all areas of your life, including personal satisfaction, enriched relationships, and a greater sense of purpose. The latter of these is perhaps optimally experienced as a result of successfully navigating difficult aspects of your relationship.

One of the least known aspects of relationships between men and women is the relationship tests women employ as a way to gauge their partner's potential. Today's female is an evolved woman whose inherent skepticism of men allows her to adapt to the ever-evolving mating rituals of men.[2][3][4][5][6] These tests are a way of keeping her finger on the pulse of how modern social norms shape men's character regarding relationships. This concept is the premise on which much of this book is written. Therefore, careful consideration of your personal relationship is paramount as you read the discussions of this concept throughout the book. Women have a psychological mechanism that naturally helps them see beyond a man's superficial behaviors. That is, his feigned attempts to represent a more committed version of himself, which seeks to engage in sexual intercourse with her.[7] To improve his mating chances, man has adapted to women's ability to see through his mating rituals, or "game." Evolutionarily speaking, this has caused women to expand their scrutinizing of a man's attempt to gain sexual favor from her. In other words, they have fine-tuned their methods—relationship tests—of calling a man's bluff during the mating ritual.

Relationship tests are disguised as misdirecting statements, questions, or behaviors by your partner that are meant to gauge your level of commitment to her and your capacity to provide for her. Gauging these aspects of you measures the nature of your responses to her tests—not the response itself. It is not the content of your responses; rather, it is the contextual meaning of them. In other words, there are significant implications of your responses to which women are much more highly attuned than men. In fact, the contrast of sensitivity to such implications is profound with today's woman and today's man. If he is to revolutionize his relationship, today's man must learn to integrate a greater sensitivity to the implications of his actions into his sense of self.

Relationship tests are designed to assess the integrity of your character, the stability of your emotional capacity, and the reliability of your purpose. However, most of the time, these tests are covert, making them difficult to detect. The undetectable nature of relationship tests is an inherent aspect of the function of covert behaviors and is achieved by concealing—at least partially—their true intentions or desires. Today's man sees this as annoying and irrational. He may even view this with moral contempt. While covert behaviors can appear cunning and dishonest, relationship tests serve to identify a man's strengths and shortcomings. However, there are times when these tests are not only intended to challenge you.

Relationship tests can also be a concealed comfort request—a type of test your partner uses to initiate intimacy by seeing how accurately you identify and how well you respond to her subtle, obscure invitations for you to connect with her. These concealed comfort requests are also used to restore the connection with you by gauging your ability to be thoughtful, romantic, comforting, and magnificent. These concealed attempts are obscured to today's man because it is the language of the ancient feminine, which he does not yet comprehend. Until he begins to transform himself, he will continue believing she is annoying, irrational, and aggressive.

Quality Responses Equal Quality Relationships

We live in a day when women have achieved more equality. The value they bring to the table has increased their ability to be more self-supporting. Their continued progress and much-deserved positive movement have empowered them in many ways. We are not living in the 1950s anymore and what defines a man's character regarding relationships with women is not what it used to be. We live in a time where women expect a different kind of excellence from men. Modern society does an effective job of calling out men for displaying their masculinity in an outdated manner and demanding that men be responsible with their masculinity. While pointing out pitfalls in men's behavior doesn't exactly provide men with a solution, it does provide a reference point as to where to move away from. And that is good!

Our responses to relationship tests dictate our experience of the relationship itself. The relentlessness of these tests—and the responses to them—alter the relationship's direction, and every test is an opportunity to adjust your aim. The direction you are heading is reflective of your responses to relationship tests. We must seek to have high-quality responses, not poor responses.

Quality responses indicate movement toward our aims—that is, a more magnificent version of our selves. Poor responses are indicative of moving away from our potential—a lesser version of ourselves. It goes without saying that; ideally, we want to make a great deal more progress toward our potential than toward a diminished version of ourselves. All this hinges on our choice of responses, as Viktor Frankl's words emphasized earlier. This is not to say the integrated man is flawless. We are human, after all, and we shift toward and away from our potential in a constant ebb and flow. This vacillation is an ineradicable aspect of human nature. We are by no means perfect. This is especially true in relationships because of the splendidly and terrifyingly fluid and dynamic experiences contained in them. They are in constant motion. This is particularly evident when our partner's emotional nuances tug at us or push us. It can be incredibly difficult to keep up with the complexities of her fluid, dynamic feminine nature. Hence, we will invariably miss the mark.

This process of push and pull is quite demanding, and such demands throughout long-term relationships can cause any man to fall short from time to time. On the surface, these shortcomings appear as general frustrations today's man has toward the challenging and cumbersome interactions with his partner. Underneath, his shortcomings reveal an acute misunderstanding of the feminine nature and, more precisely, the fundamental, biological underpinnings of her behaviors that often perplex us. The more severe a man's misunderstanding of this is, the more often he will fail. The more he fails to meet the relationship's demands, the more he might begin to question himself regarding why he is in the relationship in the first place. When today's man believes he is succeeding when he is not, he generates a false sense of security. This manifests as a complete failure to recognize his shortcoming and how they stall the relationship growth.

Rodion & Regina II

Here, Rodion's uphill climb of addressing his emerging needs and inadequacies begins to shift his view of Regina, seeing her behaviors as too irrational or too complicated and potentially as problematic. Rodion undergoes a gradual decline and begins to place more and more blame on her for the discord in their relationship. He occasionally accuses her of being too difficult to deal with, confusing her covert attempts to connect with him as outright self-centered or even malicious. This is not good. In a sense, it is easier for him to make the connection—or correlation—between the discord and Regina's self-centeredness (which is the meaning Rodion places on her behavior). He does so rather than looking at how he might have inaccurately perceived the circumstances.

Rodion's experience of Regina's emotional distress overwhelms him. Recently, she has been vacillating between shutting down in sorrow and lashing out with emotional accusations of him. Regina, with a look of contempt—unaware of Rodion's unconscious needs—says to him, "You don't even pay attention to me, and you don't care about what I need!" This strikes a nerve with Rodion. Perhaps, it is because he prides himself on being a good man who takes care of his woman. Or maybe it is because he fails to sense her pain and discomfort, placing the meaning on her behaviors (driven by pain) as being rooted as an inability for her to find satisfaction in anything.

The Precarious Path

It is easier to place the responsibility for the discord onto someone else instead of putting in the cognitive effort of the self-exploration necessary for resolving marital discord. This is not to suggest that men never put in such effort; it suggests that there will inevitably be times when the ability to manage the relationship challenges becomes too much of a cognitive strain on him. When it does, he will vacillate from a man perceived as being capable of commitment and fit for the job to a man perceived as unreliable and unfit.

This constant fluctuation creates confusion for his partner, for she cannot predict his state of mind. He may sway between these notions, vacillating from blaming her to blaming himself. Such wavering can lead to him doubting his own sense of self, further diminishing his emotional reliability, which causes him to fall short of his potential. At the core, a man's shortcomings in his relationship indicate a deeper, more profound issue of neglecting the growth and maturation of his masculinity. In short, his masculinity is reflected in his responses to his feminine partner.

Today's man might ask, "Why should I subject myself to such relentless, unbearable difficulties?" and declare that he is better off single—or, in more extreme cases, write off relationships with women altogether. However, relationships—particularly intimate relationships—are considered a basic human need. Although argued to be somewhat outdated, Maslow's Hierarchy of Needs positions intimacy and relationship needs on the third level of the pyramid, above basic health and safety.[8] Integration into our society is a necessary and fundamental part of achieving a satisfactory life for ourselves. It is important to note that we *seek* human connections because of the benefits it offers in the present, such as love, sex, or companionship. However, we *commit* to relationships to ensure the sustainability and availability of such benefits—to secure those resources, so to speak. This requires that we anticipate and predict the future of those relationships, and the future holds both threat and promise.[9]

In the context of committed relationships, we assess the potential for long-term benefits of intimacy, companionship, and family. We also assess the threat posed to the achievement of these goals. In relationships with women, the potential for connecting with them requires us to embrace and support the expression of their femininity, which can be chaotic in nature, holding both threat and promise.

Today's man is not nuanced with the nature of femininity—the unpredictability and randomness of today's woman. The unfamiliarity with the feminine nature causes men to miss the mark with tending to their partner's needs. More so, it may blind him to the fact that her dynamic and fluid experience of emotions is quite unlike his more orderly, resolution-oriented experience of emotions. Such disparity of emotional experience leads to a minimal connection beyond anything superficial. This leads to unmet needs for his partner, to which she will respond with unique ways of ensuring her needs are met, which are often frustrating for him. This pushes today's man further away from the challenges required to further develop his masculine nature. It is the refusal to assume responsibility for this that causes him to remain underdeveloped as a man. Therefore, navigating the challenges of creating harmony and intimacy in his relationship is paramount to course-correcting his development. This is most challenging in the sense that it is here where responding to today's woman is most difficult.

Today's woman has an exceptional methodology of ensuring her needs are met. She is skillful at testing the validity of a man's commitment to her and determining if he is reliable enough. The methods used by women are quite scientific in nature. It is a quality control method, per se, that is reliable and observable (to the trained eye). Their methods of navigating intimate relationships are based on the need to ensure their masculine partner is emotionally reliable and able to provide an optimal environment for her to express herself freely and fully. The more a man is in touch with his masculine nature and engages in his woman's emotional nuances, the more successful the relationship will be. Both aspects create opportunities for personal growth, challenging men to be their most magnificent self.

The opportunities for personal growth are not easily recognized by most men in the context of relationships. To some men, navigating relationships presents them with many obstacles that appear impossible to overcome, such as grasping women's emotional nuances and understanding the feminine nature to attain a deepened intimate connection. Men often avoid educating themselves on this topic. Instead, many men wish their partners would simply "act right" so that the relationship can improve, viewing her as too emotional and being fixated on the problem rather than the solution. This attempt to maintain cognitive ease, coupled with the desire for resolution, can be devastating to a man's masculine development. This is evident in his relationships with women and the emotional nuances they bring. Women generally experience emotions much more deeply than men.[10] Therefore, the feminine experience can be problematic for men. The masculine nature and feminine nature can be quite contrasting, although harmonious when the right connections are made.

Men often project their own methods of navigating relationships onto their partners, and therefore are often unwittingly dismissive of a woman's natural way of processing her own experiences. Men often naively coerce their partners into processing their emotions in a masculine way, which detracts from their femininity, leading to them missing out on the experience they intended to have. Many men fall suspect to believing that women cannot navigate the relationship with so much emotional vacillation. In fact, women tend to be much better at navigating relationships than men when it comes to the emotional nuances.[11] [12]

Men are often willfully naive toward this, frequently dismissing their feminine partner's emotional nuance as unnecessary stress. Such dismissal of a woman's emotional nuances tends to result in men viewing the dynamics of the feminine nature as mere inconveniences that are generally tolerable and worth dealing with as long as it doesn't become too demanding. This is counterproductive and generally makes the relationship difficult for him to improve or repair. This mindset is flawed, for it lacks the indispensable qualities of openness and responsibility a man must exhibit to be the best version of his self.

The unwillingness to be responsible and open-minded stifles improvements to a man's character and relationship skills by obscuring the virtues that come with navigating the chaos of the feminine. And that is not good, for it limits a man's capacity to connect with her. His own limitations—and his blindness to them—lead to the avoidance of relationship challenges, which, subsequently, halts the development of his masculinity. As a man's growth stalls, he undergoes atrophy of the qualities and values that brought him any previous success in the relationship. The attenuation of assertiveness is often the costliest, followed by a loss of frame control. Diminished assertiveness and loss of frame control cause men to sway uncontrollably from passivity to aggression. The unaddressed chaos of this vacillation leads to an underdeveloped skill set that would promote confidence and emotional reliability. When this happens, men begin to regress emotionally, eventually reverting to infantile reactions to most, if not all, of their partner's emotional distress.

The Process of Self-Improvement

The concepts for transforming into an integrated man in the context of relationships are not linear processes, and growth is never complete. Each step is the foundation for the subsequent step, and there will be a step to take as long as you live. These concepts build upon themselves. Therefore, as each concept is perpetually internalized, you can more consistently apply the fundamentals of each concept. Each concept should be contemplated and polished—careful to never neglect them. While this book serves as an in-depth guide to constructing—or reconstructing—a map for the world and for yourself, it is wise to have dialogues with others about these concepts rather than practicing the concepts entirely on your own. Processing these concepts without feedback can be detrimental to your self-improvement and, by default, your relationship. We need reference points to let us know our position in the world and the hierarchies within it. These reference points reveal the proximity of our current position to our goals. Implement these concepts in ways that best suit your purpose and apply these strategies thoughtfully. You are encouraged to philosophize these concepts with others yet declare for yourself the goals you will ultimately strive toward It is paramount that you choose your own path in life.

Understanding who you are is necessary for navigating your path in life and relationships. Setting your course of self-improvement, and doing so in the context of your relationship, requires that you first identify the type of partner you are. There are numerous ways of understanding yourself regarding your partner type, but one of the best ways is to understand your personality. Personality psychology, in this context, is an effective framework from which to understand individual differences in decision-making.[13] One of the most scientific and empirical personality models is the Big Five Aspects Scale. You can take the Big Five personality assessment at understandmyself.com (you can also have your partner take the test, then generate a "relationship report" on the website—the author has no affiliation with this website). The reports generated from this test can illuminate—with staggering precision—traits and aspects of your personality, which can help identify your partner type. Partner types are discussed in detail in a later chapter.

The next thing you must do is assess the connection type between you and your partner. Often, by gaining a more detailed understanding of your partner type—as well as your overall personality—you can gain insight into your partner's personality, which can help you assess the connection type. This is also discussed in a later chapter. From there, you will learn to master the quality of your responses in relationships by improving your assertiveness, building character, developing a strong, positive frame of mind, and increasing your confidence. You will familiarize yourself with character-building tests and covert comfort requests and become proficient with them. You will evolve as you begin to transcend your current sense of self and become a magnificent man through practicing responsible leadership and cultivating harmonious connections—but not without a descent into the darkness of your soul.

Identifying the type of partner you are brings to light behaviors that either positively or negatively impact your relationship, as well as the disparities of each other's personalities that much of your conflict sourced in. Assertiveness provides tools for managing conflict and setting boundaries. Mastering character-building tests and covert comfort requests involves unlearning certain beliefs about how men and women operate and learning to respond to your partner in new, more effective ways. This allows room for more intimacy and connection with your partner. Frame control involves becoming familiar with, building, and maintaining a strong, positive frame of mind to obtain the outcomes you want. Building responsible leadership brings out the best that both you and your partner have to offer. Finally, establishing harmony with your partner creates a more intimate and desirable connection with her. The successful implementation of these concepts will transform you into a more integrated man with a more defined sense of self.

What, How, and Why

It is essential to look at the *what*, *how*, and *why* of relationship behaviors, specifically *how* you respond to your partner's emotional distress. You must seek to understand the function of her behaviors toward you, which is perhaps best done by broadening particular personality traits. However, to better understand the fundamental nature of human behavior, we must take a look at the biological processes that consist of the *what*, *how*, and *why*. Simon Sinek's Golden Circle theory illustrates the reasons and effects of the *what*, *how*, and *why* of communication and engagement with others.[14] He posits that the part of our brain, called the neo-cortex, corresponds with the *what* level. The neo-cortex is responsible for rational and analytical thought and language. While this allows us to understand vast amounts of complex information we observe, such as conflict (what), it does not help us understand the function (why) of the behavior within the conflict. Relationship conflict is emotional, and since women experience emotions more deeply than men, it would behoove men to delve deeper into the nuances of their partner's behaviors and emotions rather than trying to intellectualize them in a reductionistic manner.

There can be dire consequences to intellectualizing the emotions of particular situations—or at least only intellectualizing them. We fail to foster the relationship when we go no further than the *what*. Additionally, with relative ease, we can understand *how* something is happening. We know the answer to *how* conflict is happening by *what* is being said or by a person's overt behavior—such as yelling or stonewalling. Although this helps us deal with *what* is happening (conflict) by understanding *how* it is happening (yelling or stonewalling), it is not so apparent as to *why* it is happening.

The *why* is the function behind the emotionally driven behavior within the conflict. Once we begin to grasp this, we can make profound, healthy changes in our relationships. Asking *why* something is happening helps us understand what drives behaviors or inspires action, positively or negatively. Once we understand *why* relationship conflict happens, *why* our partners behave in certain ways, and *why* we respond to them the way we do, we will begin to see a clearer path to an elevated version of ourselves that leads to more harmony in the relationship and a more magnificent version of ourselves.

The *what, how,* and *why* are natural parts of communication in relationships and should be observed as you master your relationship skills. The *why* is the most important question, yet we should also learn to respond to *what* is happening and *how* it is happening with focused intention. To master this aspect of relationships, you should first increase your ability to notice *what* is happening without responding irrationally. This will allow you to familiarize yourself with *how* things are happening to avoid pitfalls. The more proficient you become at this, the better you will become at knowing when to ask *why* different behaviors and events occur. As you learn to inquire *why* your partner's behavior is taking place— as well as asking *why* you are compelled to respond the way you do—you will be able to respond with valuable and attractive behaviors in ways that tend to your partner's needs and elicit more desire for you.

What

Order and chaos are fundamental aspects of human experience. There is the known and unknown. The unknown holds both promise and threat;[15] it is what lies between the familiar world and where we want to be in the future—between who we are and who we could be. When we encounter the unknown (the result of venturing toward our goals), we must first understand what we are looking at so we can know what to do with it. To know what to do with it, we must understand the contextual value of the thing we are looking at. The contextual value is the importance placed on an experience or event that is determined by the meaning of the environment in which it occurs. Its contextual value gives rise to the implications of our interactions with the thing, thereby allowing us to determine whether the thing holds promise or threat. At this point, we can respond in ways that move us closer to our desired outcomes.

Rodion & Regina III

Thus far, we have seen Rodion encounter the unknown, an anomaly in his relationship with which he must figure out what it is and what to do with it. Rodion's relationship has evolved, for better or worse. The growth relationships endure is a natural occurrence, which contains both painful and rewarding experiences. Rodion's encounter with his partner's new behaviors—existing behaviors with which he sees in a new way, or recognizes for the first time—poses a problem of the likes he has never seen. Although he did well before in identifying solutions to conflict, he is missing the mark regarding the tension he is experiencing with his partner. He knows to make sure he is doing his part, yet he never could have anticipated this degree of conflict. It is not merely the intense, volatile conflict that must be identified; it is also about understanding what lies within the obscure dynamic of the masculine and feminine connection. On the surface, Regina is upset about something she had never found problematic before. Suddenly, she now seems to be upset about it. This is the anomaly Rodion has encountered.

The anomaly Rodion has encountered is more obscure, as it does not arise from a single interaction with his partner, which would otherwise be identified based on the subject matter of the conflict. For instance, while walking on a trail one afternoon, Rodion feels challenged by Regina when she questions the kinds of things they spent money on the previous month. Rodion contends that their purchases were well within reason. In truth, Rodion is quite rational in his thought. Yet, when Regina persists with her argument, Rodion becomes frustrated about being doubted and argues even more with her. Rodion is arguing with her based on the what, which is her overt behaviors—the observable problem—rather than considering why she was upset. He refrains from arguing much further, however. Realizing he knows he is right, he concludes there is no need to argue. As the two of them walk in silence a brief distance, Rodion begins to stew on the matter.

Rodion grows more distressed. He is quite irritated at the thought of her being so stubborn and insistent on not believing him. His solution—so he thinks—is to prove himself right about their spending being reasonable. In some strange way, this is also driven by care and concern for her—he wants her to have a better experience with him. Therefore, he resumes the confrontation with Regina, to which she ultimately responds by shutting down. She picks up her pace so that Rodion cannot see her face—or so that she does not have to look at him. This only frustrates Rodion more. Unable to bear the weight of her emotional distress, and feeling a bit out of control, he apologizes to her for arguing.

From the outset, Rodion believed nothing more existed than the content of the conflict, which was about how much money was or wasn't spent the previous month. He not only escalated the conflict but also took it in the opposite direction of what was an opportunity to elevate himself to a more magnificent version. Rather than using straightforward assertiveness to diffuse the conflict and assuming happiness, Rodion felt the need to be right. In truth, this was a covert attempt to be validated by his partner, for he viewed the conflict as a threat to their relationship, or at least the harmony within it. Beyond that, Rodion missed an opportunity to see deeper into Regina's emotional world, which would have been an opportunity to support her feminine experience. He failed to identify the relationship test as a steppingstone to cultivate harmony. It is one thing to argue with her, especially when he knows he is correct. It is another thing to fail to see the implications of his responses to her deeper, unconscious needs.

When it comes to the unknown, courage is most often what produces more promise than threat. Typically, at best, a man will respond to what is occurring with a partial understanding of its contextual value. On this level, you see things at a superficial level, such as your partner yelling at you, scolding you, or ignoring you, which might lead to responding to these behaviors as a threat to your desired outcomes. Responding to threat can be profoundly different from responding to promise. Had Rodion responded to the conflict as a promising opportunity to grow closer, the outcome would have been quite different. In the context of relational conflict, responding to what is observable, absent understanding its contextual value, leads to responding to her overt behaviors with your own such responses. You might yell back, cower down, or ignore her, too. When you act in this way, you respond poorly by matching her emotional distress with your own emotional distress, failing to detect the reasons for it. You walk blindly into this pitfall because you either over-intellectualize the emotionally driven conflict or you downplay it. Your efforts to intellectualize the conflict or reduce it to mere nonsense might be fruitless and even escalate the conflict when it is highly emotional.

Your partner's emotional experience of the distressful event seeks to express itself; it does not seek to be resolved. And that is a significant distinction! If you try to make it resolvable, you will only irritate your partner, showing your inability to tend to her emotional needs. In the words of Winston Churchill, "You cannot reason with a tiger when your head is in its mouth." When you act in this way, you respond poorly by reacting to the superficiality of your partner's distress, ignoring her true needs. If you have the skills to manage such conflict, but your goal is simply to end the distressful behavior, you neglect to manage the true, deeper needs of the relationship. This approach fans the flames of discord. It is easy to see what is happening on the surface, but it takes more effort to understand how it occurs.

How

How things happen in relational conflict can be observed as your partner's criticism of you, her emotional accusations toward you, character assassination, and other negative behaviors, such as stonewalling. The unconscious narrative of this experience for Rodion says, "I sense there is discord with us. She is directing emotional distress at me right now, and that is how the conflict is being created." While this recognizes how the conflict is occurring, it does not account for the reasons why it is occurring.

Intense emotions often present themselves in an aggressive delivery. On a biological level, we deal with aggression as a threat, and our natural proclivity toward threat is to respond with aggression, defensiveness, or passivity—flight, fight, or freeze, respectively. Many of your partner's behaviors around conflict involve intense emotions on her part but are not always negative. Sometimes her behavior is highly emotionally driven and only interpreted as negative. It is not just these complexities that today's man contends with. He must also contend with the general biological disposition of women to respond with greater defensive reactivity to aversive experiences.[16] In other words, today's man contends with an unimaginable consequences of evolution. Therefore, when you respond to such stress-inducing behaviors, you are responding to how things are happening (through her negative emotions). However, it is our attitudes toward these intense, emotional behaviors that determine the contextual value we abstract from them. Your narrowed focus on how something happens (i.e., yelling or stonewalling) explains the reasons for your poor responses, such as yelling or giving your partner the cold shoulder in return. In relationships, we often respond to the how with defensive, aggressive, or passive responses. These responses are almost always of no value and rarely serve your relationship.

Why

The contextual value we place on what we encounter, coupled with courageous and conscientious effort, elicits more promise than threat from chaos, providing a clearer path to our desired outcomes. This makes it easier to respond in ways that direct us toward our goals. Observing why you behave the way you do and why your partner behaves the way she does provides the most important insight regarding the ability to respond in a quality manner.

Notably, in conflict, you respond to what she is doing or how she is doing it; the goal should be to move beyond the 'what' and 'how' and respond to 'why' your partner is doing what she's doing. At the biological level, she is doing the 'what' and the 'how' to ensure her needs and desires are met. A useful rule of thumb to remember is everything we do, we do to meet a need. The answer is that she is gauging your commitment to her and assessing your character to see if you are fit for the job of providing for her.

It is vital to respond to the what, how, and why accordingly. Respond to what is going on with an assertive curiosity. Respond to how things are happening with compassion and empathy. Lastly, learn to respond to why things are happening with magnificence. Why is she crying? Why is she testing me? Why is she angry? Once you begin to grasp her true reason for behaving the way she does, you will begin to see her as something spectacular.

Intimacy

There is a perpetual balancing of the scale of behaviors that determine the degree of intimacy in relationships. Leaning to the negative side of the scales indicates a shift toward behaviors that prevent intimacy. Leaning to the positive side indicates a shift toward behaviors that cultivate intimacy. Because intimacy is an important part of healthy relationships, this balance requires a great deal of care and attention.

In healthy relationships, the scale favors behaviors that promote intimacy and only a small number of behaviors that prevent intimacy. As you conceptualize the intimacy scale in your relationship, notice each behavior's significance—its weighted value, so to speak—which can be considered as a single item that will be on one side of the scale or the other. Many items—or behaviors—create a constant fluctuation of the scale, tilting from one side to the other.

There is an ebb and flow to this. In a relationship with little to no intimacy, the scale is weighted to the negative side by behaviors that prevent intimacy and must be tilted to the other side by modifying behaviors or shifting the significance of the behaviors to the positive side. As you implement various strategies to improve yourself in the context of your relationship, you tilt the scale more and more to the positive side. Each positive behavior, which reflects your sense of self, is like a single item moved from one side of the scale to the other. The more your body of work improves, the more the scale tilts to the positive side.

Chapter Three

Who is the Integrated Man?

Perhaps most men who take on this book once lived estimable lives and took risks, positioning themselves to climb the hierarchy of their lives. They exhibited perseverance and were often calm under pressure, needing little external validation. However, these attributes can become subdued due to the trials and tribulations of relationships and the failure to adapt to them. Although some of earlier qualities might occasionally shine through their behavior, their inconsistency contributes to unreliability, leaving too much room for doubt and skepticism. This is neglectful and irresponsible, regressing masculinity and diminishing the task of providing for their partner. Inviting someone to walk with you on your path in life inherently means assuming responsibility for that partnership, and inconsistency greatly diminishes the optimal support you are charged with providing for her.

The traits that define the integrated man are unique to each man, yet there are some underlying qualities common to all men. The integrated man behaves in ways guided by principles and values. He is rooted in a growing sense of purpose. He strives to be his best, making the world around him a better place in the process. The integrated man demands excellence of himself by asking more of himself than others ask of him— he possesses certain toughness. He does ordinary things extraordinarily well. These are traits of a leader. Of course, leadership roles aren't limited to men; women possess incredible strengths and values as leaders in their own right. The key to becoming an integrated man in the context of long-term relationships is to cultivate the masculine principles that guide you as a responsible leader.

Doing so with conscientiousness and a sense of responsibility prompts you to thoroughly examine yourself. Both a philosophical and practical inventory of your character must take place and should include seeking insight into your masculine nature, for it is a fundamental component of the connection with your partner. It is essential to your character, and there is an incredible amount of potential which lies there. It behooves you, just as it does all men, to honor your masculinity, for it opens the door to a tremendous opportunity to be the ultimate version of yourself, one which can be an enormous source of freedom.

As a masculine man, you process experiences and emotions in a way that is fundamentally unique to men. Some commonly understood terms that define this process are logical, intellectual, stoic, rational, analytical, and reserved. This does not mean that men cannot—or do not—lean toward the emotional end of the spectrum, nor does it mean that men display these common traits effortlessly and flawlessly.

While these traits are not exclusive to men, we live in a society that demands a different kind of excellence from men. There are major adjustments today's man must take to catch up with the changes in that society and become an integrated man. The process of integrating oneself in modern times—or "catching up"—sends men into uncharted territory, often confusing them about how to act. When people are uncertain about how they should behave in an unfamiliar world, they behave primitively, which appears erratic to those accustomed to this new world. The attributes mentioned above serve as principles that can guide today's man to a stable and secure sense of self and a more integrated version of himself.

The experiential process of becoming an integrated man illuminates our humanity. Today's man must adapt yet do so while maintaining the integrity of his masculinity. One of the unintended consequences of an evolving society is that the ideologies that accompany them often lead to a lopsided narrative that suppresses people's psychological development. In the context of men adapting to modern society, the ideologies that promote an improved treatment of women tend to cross over into the fallible world of devaluing masculinity. Men are told who they should not be, which can be useful. But it is not useful to neglect helping men figure out who they should be in a way that values their masculinity. Much of what defines a man is how he responds to his failures and mistakes, as evidenced most often in his long-term relationships, which have many implications. The complexities of such relationships require men to display superior masculine qualities to overcome mistakes. Therefore, today's man must become more attuned with his sense of self and his purpose.

However, a man attuned with his sense of self may deviate from his purpose from time to time, but the integrated man always returns to his center. He may fall short of his best at times, but he certainly must not assume a new, inferior role because of his shortcomings. He corrects his trajectory more accurately toward the greater outcome and does so based on the best-suited principles for the outcome he aims to achieve. His trajectory is aimed far because his life has a purpose, and he considers the long view. He does not simply fixate on correcting the current situation. This suggests that, while each experience holds its own significance, the integrated man must allow his principles to guide him in a way that considers the impact of all his actions, here and further down the road. It would be irresponsible to neglect the lessons our individual, present experiences have to offer. We must put adequate care and attention to understanding our experiences and value them accordingly. This gives us the ability to see our path's trends and patterns, which helps develop our sense of direction.

Sense of Direction

A more profound attribute of the integrated man is his sense of direction. This is a sense of self that is assertive, purpose-driven, open-minded, and oriented toward meaning. This attribute positions you toward your desired outcome. Although the integrated man is ultimately the only one who can declare his value as a man, it is wise to look to his peers as reference points to gauge the contextual value of his behaviors. Many men will deny that they care what others think of them as a way to manufacture a persona of independence and confidence. The persona is the aspect of a person's character presented to others in a way intended to only display his positive aspects. By his own outward expression of not caring what others think of him, a man indicates that he does, in fact, care what others think.

Individuals do not exist in a vacuum. Experiences are quite subjective, and we interpret events based on our individual beliefs, and the meaning we place on those events shapes our experiences of them. The human experience has been philosophized and studied for ages, particularly as it pertains to determining reality. While science can produce conclusive evidence about many theories, our individual experiences remain unique to us in many ways. As objective as we may try to be, the intrinsic nature of our experiences as men is subjective. Outwardly, this results in a wide range of subjective opinions of other men based on our own individual experiences. This also means there is a wide range of opinions that other men have of each other based on our individual experiences. Regarding mate selection, men are compared to other men as a woman searches the pool of potential males to select from. Men look toward other men's behavior in the mating hierarchy to assess their position in that hierarchy. This is how we as social creatures make course corrections.

While there is value in a man doing his own thing, if he ignores what other men are doing that is considered valuable to a potential mate, he may lack the self-awareness necessary for ensuring his value, and risks being passed up. He must find some degree of an objective view of himself to position himself in the hierarchy properly. Therefore, a man's judgment of his own quality is a subjective opinion until it is measured against the subjective opinions of other men.

The way to gain an objective conclusion about ourselves is to reflect on how our experiences of certain events compare to other men's experiences with similar events. Men need reference points to gain a sense of direction. Without reference points, a man may lack the self-awareness necessary for becoming the best version of himself. For example, how a man handles being denied a promotion can be compared to how other men have handled the same thing. A man may believe he handled the situation well if he determines how well he responded by his own subjective opinion. Suppose he fails to factor in his supervisor's and colleagues' subjective opinions of how others have responded in similar circumstances. In that case, he misses out on reference points that provide him with insight on how he can respond more effectively. This is where the ego has utility—it concerns itself with the value the group places upon him, so he is not cast out and left to die.

When we utilize such reference points, we can form an objective assessment of ourselves and how we might best respond to the obstacles in our path. We must look to other men who apply principles in their lives and who express a clear sense of direction. People do not operate in a vacuum. Therefore, if we are to gain a sense of direction, we should not isolate our experiences as a man from the context of relationships. As men, our quality can be understood in relation to others, whether it be measured against other men or reflected in relationships with women.

In these connections, we can determine our worth and value as a man, not to elevate ourselves above lesser men, but to transcend a diminished version of ourselves.

Order and direction are necessary aspects of the integrated man. We need to prioritize the tasks in our lives if we are to make progress. To advance ourselves, we must adopt proven methods and become familiar with the principles that drive those methods.

While following proven methods is paramount, doing so in your own riveting and dynamic fashion allows you to become familiar with how your own values steer you. We add our own flair to these methods, making them unique and personal to our own experiences. To optimize this process, we turn to the concepts and theories that provide us with knowledge of what to do and what not to do. These methods become meaningful and purposeful as we practice and refine the fundamental concepts and theories described in this book. This process enables us to transcend into more magnificent versions of ourselves.

The concepts and theories discussed in this book aim to broaden the masculine experience in relationships while making sense of the feminine experience. The concepts here provide us with principles that help us become aware of the fallacies in our thinking and behavior by illuminating the masculine function in our relationships.

Masculinity is best mastered in intimate relationships due to the complex array of emotional nuances women bring and the desire for excellence that women place on their men. The process of understanding masculinity in relationships can be excruciating, because it is the kind of growth that happens through the trial by fire today's man goes through before he is received by his partner truly. Through a connection with an intimate partner, our masculinity is reflected in her deeper, feminine responses to us. The more knowledge of masculinity we gain, the more useful our existing qualities will be. This implies that we already possess the qualities necessary to be a superior man; but we must cultivate them and be deliberate with them. As we master the application of these qualities, our interactions with others become more purposeful, our lives more fruitful, and our gifts more magnificent.

The Four Pillars of Masculinity

Self-discovery through the lens of masculinity is a complex evolutionary journey. Yet, the principles that guide your journey are sound and straightforward. Mastering masculinity is accomplished by focusing on four foundational areas, or what we shall call pillars. These pillars are assertiveness, character, frame, and confidence.

Individually, these pillars are self-reinforcing, which means the more you practice them, the more proficient you become at responding to your partner. In turn, your partner will improve her responses to you, and harmony will increase. Collectively, these pillars reinforce the others, meaning the more you practice one, the more proficient you become with the others. These pillars help you develop your masculinity by bringing you to a more intimate understanding of your purpose and a more secure sense of self. This gives you a point of view that enables you to behave in ways more aligned with your innate strengths and abilities.

All four pillars are indispensable, yet assertiveness is the one pillar that must be established for the other pillars to be effective. Without assertiveness, the other pillars are utilized haphazardly. Assertiveness lays the groundwork for the other three pillars by creating perimeters in which we can practice them. To exhibit your best character, you must have a fundamental ability to establish boundaries and manage conflict. Assertiveness does not need the establishment of good character to be effective. However, character is a pillar that is most effective when assertiveness is established beforehand or even simultaneously.

Assertiveness creates the environment in which others are primed to see our character assets and be receptive to us and the message we are attempting to convey. Furthermore, practicing assertiveness influences others to exhibit their own character assets, thus improving their assertiveness. The same is true of frame and confidence.

Assertiveness is the skill that strengthens and reinforces frame because we can manage conflict and reinforce boundaries in our efforts to achieve outcomes. With confidence, assertiveness can be extremely effective, for it is a skill that mitigates distractive barriers to mastery, such as reluctance and doubt.

Confidence is a feeling of self-assurance of one's own abilities or qualities. Conflict and chaos are naturally occurring phenomena in relationships, and we navigate the challenges of conflict and chaos with confidence and assertiveness skills. In other words, being self-assured in our abilities to diffuse conflict and chaos means we must be able to bring order to any situation we encounter. It brings order from chaos. The more these four pillars are mastered, the better we can do this.

Assertiveness

Honoring masculinity will be a rewarding experience if your qualities and values are developed appropriately and you are able to amend the faults of your masculinity. In other words, tending to your masculine growth—and expressing your masculinity responsibly—will lead to a more purposeful life. But how can we achieve this if chaos is inevitable? Many people believe that they must understand everything about a situation before they can successfully navigate it. This is an attempt to create a perfectly ideal path of least resistance to their desired outcomes. This attempt is rooted in a fundamentally limited view of masculinity—simply to bring order from chaos—by setting forth on the path with the least amount of objections.

However, this maligned way of thinking naively reduces the very thing that develops our masculinity. There are unintended consequences of preemptively setting things in order, removing us from the challenges that come with the chaos of relationships. Without knowing precisely what the disorder looks like, we are unlikely to master anything.

Experience is our greatest teacher; to miss out on such valuable lessons that chaos brings will prove costly. Therefore, we must assert ourselves into the uncertainty of chaos if we are to even come close to becoming an integrated man. Such a journey brings us intimately closer to our purpose. Mastering the four pillars is how we fully understand our masculine purpose and how to transform it into a gift for the world. Understand, this is not about grandiosity. As a man, this is about transcending an unhealthy, fixed sense of self into a conscientious, aware, and purposeful sense of self—one that gives freely yet responsibly. One that tends to the needs of those he values, who impact his world, and whose world he impacts.

Assertiveness is the foundation on which you build success in your relationships and your quality as a man. Assertiveness has two primary functions in relationships: managing conflict and establishing boundaries. While chaos should be courageously embraced, there is little to no order without assertiveness. Without order, there will only be chaos. And that is not good. Without boundaries, everything required of a successful relationship will be ill-managed. Thus, we behave haphazardly, potentially harming ourselves and the people in our lives.

For instance, regarding boundaries, if a man tries to bond with his partner, he must understand her boundaries, what she is comfortable with, and with what she needs reassurance. If he is not mindful of such things, his strategies will backfire.

Rodion & Regina IV

Rodion has set his sights on amending his shortcomings with Regina over the money debacle—he wants to redeem himself. He decides to take her on a weekend trip and use the opportunity to reconcile the conflict by having an open and candid conversation about the tension between them while simultaneously taking her on a surprise adventure. On the drive there, Rodion brings up the conflict and expresses his interest in coming to an understanding with each other. The conversation starts off well, as both Rodion and Regina seem to be far enough removed from the argument about money to regain a concern for each other's happiness. Then, something subtle happens. Regina begins to give shorter answers and starts gazing out the passenger window, away from Rodion. Sensing she might be losing interest in hearing his experience, he coerces her into opening up more. Although his intentions are noble, and he is speaking calmly and lovingly, her silence becomes stronger and her gaze more fixed. The more Rodion talks, the more Regina checks out. In her experience, she needs to process all the detailed amount of information Rodion has expressed to her, for it weighs heavily on her emotions.

Unbeknownst to Rodion, Regina has to consider far more implications of the conflict than he can imagine. She needs time to think, yet she feels pressured to produce answers. Although Rodion is not explicitly forcing her to talk, she feels an unwanted obligation to do so and shuts down. Torn between not wanting to hurt him and needing to process the emotional gravity of the conversation, she freezes. Rodion is frustrated by her behaviors, which leads him to arbitrarily infer her behaviors as stonewalling. He has fallen into the trap of the cognitive distortion called emotional reasoning, in which a person concludes that their emotional reaction proves something is true, despite there being empirical evidence that indicates otherwise. Therefore, he responds to stonewalling with what he thinks is an appropriate antidote by calming down and re-engaging the conversation. If this was stonewalling, this would perhaps be a reasonable response. However, since she was taking her time to process in her own way, his attempted antidote fueled her distress. Having reached a critical mass of emotional distress, Regina reacts emotionally and commences to aggressively assassinate Rodion's character. Now, they both shut down for the last hour of the trip—made mostly in silence and angst.

Rodion was not mindful of Regina's boundaries in the sense of their greater implications. Therefore, he inadvertently violated them, yet subsequently created and environment of mistrust. The haphazard violation of her boundaries is indicative of emotional unreliability, and it repulses Regina. Although connecting with his partner is necessary to build a successful relationship, there was no order in his attempts, and it led to neglecting her needs and violating her trust in him. Instead of more connection, there was more distance.

Today's man will not recognize the real conflict here. If Rodion wants to assume a leadership role in a particular situation, he must recognize the conflict when he finds himself in it. If he mismanages the conflict, his leadership skills come into question, and he cannot be relied upon with certainty. Leadership is a valuable asset in a successful relationship, yet it will backfire when misused. He must not ignore this essential building block called assertiveness. If he does, he is sure to set himself up for difficult hardships and a failed relationship.

The function of assertiveness is to manage, diffuse, and prevent various types of conflict and the discord they bring to the relationship. Invariably, relationships come with different types of conflict, many of which are nearly impossible to anticipate. Having the skills to address conflict as it arises is paramount. By practicing assertiveness, we not only develop a sensitivity to conflict, but we also begin to manage it closer to its onset, rather than after the fact. Still, conflict can catch us off guard, especially when things have recently been harmonious. The contrast between harmony and conflict is a figurative event boundary, a doorway or threshold through which we cross over from one experience to the next. These crossovers occur unbeknownst to us. It can feel like we are out of control when these crossovers happen due to the sense that we ended up somewhere other than where we intended to be.

Conflict and harmony—the diametrically opposed experiences on each side of the threshold—are in a constant dance with each other, and we are caught in the middle. This is profoundly evident in intimate relationships, for there is more at stake. Practicing assertiveness gives us control of ourselves as we suddenly pass through the event boundaries between conflict and harmony. While today's man tends to experience this as absurd and unnecessary, each encounter with either a newly emerging, longstanding, or recurring conflict is an opportunity to respond in a manner that will create an optimal environment for growth. Here, he will either prevail as a leader or altogether fail to manage the situation adequately. Mismanaging conflict delays—or even prevents—harmony. The longer harmony is lost, the more difficult it will be to regain, for time will create more barriers to overcome. Sometimes the collective magnitude of these barriers surmounts the willingness to overcome them. The more difficult the challenge of regaining harmony in a relationship, the easier it is to give up and walk away. The drive for cognitive ease becomes a priority at some point, and the temptation to throw in the towel becomes the more viable option. In other words, choosing the easier, softer way becomes appealing. While there is certainly value in knowing when to walk away, prematurely choosing the easier path is not rewarding and leaves us defeated. Ultimately, it results in a diminished version of ourselves, and we will carry this over into the next relationship, repeating the same pattern.

Assertiveness is also about establishing boundaries. As it pertains to relationships, establishing boundaries creates a clearly defined picture of your desires and what you're willing to compromise—without losing self-respect—to make room for your partner's desires to be met. Boundaries are a vital component of healthy relationships because they prevent undesirable behaviors from disrupting that relationship's intimacy and harmony. Boundaries are also perimeters in which desirable behaviors take place organically. Creating a space for desirable behaviors to take place in this manner increases the likelihood of intimacy and cohesiveness.

Character

Character is the second pillar of the four fundamental areas on which to understand masculinity. The quality of your character determines the quality of your responses and, in turn, the quality of your relationship. Your responses to your partner are a direct reflection of your character. Therefore, we must deliberately choose what part of our character to exhibit in our responses, purposefully exhibiting our best qualities. The feminine challenges presented to us in relationships—and the conflict that emerges from those interactions—expose our character defects. And this is actually good. Women have a way of demanding a particular kind of excellence from men, which comes in the form of challenges, and these challenges push the limits of our psychological development. Therefore, these challenges provide opportunities to build character and responsible masculinity. In relationships, new problems arise all the time. You may encounter obstacles with which you have little to no experience. As a masculine man, you possess particular qualities deep within yourself—that is, they exist only in your unconscious until you are primed to develop them through exposure to challenges. The more developed these qualities are, the better suited you are for responding to your partner and the perpetual unpredictability of her femininity. As these unconscious qualities are activated, we become better equipped to figure out these strange, novel problems. The degree to which we can conquer these problems is, to a large measure, determined by our conscientiousness and creativity. As you resolve the difficult challenges of embracing today's woman, you add depth to your experiences, profoundly broadening your character and personality. You learn new ways of managing unfamiliar obstacles with the experience of resolving past challenges.

Rodion & Regina V

Had Rodion been more conscientious in his efforts to mitigate the conflict he and Regina had over the money, he would have been in a better position to respond carefully and attentively by choosing which aspect of his character to display. Instead, he failed to consider the implications of his actions; they were not sourced in a deliberate practice of good character. As today's man does, Rodion's efforts were based on an attempt that sought to alleviate his own emotional distress rather than seeking to understand Regina's experience. And that is a crucial distinction to make. The truth is Rodion possesses the qualities of an integrated man, though he has yet to adequately develop them. Therefore, Regina's behavior perplexes Rodion, and the complex functions behind her behaviors elude him. To answer the call of her obscured challenges is to dig deep within and summon his unconscious masculine qualities. Although spoken in a language Rodion does not yet understand, Regina's demands will be the necessary destructive force that breaks him free of his useless, outdated skills and beliefs. Rodion must come to a place where he acts with purpose, integrity, and curiosity regarding his character.

Curiosity is perhaps one of the more useful qualities to call to mind when building character. The word curiosity comes from the Latin word *curiosus,* which means careful, diligent, inquiring eagerly, or meddlesome. It is akin to *cura,* which means care.[17] In this context, it is useful to define curiosity as inquisitive thinking, such as exploration, investigation, and learning by observing your own humanity as well as the humanity of others. Exploring innovative ideas and relevant philosophies can add complexity to your character and broaden your personality, making you more attractive. Experimenting with various behavioral practices can better equip you for managing the immensely problematic dilemmas this complex world presents to you.

For some, practicing stoicism could greatly enrich their character when circumstances are chaotic. For others, becoming more attuned to their partner's negative emotional experiences could create more space for an enhanced connection with her. For most men, becoming more playful in their interactions with their partner can make life more enjoyable when situations are taken too seriously, which they often are. Some men benefit from learning to negotiate for their needs more skillfully. Others may benefit from being more emotionally engaging with their partner. However, this is not to suggest that men should neglect their own unique way of processing emotions. It means we connect with our partner on an emotional level that allows us to understand her needs while providing a safe, reliable environment in a way that only the masculine can provide for her to process her emotions fully. This process is the thing that builds strong, masculine character. The intent is to display remarkable traits in the most valuable ways according to the given situation while also maintaining self-respect. At its most fundamental core, it is doing ordinary things extraordinarily well.

Frame

Frame is the mindset we create for ourselves that enables us to overcome objections to achieving an outcome by utilizing particular skills and insights. Frame control is the practice of maintaining a strong, positive frame when getting what we want becomes difficult or is impeded by external forces. Frame is equally vital to improving the quality of your responses as character building. Although the concept of frame is relatively abstract, it must be learned to elevate your masculinity. Frame is the mental structure we create for ourselves to achieve a goal, be it short-term or long-term. When we have a goal—and formulate a plan to achieve that goal—we are preparing to manage barriers and distractions to meeting that goal. Frame allows us to mitigate the circumstances that might cause us to deviate from the plan of achieving that goal.

Our frame is that plan; it is our preparedness to get what we want. Frame control is your ability to create and sustain a formulated plan to achieve an outcome. Learning about and practicing the concept of frame evokes a questioning attitude, which opens our eyes to how novel concepts can be beneficial. And this is useful, for it aids in improving our responses. Frame control can be observed as one displaying his life skills and value as a man, especially in the context of his relationship.

The challenges that come with relationships tend to be undifferentiated in nature, meaning they give rise to two paradoxical experiences and potential outcomes. Such paradoxes involve experiencing these challenges as either barriers and distractions to achieving desired outcomes or steppingstones toward them. It's difficult to know when these challenges serve as barriers or when they serve as steppingstones.

Differentiating these dichotomous experiences requires a strong, positive frame, and the particular skills we use are determined by how we implement frame control. What today's man sees as barriers will be seen by the integrated man as steppingstones.

Rodion & Regina VI

Rodion exhibits a severe lack of frame, which can be observed in how he handled Regina's confrontation about the money. Not only did he not have a good plan for handling this kind of situation, but he also did not have a well-defined goal regarding how he would handle such confrontations. Rodion's weak frame was no match for Regina's frame, which she used to challenge him about the money. He deviated from what should have been done, which was to have a sort of "plan of action" at his disposal, such as simply being assertive and showing good character.

Furthermore, Rodion's lack of frame control prevented him from seeing that the distress did not, in fact, lie with the money issue itself. The real issue hid behind the veil of superficial emotional distress; the distress about the money was a manifestation of a deeper emotional need. Rodion simply failed to detect this. Regina gave Rodion the key to her heart, but that key appeared as a dagger to him, and he responded accordingly. Rodion was not ready to see things as they really were. Rather than seeing her confrontation with him as a steppingstone—a key—Rodion's frame of mind only allowed him to see her challenge as a barrier—a dagger. He failed the test. Again, Regina is speaking an ancient language that Rodion only perceives as annoying and aggressive. But Regina is not willing to slip back down into her proverbial cave and return to her slumber. No, she will only continue to emerge with more ferocity as she calls for the ancient masculine within Rodion to awaken. First, however, he must realize his position in the hierarchy of his own masculine development. Up to now, he does not realize he is at or near the bottom.

The man at the bottom of the hierarchy, fighting for position, will view challenges as barriers; naturally, he will respond to them as such. The bottom of the hierarchy is a precarious and unpredictable place—one wrong move could be the end of you, or, at least, the death of a goal. It is not a matter of being methodical with navigating barriers when near the bottom. In fact, much to his dismay, such navigation requires an extraordinary amount of conscientious effort for today's man. The integrated man is as methodical, yet he is much more proficient in the sense that he does not try to engage in easier challenges. Rather, he strives to become better at doing hard things. It is easy and appropriate to see barriers as steppingstones when things are going quite well for you. Yet, when you have suffered too many hierarchical defeats—and things are going poorly—some challenges literally are barriers and must be responded to as such. This is especially important to know when you are mending your relationship and attempting to transform yourself.

For some, it is clear to them that they are at or near the bottom of the hierarchy. Therefore, they can set their trajectory in an obvious direction. The thing with hierarchies in this context is that when we reach that optimal place at the top, our potential expands even further. This expansion repositions us in the hierarchy. Note that this is an indication that the hierarchy has increased in size, with the epicenter of its growth being where we currently stand. That is, we do not move; rather, it is our potential that has increased, and, by default, our position has changed in reference to the top and bottom. In other words, we are no longer at the top—we are once again a small fish in a big pond. Regardless of where you are in the hierarchy and why you are there, frame is an indispensable pillar you must master before you can climb.

Confidence

Confidence results from becoming proficient at something and being assured of one's abilities and qualities with reliable certainty. It comes as a result of practice. This could be practicing a sport, such as baseball; a philosophy, such as stoicism; a hobby, such as woodworking; or practicing any behavior or way of thinking. Confidence plays a significant role in attraction because it signifies a man's trustworthiness in his own abilities. If a man cannot trust himself, how can he expect anyone else to trust him?

A confident person can often be the only source of assurance in the presence of those who are uncertain of which direction to go. When others are experiencing tremendous uncertainty, being around someone who is self-assured creates a calming effect. People need a proportionate amount of certainty; therefore, any degree of certainty is valuable when they do not have it, even if it is someone else's feeling of certainty.

A person's confidence—combined with assertiveness, character, and frame—displays emotional regulation and mental stability. Everyone experiences chaos in their lives, and oftentimes a person's confidence can inject order into that chaos. When someone emanates an air of confidence and walks into a room full of disorder, it is as though you can feel the chaos dissipating almost instantaneously.

There is something about a person with genuine confidence that can establish peace in the midst of conflict. Winston Churchill was considered by many to be an arrogant man. However, from the perspective of confidence, he was brimming with it. It was this confidence that instilled hope and comfort that Nazi Germany would be defeated and that Britain—along with the rest of the world—would prevail.[18] In the film *Darkest Hour*, Churchill's confident demeanor was portrayed in just this way, as he stood assured in the face of tremendous adversity, and this had a profound effect on those around him.[19] In relationships, responding to your partner with confidence creates an environment of stability and trust, which promotes intimacy. Confidence allows us to be our best because safety and security have been established, which reduces the need to act strictly on survival instincts. When we establish our basic human needs, and do so in order, we can confidently focus on the next level of needs. As a result of establishing safety and security needs, we can then focus on our relationship and intimacy needs.[20] [20]

You cannot have confidence in something you have never done. Confidence must be built and is done so by achieving victories. Confidence is also correlated to serotonin—which is correlated with happiness, well-managed neuroticism, and an overall sense of well-being. Biologically, confidence is the difference between surviving and thriving. From a hierarchical perspective, confidence contributes to achieving dominance, or status, as a way of securing needs and resources. It correlates with stability and growth. In the role of a leader, confidence makes it easier for others to have faith in where they are being led. The integrated man exhibits this quality and tends to draw others into his presence, and those people will follow him to the ends of the earth. Of course, we must have a keen eye for narcissists and those with antisocial personality disorder, for they are masters at feigning empathy and gaining your confidence for darker, more deceptive reasons.

Rodion & Regina VII

Regina's increased emotional distress, as well as her eventual shutting down, is an indication of a rapidly diminishing trust and assurance in Rodion. While he is not entirely without confidence, it seems to elude him when things get to be too much—when it matters most. Rodion's struggles, in this regard, have taken a toll on his confidence. In a way, Regina's trust in him—unbeknownst to both she and Rodion—has been growing smaller for quite some time. Perhaps a more confident Rodion would have been a source of assurance for Regina when she was experiencing uncertainty around her level of safety and security.

Instead, his lack of confidence negatively exacerbated her sense of worry, and the growing sense of instability she carries indicates they are moving away from intimacy. In Rodion's defense, he has never been here before. This is all new to him, after all. Yet, this does not absolve him from the responsibility of practicing assertiveness and good character while maintaining a strong frame, for it is in those pillars that confidence is most optimally gained. Developing his unconscious masculine aspect does not come easy. Awakening the ancient masculine within is grueling.

At the core, today's man experiences neuroticism and a severe lack of confidence and assertiveness in at least one or two aspects of their lives—most often, regarding their relationships with women. The antidote to this is to behave in ways indicative of a more confident version of himself.

When it comes to relationships with women, men are judged in large part by their level of confidence. Women have a biological proclivity to gauge a man's potential to fulfill the role of her mate—the self-assurance in his own abilities carries an enormous amount of weight regarding a woman's assessment of his character. She wants to know if he is fit for the job. If he is not confident, then she cannot conclude with any certainty that he can reliably meet her needs.

Connection and Responsible Leadership

Seek to be emotionally reliable for your partner and trustworthy with her vulnerability. Understanding this with greater depth is important, for the two aspects of relationships are the bases on which today's man can create a more integrated version of himself. The word emotional refers to one's emotions or the notion of being affected by emotions. Reliability is the characteristic of being safe and dependable and behaving so in a consistent manner. Emotional reliability is being consistently safe and dependable in emotional situations and with the emotions of others. Improving your sensitivity and responsiveness to others' deeper emotional needs must be one of your primary goals as you work to transcend into a more remarkable version of yourself.

The call to improve your sensitivity does not indicate that you are completely insensitive to others' needs, but that there is value in gaining a more nuanced understanding of those needs. Men are typically lower in agreeableness, which is the personality trait that drives people to tend to others' needs more than their own.[21][22] People lower in agreeableness do not have as much of a disposition to do so—yet they do tend to negotiate well for their own needs.[23] Men are also typically lower in neuroticism,[24][25] the personality trait that largely determines the sensitivity and reactivity to pain and discomfort.

Men who are on the lower ends of agreeableness and neuroticism are generally not naturally oriented to their partner's emotional needs, especially as it pertains to pain and discomfort. These men have a limited proclivity to detect another person's unmet needs and their struggles to meet them, causing the appearance of insensitivity. Understanding your personality will be especially helpful when assessing your partner type.

While most men are lower in agreeableness and neuroticism, plenty of men are relatively high in these personality traits. This might be suggestive of traits of the so-called nice guy. Men who are higher in agreeableness or neuroticism tend to experience their partner's emotional distress differently. Agreeable men may be more attuned to their partner's emotional needs. Yet, they often take their partner's negative emotional experiences too personally and fall into the trap of allowing this to induce too much emotional distress in themselves. This leads to feelings of inadequacy or inferiority. Taking on too much of your partner's emotional distress can easily result in your needs being neglected, which will lead to your own unbearable emotional turmoil.

Men who are high in neuroticism have the proclivity to be sensitive and reactive to their partner's emotional pain and discomfort—or the potential for it. This translates to a man shutting down when he senses the onset of her emotional distress or having a volatile reaction when her emotional distress occurs in full effect. While being sensitive and reactive to your partner's emotional distress is necessary, being too sensitive and reactive to it will cause you to be volatile and emotionally unreliable.

Rodion & Regina VIII

For all intents and purposes, it is only in the past several months that Rodion has become so ill-equipped to navigate Regina's emotional distress. Up until then, he appeared to be optimally matched for her emotional experiences, including her emotional distress. It is confusing trying to assess Rodion's personality here. Is he lower in agreeableness than we initially thought? Or is he higher in neuroticism than we first believed? One might say his personality changed, and he could no longer respond well to her distress. Although personality doesn't change, what can be said is that his circumstances changed, and he was no longer optimally matched for his current environment. As the relationship has evolved, so have Regina and Rodion.

Research shows that as "human capacities, needs, and activities change across the life span, relationships change as well."[26] With growth and change come new aspects of ourselves, some of which may present varying degrees of compatibility—or incompatibility—with our partner. This new environment, created by the evolution of their relationship, contained obstacles to Rodion's own emerging problems with which his personality was not equipped. Coupled with Regina's new problems—likely from her own emerging needs and her recent distress and skepticism of him—Rodion was declining in his ability to navigate the relationship.

There is a range of circumstances or problems with which our personality is well suited. When we encounter anomalies—or problems outside that range with which we are unfamiliar—our personality may not serve us well.

Therefore, we can assume that Rodion's personality finally meets its match, so to speak. This was, in all probability, inevitable, for long-term relationships have a way of exposing our character over time, for better or worse.

If it is the case that Rodion is low in agreeableness, he will benefit from practicing more compassion and considering her needs more. This would serve to provide an optimal environment in which Regina's needs could be met, reducing the emotional distress in the relationship. This would make resolving his emerging problems a more manageable task. If he is not low in agreeableness, he should learn to meet his own needs with more efficiency than he currently does. He would then be less frustrated about his own lacking needs and more confident with addressing Regina's.

If it is the case that Rodion is low in neuroticism, it is likely that he does not have a well-developed sensitivity to Regina's pain and discomfort. Without realizing there are wounds to tend to, he will miss the mark. His blindness to Regina's pain means his experience will be that there is nothing wrong. Such a point of view often leads to moral contempt and resentment on the part of the one whose needs are going unmet, both of which are quite detrimental to relationships.

If Rodion is high in neuroticism, he detects Regina's pain and discomfort, although he reacts in fear and distress. The problem here is there is that the sensitivity and reactivity tend to be disproportionate to the actual degree of pain and discomfort. That is, Rodion would take on a view of her pain that is too severe for him to be confident with managing. He would also believe that she cannot sufficiently cope with the pain and discomfort and he would overly tend to her, robbing her of the opportunity to develop coping skills for herself. This is a common problem with men, although often too obscure to easily identify. In this case, Rodion would become overwhelmed with her pain and discomfort; it would take up the majority of his field of view, and he would respond as such. If he is high in neuroticism, Rodion would need to learn skills for stepping back from the pain and discomfort enough to gain more of an objective and manageable view. On the other hand, if he is low in this trait, he would need to make a conscious effort to identify the pain and discomfort that underlies her behaviors.

Perceiving your partner's emotional state more accurately gives you incredible insight into choosing a response that leads to a better connection. Connecting with your partner involves understanding her in ways you never experienced—and doing so in ways no one else has—will elevate that connection to unprecedented levels. This is true when it comes to your partner's feminine nature. Your partner will experience emotional distress in her life; it is an ineradicable part of her.

Weathering these emotional storms enables you to create an environment conducive to intimate connections. There is something to be said about a man who can take on emotionally distressing situations and transform them into something meaningful. We become emotionally reliable and trustworthy for a woman to process the emotional gravity of her experiences in an optimal place—one in which her femininity is embraced and supported.

Creating harmonious connections calls upon your assertiveness, character, frame control, and confidence, and creating such connections with your partner gives you a chance to display your qualities as a man. Responsibly tending to her emotional needs sets you apart from other men in her eyes. More importantly, it shows you how attuned you are with your masculinity, and as this is reflected in you, it will lead to a greater sense of self.

To reach a place of harmonious connections, you must be a responsible leader, creating ways to get what both you and your partner want. Responsible leadership is about taking corrective actions to make things work in the most wholesome and meaningful ways. It is about taking the initiative to do what needs to be done. Responsible leadership is also about enabling people to do what they are best at and valuing their capacity to do a good job. Being a responsible leader in your relationship—and cultivating a harmonious connection—reveals your worth to your partner, but, more importantly, it reveals your worth to yourself.

Self-Worth

As a man, self-worth is about valuing our intrinsic worth and the gifts we give the world as well as living out a life that is sourced in a deeply rooted sense of self. In our quest to become an integrated man, we have a particular mindset regarding what it takes to be one. We set out to achieve our goals by behaving in ways that move us toward that goal. We therefore must practice valuable behaviors that drive us closer to being that man. Such displays of value also serve to sustain our self-worth. Looking at what personal struggles you have previously overcome throughout your journey provides insight into your self-worth. The general experience of gaining some degree of mastery over previously encountered adversities gives you confidence to do so once more. The success you achieve on your journey, and the obstacles you overcome, will determine the contextually relevant behaviors you must display. This indicates your self-worth by showing that you can transform difficult circumstances into meaningful experiences.

Experiencing failure is not an indication of low self-worth. Failure will happen. It is a necessary, ineradicable part of life. What determines your self-worth as a man is the quality of your responses to those failures. The value you display when you encounter challenges is a measure of your self-worth—at least at that moment. When you make a mistake, your self-worth can be redeemed by taking responsibility for them, enabling you to atone for your shortcomings.

It is in our redemption that we are most able to showcase our best qualities. This aspect of course-correcting suggests that it is also important to recognize what you do well so that you may continue doing well.

Identifying the behaviors—and the function of them—enables us to bring about positive, rewarding experiences more deliberately. By understanding our own behaviors, we gain insights into controlling our lives that we would otherwise never attain. Fortifying and implementing our process of acting deliberately reinforces confidence and broadens our perspectives, which are qualities of an integrated man. This is positive reinforcement.

The Essence of the Masculine in Relation to the Feminine

Regina serves as a barometer that reflects changes with Rodion, especially whether he is moving toward his potential. This can be observed in her actions in relation to him. If Rodion is moving toward his potential, he experiences love and appreciation from Regina. If he moves away from his potential, he experiences challenges and tension with her. Neither of these experiences is a bad thing; they are gifts. The challenges and tension Rodion experiences with Regina when he is moving away from his potential means that she has high standards and expectations for him, which means she believes in him. If Regina values herself enough, she will challenge Rodion relentlessly and do so with an unforgettable fierceness. The key to Rodion's success in the relationship is to respond to such challenges with his most magnificent self. The key to Regina's success in the relationship is to value herself enough to not settle for anything less than him giving her his most magnificent self.

Chapter Four

Partner Types

Rodion & Regina IX

Long-term relationships are fluid and ever-changing in many respects. The man and woman Rodion and Regina were when they first met have changed throughout their young relationship. Their earlier identities have progressed over the years. This is an indication of normal relationship development, for we commit to long-term relationships primarily for who we could be—not just who we currently are.

By now, there are many ways in which they both have changed. Although many of these changes are positive, some of these changes have been negative in that they have exposed disparities in their personalities and how they navigate them. That is, ares of incompatibilities that were once unknown have surfaced. Some of the negative changes happened subtly—unbeknownst to Rodion—which have impaired his relationship skills. These changes undermine who he is and with what he is skillful.

It is possible that he has not noticed the subtle changes in how Regina responds to his jokes. He may have overlooked the way she responds to his flattery, not knowing that the frequency of his flattery has become erratic, causing an unconscious skepticism toward the inconsistent nature of his attention to her. However, some of these negative changes are more obvious.

There are many ways in which his negative changes have altered his connection. The way things are going, the contentious money issue could soon be considered a minimal source of discord in their relationship— low hanging fruit, so to speak. He and Regina argue more frequently than ever. The fights cause more distance, and they aren't as close as they used to be.

At this rate, they are headed toward the place they swore they would never be—in a disconnected relationship. In the past, they have been appalled by stories within their social network of failing relationships that entailed couples sleeping in different bedrooms—or even having affairs. They swore they would never allow themselves to get to that point. Yet, here they are, staring down the barrel of a failing marriage. It could well be the case that Rodion and Regina's sex life is beginning to suffer. Little to no sex could be a real issue, which is often an accurate indicator of an unhealthy marriage.

The life Rodion arranged for himself no longer seems to fit what he believes is good for him. Underneath, he has been losing control of his happiness, and the joy life used to bring him is now scarce. Things are no longer going his way, and something needs to change.

In Rodion's hidden thoughts, ending the relationship seems to be a less painful direction than figuring out how to conquer this indomitable mountain of challenges—it is the beastly dragon that stands between him and who he could be. The dragon is that terrible chaos of the things we fear and despise, which is the place where he will find the truth he needs, even though it is filthy. The problem is that he is unconsciously avoiding his inadequacies and the terrible things of which he is capable, which he must confront if he is to have real control over himself. Rodion is unaware of this, let alone does he comprehend it. Yet, he gets the feeling that he must face his relationship problems head-on if he is to emerge with something valuable.

Fortunately, Rodion is more inclined to see the relationship through. He is determined to figure it out, even though he does not know what else he can do.

People can usually become more effective with cultivating a harmonious relationship, even if they feel they've done all they can do. That is not to say that ending a marriage is never the best option. Ending relationships might be reasonable under particular circumstances, but it is usually messy. Before you can walk away in good conscience, you must know for certain that you have done all you can do.

This means that you must strive to improve yourself as a man. Improving yourself requires that you look within to assess your shortcomings and why you need to change. In the context of a relationship, taking an inventory of who you are as a partner is key to unlearning unhealthy habits and creating space to adopt healthier habits.

Our quality as men is profoundly reflected in our intimate relationships. As today's man strives to transcend his current sense of self into a more remarkable version, it is helpful to determine his baseline sense of self. As you read about the different partner types, listen for clues about yourself to gain insight into where you fall in this matrix.

There are three types of partners: *former alpha, nice guy, and unprincipled leader.* Few men fall solely into a single partner type. Most men meet criteria for at least two partner types, and some meet criteria for all three. However, most men can easily identify one of the three partner types as the more prominent. This crucial first step of identifying your partner type requires that you be willing to take an open, honest look at who you are as a man. Judge yourself fairly and remain as truthful as you can.

You might ask trusted friends for their opinions of you based on the descriptions of each partner type. Take great care if you decide to ask your significant other for her opinion on this, for this will likely backfire at this point in the process. You do not want to die on this hill.

This chapter does not serve as a personality assessment. As mentioned previously, you are encouraged to visit understandmyself.com to take the personality assessment offered there. This book is not intended to reinvent the wheel with such an area of study, especially when there is one as empirically valid as the one referred to here (although this book may add useful anecdotal observations relevant to the study of personality psychology). The partner types described in this book serve more as archetypes that help illuminate what our experiences and behaviors can be attributed to so that we may improve ourselves with great clarity.

The Big Five Aspects Scale provides detail into our traits and the underlying aspects of them. However, to incorporate them into the specialized, abstract nature of the subject of this book, it is useful to have a set of identifiable examples that are comprehensible and relatable. The partner types described here attempt to clarify the abstract concepts in this book while making the rather vast amount of detailed information much more manageable.

These descriptions serve as an intermediary between the abstract, vague ideas and the innumerable nuances of the specific implementable actions required to improve yourself in the context of your relationship.

Partner Types Explained

The use of the word *alpha* often carries a negative connotation with people. However, it is used here because the term alpha pertains to dominant men and is universally understood to represent men who are powerful, socially superior, fit, funny, outcome independent, persuasive, callous, ruthless, aggressive, and predatory (although not necessarily pathological in nature). Another reason for its use here is that it is a word men can connect with while not requiring extensive research-based knowledge on the word. Instead, they can infer its general meaning based on the contextual significance it holds within this book. Its use here is concerned with helping men understand themselves deeply and in a way that allows them to begin a transformation.

The same goes for the use of the term *beta*. Although a less universally understood word, it represents men who are sensitive, romantic, value honor, dignity, and friendliness, and who provide more of an emotional connection. Beta also refers to "nice guys" and pushovers. It seems to be the case that people who identify with one of these two terms hold some measure of disdain for the other type. There are levels of debate between the value that these terms hold in relation to each other as well as their collective meaning overall. This book does not intend to be an extension of that argument. It intends to use terminology that is already in the common vernacular.

From a personality perspective, alpha traits are somewhat at odds with the nurturing aspects of the trait agreeableness. They align with the aspect of the trait extraversion, known as assertiveness. A third, and perhaps less obvious observation, is that the term alpha is analogous with being on the low end of the trait neuroticism. Men score lower than women in agreeableness and neuroticism while usually scoring higher than women in assertiveness.[27]

Experts suggest that your personality does not change much at all, having only minimal changes over long periods of time as we age. Personality traits are stable patterns of emotion, motivation, cognition, and behavior, in response to particular environmental stimuli consistent over time.[28]

This notion leaves some unanswered questions of what explains changes in the behaviors of men in long-term relationships. Just as we have conceptualized Rodion's personality in the last chapter, it is altogether useful to understand yourself in the context of your environments, for they provide critical reflections of your personality regarding what you are well-suited for and for what you are not. You were once able to navigate and overcome the challenges of relationships; however, you now experience great difficulty with those same challenges.

Yet, today's man must not despair. Such contrasting experiences provide a broader understanding necessary for becoming an integrated man. In this kind of understanding, we can best set our trajectory regarding our personal growth and how we add value to the world.

What seems like a shift that can only produce detriment can, in fact, be used to revolutionize yourself and your relationship. If your temperament is more aligned with alpha traits that produce your ability to negotiate for yourself, establish social status, and maintain outcome independence, yet you no longer display these traits effectively, it is not indicative of a shift in personality traits. Rather, it is an indication that you are not behaving in accordance with your own personality and that you need to broaden particular personality traits. Furthermore, it could also indicate a need to improve the circumstances of your current relationship environment.

Not understanding your personality can have negative implications. Unexplored aspects of ourselves can lead to moral contempt on the part of our significant other. We often see things dichotomously—or as black or white—especially with morality. Our personalities shape how we see and handle the complexities of the world, so it's hard to comprehend others who act differently due to varying personality traits.

For example, agreeable people may not get why disagreeable people prioritize themselves. This can lead to cognitive dissonance and assuming contempt instead of being open to the good in the personality in the other.

To ease the cognitive dissonance caused by such false dichotomies, we tend to moralize the other person's behaviors. This type of thinking can harm us when we arbitrarily judge the actions of others without first acknowledging the faults of our own thinking and actions while considering the circumstances with which we might be ill-suited. Just because it doesn't make sense to us doesn't necessarily mean that people's actions lack a moral foundation.

People high in agreeableness, which is composed of compassion and politeness, are interested in others' needs and problems.[29] They are sympathetic and generous with their time, and they are more likely to take others' interests into account. They have respect for authority. They are not pushy or insulting and are careful with their words. If your temperament is more naturally aligned with beta traits that drive your ability to be sensitive, romantic, and friendly, having a morally black and white view of your behaviors can betray you in ways that differ from how they do an alpha male.

Failing to display behaviors and characteristics that lie outside your range of each trait indicates a neglect to broaden your personality traits, which entraps you into a narrow and costly methodology of managing relationships. Refusing to explore behaviors and characteristics outside of your natural temperament will catch up with you. That is, with overly narrow personality traits, you can find yourself in too many environments that are too difficult to traverse.

We can see this with Rodion as he is declining in his ability to respond well to the challenges that come with the evolution of his relationship with Regina. When both his and Regina's needs evolved, it brought new circumstances that Rodion was not equipped to manage. As time went on, he became more overwhelmed and lost regarding how to recover himself and his relationship.

In general, he knew he wanted a successful relationship with Regina. And that is good, if only for the fact that he at least had an aim. But as the hierarchy of his life and marriage expand, his aim must become truer. Yet, when it comes to the implementable actions it would take to get there, he has become paralyzed by the limitless choices of the innumerable forks in the road.

Rodion must get an idea of what kind of partner he is so he may begin narrowing the vast amount of actions to a manageable degree, which will make the direction he must go less vague.

The following types of partners highlight why you have found yourself in need of a drastic improvement.

The Former Alpha

If today's man is a former alpha, he was once able to demonstrate alpha traits, and he has become either an overly apologetic partner, an angry, frustrated, and defensive partner, or a passive partner who often gives the cold shoulder when conflict is too intense and difficult. Initially, he displayed alpha traits that attracted his partner to him. He carried himself with genuine confidence and was unflappable. He emanated an air of stability wherever he went. Now, he is indecisive, which leaves his stability in doubt. He used to be independent and goal-oriented, yet he is now unable to maintain frame control with his partner. He seems to wake up each day feeling a bit lost. Where he once provided an endless sense of security for his partner, he now overreacts to her slightest distress.

As a former alpha, you have likely experienced moments of confidence, dominance, and standing tall. Your risk-taking behavior may have allowed you to climb the hierarchy of your own life and position yourself to achieve your goals. You valued yourself too much to engage in petty drama and were in pursuit of bigger things. You were able to remain calm under pressure, needed little external validation, and displayed the value of perseverance. While these traits may have been subdued due to a detrimental change in your environment or a failure to adapt your personality, they are not absent. Occasionally, you may still exhibit these traits, albeit to a lesser extent.

However, the inconsistent nature of your behavior can lead to doubt and skepticism from those around you, including your partner. If you are unreliable, your partner cannot feel safe with you, and your masculinity may regress. Remember that when you invite someone to walk with you on your path in life, you assume responsibility for their well-being. Your inconsistency greatly diminishes the optimal place you are charged with providing for your partner, which is neglectful and irresponsible.

In the context of relationships, alpha traits alone will not suffice. So-called beta traits have their place, too. Beta traits include sensitivity and romance, enabling betas to provide more of an emotional connection than alphas.

Broadening your personality traits allows you to utilize both your alpha and beta traits, improving your responses to your partner. As a former alpha, you may have had some realization that exhibiting alpha traits may have gotten you the girl, but they weren't going to keep her. In your attempts to be an excellent long-term partner, you moved away from your alpha traits, hoping a decreased prevalence of them would make you appear to be a good, committed man for your partner.

Although showing commitment in a relationship is necessary, doing so at the expense of your alpha traits dismisses an essential part of you, one that provides evidence to your partner that you are fit for the job of providing particular needs of hers. This fluctuation reflects a simpleminded attitude toward masculinity.

Naturally, today's man must learn emotional nuance if he is to connect with his partner in a wholesome manner. When you dismiss such a major aspect of your personality, you don't achieve balance. Rather, beta behaviors become your default, which leads to an unbalanced sense of self. It would be best to learn to operate from both alpha and beta traits simultaneously. It might be the case that for men to mature in their masculinity, they must first integrate both the alpha and beta persona.

Operating from a defaulted sense of self cannot lead to a greater sense of purpose. You resist exhibiting alpha traits in fear of pushing your partner away. This is an avoidance-based motivation, not a rewards-based motivation. The misstep here is ignoring your capacity to lead through charisma and confidence.

Neglecting alpha traits and defaulting to exhibiting beta traits is all or nothing thinking. It is lazy and uncreative. It would be best if you learned to honor your alpha traits while practicing beta traits, especially when they seem to contradict each other. We often fail to see how two opposing ideas can work together cohesively.

If we give a valiant effort, we may be surprised with how well we can integrate polar opposite traits. We begin displaying a more remarkable version of ourselves when we achieve this. More profoundly, those with whom we interact become the beneficiaries of the value we bring.

The idea of behavior modification is to replace negative behaviors with positive behaviors. If you remove a negative behavior without purposefully replacing it with positive behavior, the void left by its displacement will fill itself with yet another negative behavior. For the former alpha, this may be difficult to comprehend.

You might argue that you did, in fact, replace negative behaviors with positive behaviors by becoming more thoughtful and sensitive. You replaced your old alpha behaviors with behaviors indicative of a good partner, or a nice guy, by acting on your beta traits. The fallacy with this is that alpha behaviors were, by default, looked at as negative behaviors. This dichotomous, morally black and white view of such traits blinds us to the virtues of alpha traits, leaving only the faults of alpha traits in view. When we fail to understand the virtues of alpha traits, we risk labeling them as immoral. And this is an incomplete view, for all traits contain faults and virtues. Morality does not lie in alpha traits in and of themselves. Instead, morality lies in how we utilize alpha traits.

The alpha behaviors you sought to extinguish had nothing to do with neglecting your partner's emotional connection nor your sensitivity to her feminine nature. This is a common mistake with men. They tend to assess the problem as alpha behaviors rather than the particular misuses of them. These men often abandon alpha traits for more beta traits; neglect social skills, assertiveness, strength, and providing assurance through confidence; or move from one end of the spectrum to the other.

There is a possible contradiction here, for we have learned that our personality does not change. The real problem is by attempting to shift our personality—neglecting alpha traits in this example—the former alpha strips himself of the skills that come naturally to him for navigating the world. The key is balance. Rather than exchanging one set of traits for another—or attempting to—the goal is to broaden ourselves to the point where we encompass all traits. We must exhibit both alpha traits and beta traits appropriately.

When the pendulum swings from alpha traits to beta traits without creating a more sustainable ebb and flow, your behavior and mood will appear chaotic. A man's own chaos is not an optimal place for his partner to express her femininity.

Men are confused and frustrated when their efforts to change yield no positive results or, worse, backfire, causing more disconnect in the relationship. You thought you were doing the right thing. You thought you were doing what she wanted, but the connection worsened. Do not abandon any of your traits. Instead, learn how to integrate all of them into your frame of mind in a way that makes you more psychologically well-rounded in your relationship.

From a personality perspective, the former alpha is a disagreeable man who has committed two transgressions: neglecting to broaden himself and changing his circumstances. The first transgression is that he unwittingly abandoned his natural disposition of being on the low end of the trait agreeableness (negotiation for self) while failing to master the nuances held in the high end of the trait (nurturance and compassion).

He neglected to maximize the virtues and minimize the faults of disagreeableness. Little did he know that he was trying to be someone he is not by abandoning those faults and virtues. He cannot outrun his temperament. An attempt to do so will leave that aspect of himself to come out unconsciously.

This unconscious manifestation will usually occur as faults rather than virtues. The irony with the former alpha is that, because he unconsciously declared that low agreeableness holds nothing but fault. He tried to move away from that aspect of himself to become more agreeable in an attempt to keep his partner.

In other words, the problem is that his behaviors are now sourced in the faults that come with both ends of the agreeableness spectrum. But what is the greater sin here? Is it to fail to have more virtues than faults with his low agreeableness, or is it a failure to adapt to the world of compassion and nurturance? Perhaps, it is the former. If we are not well established in our personality, how can we expect to establish ourselves in an area more difficult to master than our own temperament? While his efforts to connect emotionally is important and well-intentioned, the former alpha must first reconnect with his natural disposition of low agreeableness.

The latter transgression is about the failure to adapt to or change his circumstances. This is quite the predicament because of the additional barriers that come with differences in personalities with other people. Changes are disruptive and usually met with resistance. The notion of changing his circumstances in his marriage might bring an acute awareness to the possibility that his partner might be resistant to them and possibly leave the relationship. After all, relationships come with terms and conditions, and relationship changes are often seen as violations of them. Yet, this view assumes the worst and only the worst.

While it is possible that his partner could leave, there are many other potential outcomes that are contingent on what changes he makes. Even the subtlest of changes can come with resistance and disruption, but it is more important that our environments are optimally matched for our personality if we are to stabilize the chaos in our relationships. We must push past this resistance to change, leaning beyond the edge of fear and discomfort, constantly; in everything we do.[30]

Suppose today's man remains positioned in an environment unsuitable for his personality. In that case, he will never be able to reach his full potential, making it impossible to develop a sense of purpose and, inevitably, this will impede the process of integration. Of course, his partner has the same need for an optimally matched environment, too. Therefore, any proposed changes to modifying the environment (relationship) and its conditions (boundaries) must be agreed upon in a way that both of them can sufficiently have their needs met.

The Nice Guy

The thought of being this type of partner may be a hard pill to swallow for today's man. He differs from the former alpha in that he has been rather agreeable, and the lack of alpha behaviors has caught up with him. As a nice guy, you strove to be unlike other men, particularly those you perceived as self-seeking.

You focused on being a good, upstanding person in a world where men seemed to mistreat women. You worked hard not to be a jerk. This has served you well in many aspects, yet you fall short of your relationship goals.

How can this be? The nice guy often struggles to understand why his strategies are ineffective, yet he continues to repeat those same failed methods. All behavior serves a purpose; hence we repeat the behaviors that seem to work for us. In many cases, such behaviors worked for us until life became too complex for them.

Yet, even when our behaviors are not working, we find it difficult to change them. As with most problems with which we are unfamiliar, we tend to take on dichotomous views of the solution. Typically, these views are looked at in general categories, such as good and bad.

Because our behaviors are largely driven by our personality and the values that are sourced in them, our views conclude that one way of behavior is good and the other way is bad. Naturally, we believe our way of perceiving and doing things is the right way. Therefore, any other way must be wrong. Hence, as we look to change our behaviors, we are blind to other alternative good ways because our biases cause us to only see what confirms our initial position. And this makes it difficult to see how these traits can cause problems in relationships.

Early on, the nice guy intended to sweep some girl off her feet and show other men how to treat a girl. Yet, he often found himself in the dreaded "friend zone" with women, and he would frame it as though he didn't want anything more than a friendship with her in the first place.

Regardless, this caused unnecessary suffering. Identifying with these experiences indicates that you are, in fact, similar to those men who come across as overtly self-seeking, only you were covertly self-seeking. This is why it is a hard pill to swallow—at least the other guys were honest.

Nice guy traits include honor, dignity, friendliness, and whatever you thought was admirable. These traits are rooted in a deep part of the unconscious from which all things are sourced. Yet, the nice guy will only extract the parts of those traits that fit his personality. That is, he takes from it a partial meaning and tries to make it do everything for him—a one-size-fits-all approach. This could be indicative of low conscientiousness—or the failure to broaden that trait. These incomplete abstractions from the whole leave a man ill-equipped for his relationship challenges. He has half the truth; therefore, he can only live half-truths. He is, in essence, a naive deceiver and dishonest.

Understand, this is not about casting him in an immoral light. He is not entirely to blame here. After all, it is difficult to outrun our personality. However, we do have the capacity to develop aspects of ourselves not yet realized. We are born undifferentiated. Therefore, regarding those undifferentiated aspects of ourselves, our personalities lead us to a partial abstraction of human traits as a whole, and this produces an ideological frame of mind that leads to dead-end paths.

Abstracting a partial truth from the whole—or neglecting it—corrupts it. When those deeper aspects of ourselves have been differentiated, we can make them work for us on a conscious level more cohesively, which will produce more wholesome outcomes. That it, the nice guy has not differentiated his principles.

Although principles such as honor and dignity are deemed valuable by him, they alone will not suffice as strategies to navigate relationships successfully. Therefore, the fact that the nice guy places value on a principle—then declares that it is good—is arbitrary and incomplete. There are times when some principles are not applicable and even counterproductive. The nice guy arbitrarily declares that particular principles are good and applicable, neglecting to understand that it is the application itself that determines the goodness of the outcomes. Such a declaration moves him further away from the potential truths that lie in the opposing side of his traits.

As a result, the nice guy cannot make honor and dignity work for him when it matters most. If you are the nice guy type, it was likely that you eventually got into a relationship through happenstance. It is also likely that you saw her as the prize and that you hit the jackpot. It is highly probable that you came into her life at an opportunistic time and were able to win her over due to underlying circumstances, of which, in reality, you had no clue. This is not to say there was no genuine attraction.

Still, if today's man is going to break from his dysfunctional approach to life, he must look at all potential aspects that contribute to his relationship's demise or success. So, you felt like you had hit the jackpot, and now you are often frustrated with your connection with her. But it is your lack of assertiveness or ability to negotiate for your needs that causes this frustration.

Tragically, you sacrifice your self-respect in your attempts to keep from losing your partner. You give up aspects of your life that are valuable to you to appease her, and even that doesn't seem to be enough. She might even seem selfish and ungrateful at times. You end up blaming yourself, and your solution is to be nicer to her, which fails to achieve your desired outcomes. In fact, she might respect you less.

Seeing yourself in the description of this partner type can be painful. Cognitive dissonance can set in as you encounter the novelty of the perspectives discussed in this section. The struggle to understand why you desperately need to improve yourself when you are already noble and admirable contributes to that cognitive dissonance. You have worked diligently to carry yourself with a great deal of morality and selflessness. It is even more difficult to understand how your morals can inadvertently lead you to failure.

It doesn't seem to compute that your inflexible morality can blind you to the deeper, underlying principles of navigating relationships that lead to success. Overcoming this morally fixed sense of self requires that you gain a deeper understanding of the difference between morals and principles. To illustrate, look at how morality often leads people to steer clear of self-praise because they strive to be humble and avoid coming across as boastful and arrogant.

However, based on the principles of positive reinforcement, self-praise can encourage us to continue particular behaviors that lead toward the greater good, such as a harmonious connection with our partner. If we act based on the oft-misunderstood morals of humility, we fail to positively reinforce the behaviors necessary for achieving our goals by preventing us from patting ourselves on the back.

Our brain's reward system plays a vital role in our behavior patterns. When we do well, we must acknowledge it to ourselves—consciously or unconsciously—before we can feel good about it. And we need to feel good about moving toward our goals. This inspires us to continue doing the things necessary to reach them.

Part of the nice guy's problem is that he feigns humbleness. He wrongfully understands humbleness as downplaying qualities, especially ones he naively deems immoral. Humility is not about downplaying your qualities; it is about acknowledging them without acting as though you deserve special treatment because of them. The nice guy believes that he will be viewed as noble and selfless by emanating an air of moral superiority. In the long run, this prevents him from displaying true, genuine confidence, an indispensable quality of the integrated man. And this is paramount to comprehend!

You must understand that your partner possesses a degree of healthy skepticism of you, which partly serves to gauge your confidence and how much she can trust you. By acknowledging your worth and value as a man, you position yourself to experience the necessary victories that build confidence.

Where morality can cultivate many positive qualities in a man, principles guide him toward manifesting those qualities in his relationships. At best, failing to figure out how to exhibit these two paradoxical ideas of morality and principles leads to mediocre relationships. At worst, they may lead to its demise.

Finding yourself as a nice guy can be an unpleasant awakening. Small wonder that denial often creeps in—even after one believes he has accepted this unpleasant truth about himself. The description of the nice guy has been rather unvarnished up to this point. We must once again turn to personality to understand this partner type. The nice guy tends to fall on the higher end of agreeableness. He, too, has committed transgressions regarding his development.

The nice guy did not expect that his partner's feminine challenges would confuse him as to why his noble ways are not eliciting from her more love for him. He does not realize that his noble ways are incomplete and that he has failed to make her feel safe in the most important ways, which would elicit more love and appreciation for him.

This confusion is deeply rooted in an insecure sense of self. However, his glaring transgression is in his unwillingness to broaden his personality so that he may better understand his partner in this regard. The nice guy tends to exhibit high agreeableness, high neuroticism, and low assertiveness. However, the degree of these will vary for different nice guys. While it could be considered that being high in agreeableness equates to negotiating for other people's needs, there are multiple variables at play here.

One might assume that because they are inherently driven to put others' needs before their own, they are, by default, good at advocating for the needs of others. The successful advocacy of other people's needs relies on two variables: the trait neuroticism and the aspect of extraversion called assertiveness. Neuroticism is the sensitivity and reactivity to pain and discomfort, or the potential for them, to occur. It is the experience of negative emotions.

Generally speaking, neuroticism is not necessarily projected in any specific direction; its direction in this regard is determined by the trait agreeableness. It seems to be the case that the more agreeable a person is, the more their neuroticism will be directed toward the pain and discomfort of others. Whereas those low in agreeableness will find that their neuroticism tends to be directed toward themselves.

This suggests that if the nice guy is rather agreeable, his neuroticism will be directed toward his partner's pain and discomfort. There are two diametrically opposed experiences that his partner could undergo as a result of this. She could simply feel "tended to" or she could feel skepticism about his reasons for tending to her (such as to alleviate his own emotional distress rather than hers) and his ability to stand up for himself, which would have implications on his capacity to make her feel safe.

This brings us toward the aspect of assertiveness. Assertiveness, in this context, generally means effectively advocating for needs, be it your own or your partner's. Agreeableness and assertiveness are an optimal combination (if neuroticism is not too high) for making your partner feel tended to in a way that makes her feel safe.

However, suppose it is the case that he is low in neuroticism. In that case, it may cause him to be insensitive to her negative emotional experiences, resulting in failing to see the needs that require attention. In order that he may tend to her wholeheartedly, he must broaden his trait of neuroticism to either be more sensitive and reactive to her pain and discomfort or in a way that ensures it is truly about her and not to alleviate his own emotional distress.

Suppose the nice guy is rather high in neuroticism. In that case, he must focus on broadening that trait to be less sensitive and reactive to her pain and discomfort to see the whole of the situation so that he may better provide for her. If it is the case that he is agreeable and low in neuroticism, yet also low in assertiveness, he must seek to broaden his assertiveness with a sense of urgency. Then he must evaluate the need to broaden his neuroticism trait.

If the nice guy is low (or even average) in agreeableness, he is likely to be found to have low assertiveness. While neuroticism must be evaluated here, it is a secondary concern when assertiveness is low. Passivity is a common characteristic of nice guys. They often experience the most frustration of all nice guys because of their severe inability to be open with what they need and want.

As with the four pillars, assertiveness must be ensured before other traits and qualities can be optimized. The nice guy is deficient in having his needs met and in his capacity to provide a safe and optimal environment for his partner. He is notably defined by a high baseline of frustration. And frustrated men are not good leaders!

The Unprincipled Leader

An unprincipled leader is a man who, early in life, observed men who seemed to have a command of their relationship. This partner type took this idea and ran with it in their own relationship. If he had questioned what this meant—by differentiating it—he would have, perhaps, recognized the nuances of such a man's command. He would have seen that such a man's personality was broadened by his life experiences and guided by principles he learned through his successes and failures.

Nevertheless, the unprincipled leader did not and does question the nuances of what afforded that man to lead his relationship thoughtfully. He mastered few, if any, valuable relationship skills and never reached his leadership potential. Instead, he is careless and inattentive with his approach to being the 'man of the house'. The unprincipled leader can be the former alpha or the nice guy, although likely the former.

Yet, what sets him apart is that his attempts to establish himself as a leader is too often driven by ego. This does not evoke genuine love and respect from his partner. His plan to lead is not properly designed. This may result from having built confidence without considering its implications on his relationship. In other words, his confidence serves *him* well; yet he does not consider how his confidence should benefit his *partner*.

Instead, his self-seeking confidence denies her the promise of harmony and intimacy. This type of partner struggles to see his shortcomings, usually deferring blame and fault to others rather than taking responsible actions to improve himself. Denial and ego are two of the problematic issues to overcome for him. Denial is a defense mechanism with which one fails to acknowledge and accept difficult truths and make himself conscious of them. Denial is not knowing how fallacious one's thinking and understanding are of his current circumstances.

If you believe you fall into this type, you will find that you tend to operate from an authoritarian approach within your relationship, even if your intentions are noble. You elicit obedience rather than cultivating negotiated agreements. Instead of an accepted consensus on the conditions of the relationship, your approach to the relationship seems to result in forced compliance from your partner. Forced compliance is when an authority figure—real or imagined—coaxes another to assume a position he or she does not believe.[31]

You are even quite sensitive to criticism and resistant to being held accountable. Thus, there is a high probability that you don't contribute to the relationship as much as you think. It is useful to consider the unprincipled leader type as a modifier of sorts. He can be a nice guy or a former alpha and exhibit tendencies of this partner type. The unprincipled leader can be overt with his authoritarian style of relationship behavior or rather subtle and covert, using deceptive manipulation tactics.

The authoritarian man is more likely to be a former alpha who forces his partner into submission with fixed, stubborn methods of getting what he wants while dismissing his responsibility to tend to her needs. He takes advantage of her need for approval, especially if she is quite agreeable.

The unprincipled leader, who is more of a nice guy, can recognize his partner's needs yet exaggerates his own needs as if they are far more important. This is a fear-based response. He prioritizes his problems over everyone else's, and rarely tends to his partner's needs and desires.

A peculiar feature of the unprincipled leader is that he has no tendencies that are not easily attributed to his personality. He can be anywhere on the spectrum of agreeableness, assertiveness, and neuroticism.

One possible explanation for how a man emerges into this type is ideological thinking. Ideological thinking can be powerful and dangerous.[32] The danger is that ideological thinking derives part of the story but understands it as if it were complete. It does not take into account an extensive amount of aspects of how ideas, concepts, and philosophies work.

It is reckless to act with such half-truths in relationships, especially when it involves those who willingly and faithfully put their well-being into our hands. Failing to see the wholesome and integrated nature of those who thoughtfully lead their relationships leads to erroneous and incomplete conclusions of how to manage relationships. If there is one personality trait that explains the greatest transgressions of the unprincipled leader, at least in part, it is conscientiousness, particularly the aspect of industriousness. The sheer lack of effort given to broaden himself and seek the whole truth of the relationship ideas that appeal to him makes him susceptible to becoming stuck in his ways. His stubborn refusal to work more than what he feels he should locks him in an incomplete and dangerous relationship ideology.

On the other hand, high orderliness (the other aspect of conscientiousness) might also contribute to the behaviors of this type. If this is him, it could be the case that his disgust for chaos drives his leadership style to the inflexible point of only seeing his partner as someone who needs to behave in accordance with what he deems appropriate. And that is not good!

Identifying Your Partner Type

Regardless of what partner type you identify with, there is room for improvement. Consider each of these partner types as you seek to understand yourself better. Some men may have lost their touch or gotten a little rusty, while others may have dug themselves a rather deep hole. The former alpha might only be falling slightly short in a few major areas in his relationship, or he may have lost sight of his masculinity and regressed into a lackluster, frustrated shell of the man he once was. The nice guy might be a little too passive here and there and maybe experiencing a few minor insecurities, or he may be realizing that he has become a doormat in his relationship, overly apologetic, and susceptible to critical failure.

The unprincipled leader might only need to take the initiative with a few simple tasks to improve his situation. For instance, he may need to complete a few projects around the house with which he has delayed for some time or start helping with planning trips and events with his partner. On the other hand, the unprincipled leader might be severely lacking in many areas, not knowing he is failing miserably, resulting in a poorly run household and, inevitably, a failed relationship. Thus, he would need to undergo a profound transformation.

One of the most poorly managed households is those run as a dictatorship. This style of leadership is prone to severe dysfunction. A dictatorship-run household is led by an authoritarian leadership style in which one person possesses, or seeks to possess, absolute power without effective limitations. This is an absolutely unhealthy style of leadership in a relationship. Not only does the unprincipled leader attempt to lead this way, but he is also in denial about the ineffectiveness of his attempts at control.

This type of unprincipled leader is likely to be low in agreeableness and neuroticism while extremely high in orderliness and assertiveness. Alternatively, another common type of unprincipled leader is one who is driven by a low conscientiousness overall. Slothfulness and disorderliness are his defining characteristics, followed by a baseline disregard for others' emotional needs and a low sensitivity to pain and discomfort for both him and his partner. Upon reading this description, one might wonder how this man got into a relationship in the first place.

Perhaps, the arrival at such a state is indicative of our inherent longing for lifelong intimate companionship. Thus, its importance implies that there is a great responsibility that comes with it. Assuming responsibility for your relationship cannot be fruitful if you do not know who you are. If you cannot be truthful with yourself regarding your unfavorable aspects, you will struggle to live a purposeful life and have meaningful relationships.

Sexless Relationships

One of the most embarrassing and least talked about issues found across all partner types is low sex or sexless relationships. Many men experience the withholding of sex from their partners, which is usually correlated to the attraction level she has for him. Women want to have sex with a man they find attractive, not a man they find unattractive. This dynamic is found in all three partner types.

It is a sensitive topic, and most men will refrain from engaging in a healthy confrontation with their partner about sex. Instead, they ignore the issue, failing to respond assertively and confidently. It can be painful to admit that your partner is not as sexually attracted to you as you'd like her to be. Just as we learned that Regina serves as a barometer that reflects changes with Rodion, especially regarding whether he is moving toward his potential, we must courageously look to how our partner's behavior indicates in us a severe lack of magnificence.

We can only transform ourselves as far as our denial will allow us. Understanding the type of partner you are breaks down the walls of denial, providing insight into the areas of your life and relationship that need improvement and how to begin restoring sexuality, if necessary. Depending on your partner type, certain strategies are more effective than others. However, these strategies are only effective once your foundational body of work has been established. Using the four pillars as a guide, you can identify where you fall short and how practicing these concepts can profoundly increase your attractiveness.

Speaking of denial, if a man is honest and unbiased, he will admit that he wants sex. Most men struggle to acknowledge the lack of sex in their relationships. Acknowledging this can be quite difficult for men, and many may even experience it as shameful. Men will often frame the lack of sex in their relationship as simply not being a priority.

The nice guy will dichotomously frame this as respect for his partner's wishes, believing that expressing a desire for sex is somehow incompatible with respecting her. Such ideological narratives seek to eliminate the possibility that a man can express his masculine sexual desire while simultaneously being respectful.

When the former alpha frames sex as not a priority, it is usually because he does not understand that he cannot ride on the coattails of yesterday's magnificence. He assumes he already earned a lifetime's worth of sex by the value he brought previously, naively believing that he does not have to elevate himself as his partner's needs deepen and broaden. In essence, he places full responsibility on his partner, which is the exact opposite of what he should do in this situation.

Both of these partner type experiences indicate a weak frame because they only adopted their beliefs on the matter *after* the sexual intimacy decreased in frequency and intensity. It is easy to assume a stance on something after the fact. This is called hindsight bias; we adopt a certain belief or viewpoint on something only after it has happened.[33]

Additionally, men will frame this issue as though they are 'focused on other areas in the relationship that are far more important than sex'. As elaborated on in the chapter, Frame Control, improving frame can help overcome this kind of denial. The man who says that sex is not a priority typically only assumes this stance once he has given up on being sexually appealing to his partner, and his partner limits the sex she will have with him. This happens due to having neglected his personal development as a man, essentially giving up on himself before he has become integrated. Strategies for overcoming low sex relationships are covered later in this book.

C h a p t e r   F i v e

Connection Assessment

Rodion & Regina X

Let us return to Rodion and Regina. Through the course of recent events in his marriage, Rodion realized he has much to learn if he is to elevate his relationship. This realization has awakened him to a need to understand himself more deeply; he knows he must turn inward and face his demons—his Shadow. Although he senses this on a more superficial level, Rodion does not quite understand what he has encountered in Regina. His unconscious Self gravitates toward her, even though he does not comprehend why. You might say his inner feminine aspect—his anima—is leading him toward a place he must go so that he may develop a more integrated Self.[34][35] He is sensing, unconsciously, that there is an ancient language being spoken by Regina. Consciously, Rodion only perceives this as hearing something different, something novel. He does not yet know it is a peculiar language, only that something is tugging at him. In a way, all he knows is that he has to figure out what it is and what he must do. With this calling, so to speak, Rodion turns to books, online forums, podcasts, and other men to hear their stories, methods, successes, and failures of self-improvement in the context of their relationships. In doing so, he begins to establish a baseline sense of self by developing an understanding of what type of partner he is, and he is motivated to move forward and begin understanding the dynamics of the connection between him and Regina. Assessing his connection with his partner illuminates the direction he needs to go regarding his transformation as a man.

One of the advantages of Rodion assessing his connection is that Regina is the most accurate reflection of his leadership and direction. A man's partner is usually much more in tune with his idiosyncrasies than he thinks she is. Rodion's reactions to this aspect of Regina are a direct result of how well he carries himself. She either connects well with him, or she is repulsed by him. Her repulsion of him is an excellent indicator of discord in the relationship. Gaining insight into the connection with his partner allows Rodion to understand the severity of that discord.

Utilizing the right tools to assess yourself and the connection with your partner involves the serious application of the resources this book directs you to. This includes assessing the relationship power gradient (the degree to which each partner is equally balanced with committing to the relationship and providing intimacy and sex) and identifying covert contracts (manipulative and discrete methods used to negotiate desire, such as sex or approval from your partner). If you want to be effective, take the Big Five Aspects Scale assessment. Having your partner take this personality assessment and generating a relationship report would also be useful.

While both men and women can land anywhere on the relationship power gradient, the following concepts will be from the biological perspective and evolutionary psychology that suggests women want commitment and men want sex. Incorporated in this is a behavioral economics perspective to illuminate how behaviors can be assessed and modified in this context. Furthermore, to focus on the topic at hand, his/her pronouns will refer to masculinity (although some women may identify as more masculine). She/her pronouns will refer to femininity (although some men may identify as more feminine). Combining biology, evolutionary psychology, and behavioral economics in this context allows these concepts to maintain the integrity of evidence-based science while providing an appropriate amount of flexibility that allows these concepts to illuminate some fundamental differences between men and women. .

While this book often draws from these and other perspectives, there is no intentional discrimination. However, as you grasp the four pillars, interpreting anything in this book as personally discriminatory perhaps indicates the need to read this book.

Error Management Theory and Pair-Bonding

Perhaps, the most integral theory regarding male self-improvement in the context of relationships is derived from a theory founded by David Buss and Martie Haselton called Error Management Theory. Buss and Haselton discovered what perhaps the most important theory is regarding male and female differences in intimate relationships and the problems that arise from them. This theory is called commitment-skepticism bias, an evolved psychological mechanism in women designed to substantiate her partner's commitment to her.[36]

This is essentially an error management system, which assesses which error is more costly given the options one faces. This is a natural way for humans to make decisions based on risks. From both evolutionary and biological perspectives, women rely on this error management system to assess false positives when it comes to pair-bonding. She cannot afford to make the wrong error. Therefore, she must ensure she secures a partner who supports her needs and desires while maintaining an unwavering commitment to her. Women are biologically more vulnerable, especially when pregnant and when nursing a child, so it benefits them to have a partner who fulfills his commitment to her. Women also tend to be perceived as less attractive as a mate when raising a child from a different man.

On the other end of error management theory, men have an evolved psychological mechanism called sexual over-perception bias. Men do not share the same biological needs and vulnerabilities as women. In fact, the error management system for men in this context assesses for false negatives. They err to the side of overconfidence: they must assume a woman wants to have sex with them or will eventually want to. If they default to the notion that women do not want to have sex with them, the odds of ever having sex greatly diminishes.

In contrast to women, men are not biologically geared for the same mindset as women when it comes to mate selection and pair-bonding. They don't have the same burdens of pregnancy and nursing children; therefore, they do not experience the same kind of biological obligations and vulnerabilities. This theory supports the effectiveness of attaining balance in the Relationship Power Gradient, a way to gauge how naturally balanced the relationship is and what needs to be done to restore that balance.

Relationship Power Gradient

Assessing the relationship power gradient, along with understanding your partner type, will enhance your strategies for self-improvement and increase the probability of restoring harmony and intimacy in your relationship. Men have an inherent proclivity to be more concerned with sex with a woman than a commitment from her. From this perspective, women have the power to give and withhold sex. While this could be perceived as a bargaining weapon, it would be narrow-minded to only see it in that way. It would be wise to also consider this from a biological framework that supports creating polarity in relationships.

Conversely, women might have the inherent proclivity toward a man's commitment more so than sex from him. This indicates that men have the power to give and withhold commitment. As you can see, the power can go both ways. It does not mean that men don't want commitment or that women don't want sex. From an evolutionary point of view, this is suggesting that men and women seem to gravitate toward sex and commitment based on their respective biological drives. This creates a dynamic in pair-bonding or long-term romantic relationships, which seems to be universally experienced by most couples. Rodion's unfamiliarity of this dynamic obscures the contextual value of basic, fundamental drives in relationships and the insight he might gain when he if he understood them. Understanding the relationship power gradient illuminates how much power each partner holds over the other regarding the invitation for sex and the promise of commitment, for better or worse. More importantly, it illuminates the importance of equity in relationships.

Relationships require equitable value and effort. When various aspects of Rodion and Regina's relationship experience an imbalance in this regard, there is discord. Conflict inevitably arises from this inequity, and the only resolution for the relationship to be successful is to restore balance. Understand that *equitable* value and effort are not the same as *equal* value and effort. Rodion and Regina possess their own respective strengths and qualities. When they bring their strengths together harmoniously, it opens the door to wonderful experiences in the relationship. What matters is that they both give their best effort, regardless of who can do more. Perhaps Regina is better at planning and organizing than Rodion.

Although he doesn't necessarily have to be as capable of this as Regina is, she will see his efforts and appreciate them when he shows conscientiousness with planning and organizing. The same goes for Regina. Maybe Rodion is a better cook than she is, but if she gives a great effort to cook a delicious meal for him, he will appreciate her efforts, and the two of them can enjoy a pleasant dinner together. Of course, acknowledging each other's efforts is equally as important as the efforts themselves. Cultivating each other's best can be optimally achieved by giving praise and thanks, which is nourishing to the relationship's growth. The absence of effort leaves too much of a void between them, making it difficult to connect. When a significant aspect of the relationship (or the relationship as a whole) experiences disparity in the equity of effort and value, the relationship power gradient must be assessed and restored.

It is often easier to identify the inequity in a relationship by looking at the actionable effort, specifically regarding the degree of sex versus commitment. While relationships are obviously much more complex than this, there is a necessary simplicity here that illuminates the importance of giving the proper amount of effort that meets your partner halfway—no less and no further.

There is no coincidence with where you are on the gradient. Women who withhold sex from their partners often display more power in the relationship. Your partner's display of relationship power is not random. It is usually linked to her attraction to you and respect for you, which is determined in large part by your efforts. If your partner withholds sexual intimacy from you, she does not value you enough to give you the gift of her intimacy or her body. This is generally an indication of a lack of commitment or fitness for the job on the man's part. By the same token, men can withhold commitment in displays of power. This can be detrimental to a relationship. If he is receiving sexual intimacy from his partner yet not reciprocating with an equitable amount of commitment to her, there is an imbalance, and harmony is lacking. These behaviors are often correlated with failing character-building tests, lacking frame control, or overall poor responses to your partner's needs or emotional distress. These concepts are covered in depth in the chapters, Character and Frame. A healthy balance in this dynamic consists of earning the gifts of intimacy and commitment from each other in a manner where the masculine meets the feminine, creating a harmonious connection between the two partners. This topic is covered in detail in the chapter, The Achievement of Compatibility.

The Former Alpha and the Relationship Power Gradient

Men have gone to great lengths to have sex with women, and countless methods have been used in this pursuit. Historically, the more alpha traits a man displays in this pursuit, the better his chances of having sex. Behaviorally, this consists of displaying traits that indicate confidence, reliability, strength, and social/socioeconomic status. This is consistently observable—many books have been written on pick-up artistry and what women look for in a man, not to mention the scientific research on the matter. Alpha men, to some degree, have figured out the dynamics of mating rituals enough to achieve varying success with having sex with women. While many self-identified alpha men have attained indisputable levels of mastery in mating rituals, many have inevitably encountered a woman with whom he surrendered his alpha qualities in hopes of securing her indefinitely. In other words, he finally met his match. He either secretly wanted such a woman and feigned his alpha persona, or he suddenly changed his approach once he happened upon a woman he viewed as the ultimate prize.

Perhaps we all have our threshold of maintaining a particular persona, such as the alpha does, and we inevitably meet our match, which comes in the form of today's woman, whose ancient feminine draws us near. Once this alpha had committed to a relationship with this prize of a woman, he would have deviated from the qualities that initially attracted her to him.

Understand that we must adjust our alpha behaviors accordingly as we evolve. Yet, we must do so in a manner that honors our true nature and uses those qualities as a conduit of giving our gifts to the world. This is living with a deep sense of purpose, while those around you are the beneficiary of your purpose. In relationships, we must grow and evolve in our qualities as a man; but we must never neglect the underlying principles of the alpha qualities that got us here. That is irresponsible and unwise. Dance with the one who brought you.

The former alpha is a man who once identified with the qualities mentioned above and is currently experiencing an imbalance in the relationship power gradient. He struggles to restore balance in ways other than being an alpha. That is, he fails to incorporate a broadened set of personality traits. Rather, he blindly abandons his alpha traits, which he labels as his "old, egotistical self." Because of the dramatic shift of ignoring his alpha traits and only practicing beta traits (with which he is not masterful), he experiences a regression in the quality of his responses to his partner's distress with his own impulsive, emotional behavior.

In essence, his plan backfires. Without his alpha qualities, there is little to no internal guide to ensure the kind of assertiveness and confidence needed in his responses. While tenderness and compassion are necessary for connecting with your partner's emotional experience, these aspects cannot be adequately carried out unless it is from within the pillars of assertiveness and confidence.

This is another example of a man failing to honor his own masculinity. Instead, he may forfeit and succumb to the misconception that he can do nothing, surrendering to defeat. And that is not good. He may be oblivious to, or lost sight of, what attracts his partner to him sexually. If he is to elevate himself and his relationship, he must accept the challenge of facing the repressed aspects of himself he now finds to be the darkest and most detestable. He must enter the cave he fears.

If you recognize this experience as your own, equalizing the relationship power gradient likely requires restoring some of your alpha traits, recalling the skills you inherently possess to negotiate for your needs. This must be done while emphasizing a connection to your partner's feminine side and practicing empathy in communication.

For example, practicing assertiveness can help naturally restore an appropriate amount of attractive alpha traits that signify resolve and stoicism while simultaneously showing your compassionate side. Being intentional with particular aspects of the character you exhibit can improve your ability to be trustworthy and romantic. Maintaining a strong, healthy frame can aid you in your efforts to lead responsibly in a manner indicative of ambition and determination. Practicing confidence brings back your emotional reliability, which provides a sense of safety and security for your partner. All these aspects can exponentially bolster your attractiveness with your partner and, in turn, restore balance and harmony.

Regarding personality, the former alpha must first evaluate the aspect of assertiveness. For restoration of the power gradient to occur, it can only be effectively done in an appropriate orderly environment. Suppose it is the case that he is deficient in assertiveness to any significant degree. In that case, he must first set out to broaden this aspect so that he may establish a more secure sense of self and, in turn, shore up the environment in which his relationship exists.

If it is the case that he is inherently assertive, the former alpha must evaluate himself as to whether or not he is living in accordance with that aspect. If he is not, then he must reestablish this aspect of himself by elevating his practice of being assertive. Once this has been evaluated, he must then look to his trait of agreeableness. This trait is strongly correlated with the pillar of character.

Suppose the former alpha is of average agreeableness. In that case, he must take an inventory of himself regarding his ability to negotiate for himself without doing so at the much expense of others. He must courageously venture into the world of uncertainty, which lies on the low end of the agreeableness spectrum. He must familiarize himself with the nuances of that world if he is to broaden himself enough to manage the complex nature of relationships. If it is the case that the former alpha is low in agreeableness, he will do well to consciously seek to understand the emotional nuances of his partner and of relationships.

Regarding neuroticism, the former alpha can fall anywhere on this spectrum, although they are usually not high in this trait. The lower he is in neuroticism, the less sensitive and reactive he is to his partner's pain and discomfort. Therefore, the lack of its recognition causes him to appear cold and calculated, to which his partner will infer terrible implications. He must condition himself to detect her emotional experiences, both positive and negative. If he is higher in neuroticism, it will bode well for him to develop skills for reframing events in which pain and discomfort take up most of his field of view. That is, he must learn how to take a step back from the negative emotional experiences of both himself and his partner so that he may gather a more accurate representation of the situation. This will help him make a better-informed decision when times are emotionally charged.

Last but not least, the former alpha must assess his trait of conscientiousness. The two aspects of this trait, industriousness and orderliness, can help him understand his efforts in the relationship and get his finger on the pulse of their effectiveness. There are no obvious markers in the former alpha that suggests they lean to one side or the other in conscientiousness. Therefore, it is worthwhile to touch on the different types of behaviors and experiences that can be attributed to industriousness and orderliness. We will not go into much technical content here.

However, if there is one thing more than anything else to pay attention to regarding the faults of this trait, it is when the former alpha is rather low in industriousness. In this case, he may recognize the need to broaden himself so that he may be better equipped for a diverse range of challenges. Yet, it is another thing to follow through with that broadening. In other words, making a decision about something does not equate to taking action with that decision. This is the crux of being low in industriousness. Relationships are complex, and they require a great number of implementable actions, meaning a significant amount of effort must be exerted. Thus, he must expand his capacity to work persistently and diligently with elevating his relationship skills, especially those with which he is not well-versed.

Even if he is highly efficient with his efforts in the sense that he can get the most with the least (which is often the case when people are low in industriousness, yet high in orderliness and intellect), the display of effort is not apparent to his partner. As you will see, the consistency of the quality of our responses to our partners can only be as good as our clearest understanding of their desires. Likewise, the attraction of our partner to us can only be as great as the visibility of the effort we display. That is, it is paramount that we make our efforts overt.

Both the former alpha and the nice guy will often counter this notion with the narrative that says, "One should simply do what they need to do without making a show of it, for it comes across as attention-seeking." This school of thought is too ideological in nature to be effective in relationships. Believing that overtly making your efforts known to your partner is weak or dishonorable risks failing to ensure she notices them, ultimately reducing her chances to see your efforts. Her experience will be such that you do not care enough about her or the relationship to give effort. Just as it is helpful when she clearly expresses her desires to you so that you may respond to her with more precision; it is helpful for her to clearly see the efforts you put forth. Efforts in relationships are highly attractive, and it is often necessary to verbalize them to each other.

If the former alpha is relatively industrious yet is low in orderliness, he may experience an imbalance of chaos and order. Although the feminine is chaos, your partner needs an optimal orderly place where she can experience the fullness of her feminine. This orderly space consists of everything from having a clean and tidy house to a safe and reliable place within you for her to express the emotional gravity she is experiencing at any given moment.

If the feminine woman has to create her own orderly place to express her feminine, she will have to operate from her own inner masculine to do so. She will then find you lacking in that capacity, a proficiency in which she would much rather see you possess. The more she has to operate from her masculine, the less she gets to express her feminine nature. Both of you miss out here because she does not get your true masculinity, and you do not get her femininity, and the relationship will not make sense. The reasons you got together will have been dangerously obscured and subdued, and the connection will be compromised.

Conversely, high orderliness may cause problems for the former alpha in his relationship. Too much order suppresses the feminine, preventing her from fulfilling her purpose of bringing creation and regeneration to the relationship—and the world, for that matter. If orderliness goes too far, stagnation sets in and stalls creative achievement, for when the feminine is locked away in her dungeon and written out of history, the masculine will have nothing more to conquer, and he will cease to have purpose. Without the ability to express her feminine nature, his partner will begin to wither away until she will either succumb to the slavery of permanence or rage against you, to which you will either wake up or be driven away.

The former alpha who is high in orderliness must work to ensure the chaotic feminine has an optimal place to express herself in a creative manner. He must not resist that chaos; rather, he must conquer it. To resist it is to wish it away. To conquer it is to bring it to its fullest potential.

The Nice Guy and the Relationship Power Gradient

Plenty of men have been on the other end of the spectrum, having the opposite experience, which resulted in unsatisfactory results in their pursuit of sex. These men used the approach of loyalty, sense of honor, dignity, friendliness, and faithfulness, to name a few. They held true to their gentle qualities and found solace in them. These qualities are noble. However, despite these admirable traits, they covertly longed for intimacy and sex. Their approach to the mating ritual would be to shroud their intent with vows of treating the woman with respect and, perhaps, unknowingly, concealing or downplaying their truest intention, which was the pursuit of having sex with her.

These men truly believe in their persona of nobility, which are not, in fact, almost entirely feigned. Such characteristics typically have been ingrained since childhood and are driven by their temperament. However, because of the conviction such men carry with these traits and characteristics, it can be difficult for them to explore additional qualities to exhibit, such as alpha male qualities.

The nice guy sees alpha males as disrespectful, cunning, and ruthless. However, they may unconsciously covet the alpha's skills, possibly indicating weakness in true mating strategies. Yet, overall, the idea of behaving like an alpha male seems to contradict the nice guy's core values. To put it simply, he does not know how to be direct without being disrespectful and aggressive. This is the crux of the nice guy: he cannot figure out how to maintain the integrity of his values and practice alpha behaviors. This paradox causes cognitive dissonance for the nice guy, which can be too much to bear, so he chooses to ignore the value of alpha traits.

The paradoxes of life it is not a matter of choosing which side to make work (though that seems easier); rather, it is a matter of making both sides work together despite how diametrically opposed they appear. This is integration. We are called to move beyond the false limitations such paradoxical beliefs, self-imposed by the ignorance of our own experiences. Moreover, the nice guy errs on the side of fear and inflexibility in the name caution and righteousness. His fixed, moral beliefs deter him from overcoming his narrow sense of self.

The nice guy is a man whose sense of self is deeply rooted in the previously mentioned characteristics and personality. He has experienced a degree of imbalance in the relationship power gradient. That is, he offers more commitment than she offers sexual intimacy. Deeply rooted beliefs can result in denial when pitted against our deeper unconscious drives, which can hinder progress. Because society often views nice guy traits as admirable, it can be most difficult to see himself adopting other approaches in their pursuit of sex, even within their own relationship.

Typically, the initial barrier is (falsely) admitting to himself that sexual intimacy is a high priority for him. Of course, there are many more barriers to overcome as he makes the conscious decision to restore balance to the power gradient. Yet, the nice guy's efforts to restore balance is incorrectly based on the premise that he must refine and amplify his beta traits, neglecting to hone his alpha traits. By refusing to cultivate alpha traits, he experiences continued frustration with his partner.

This frustration leads to acting impulsively and becoming emotionally volatile, furthering the imbalance. Without alpha qualities, there is little to no emotional regulation in his responses to his partner's more intense emotional experiences. When his partner's emotional distress escalates, he inevitably regresses to his baseline submissive state.

If you recognize the Nice Guy partner type as yourself, restoring balance to the relationship power gradient will be similar to the former alpha. What differs from the nice guy's approach to restoring balance is that many of the alpha qualities he needs must be summoned for the first time, whereas the former alpha recalls them. It is sort of like muscle memory. If you have a history of working out, you will regain strength and power with relative ease. If you have little history of working out, there is little to no muscle memory, and it will be difficult to build muscle, although it is possible. Summoning alpha traits can be awkward for a nice guy, and alarming for his partner. If she is accustomed to a more passive version of you, you must: understand that asserting yourself may appear as aggressive behavior; establish boundaries while emphasizing assertive communication skills; let your partner know that you are attempting to make positive changes; be sensitive to her emotional experiences; and consciously display good character in response to her emotional distress.

Developing a healthier, stronger frame can help you in your efforts to have your desires met while continuing to support hers. Practicing confidence brings your partner a renewed and more trustable sense of safety and security. These aspects can transform your qualities as a man and excite your partner in ways the two of you have rarely experienced, if ever.

Like the former alpha, the nice guy's personality affects his behaviors and experiences within his relationship, particularly with its power gradient. In keeping with the notion that assertiveness must be substantially present, the nice guy often finds himself deficient here.

Even with those high in assertiveness, there will be a range of people with whom they must work harder than usual to be assertive. The nice guy finds it difficult to be as assertive as he needs to be with his partner, even if he is not deficient in assertiveness overall. He must move beyond the fear of coming across as aggressive if he is to land in the assertive middle of the spectrum. Even if he is assertive with most things with his partner, the nice guy struggles with the things he most needs to be assertive. Even if there is a single dynamic with which he is not assertive, it weakens his overall magnificence. Of course, if he is low in assertiveness, he must broaden that aspect within himself overall. One positive note here is that such broadening creates a rather profound and contrasting change that can serve as a refreshing and novel experience for his partner.

Having set a course with broadening and deepening his assertiveness, the nice guy must look to his trait agreeableness. If there is one trait that signifies a nice guy more than any other trait, it is this one. If he is above average in agreeableness, the nice guy must make a conscientious effort to become nuanced in the art of negotiating for his own needs and getting what he wants.

Many agreeable men balk at this solution out of the fear of appearing to be calloused and self-centered. The irony is that becoming calloused and self-centered is one of the last things he should be worried about. That is not to say that if he was prone to ideological thinking that he could not go too far. But he would not get terribly far before seeing the error of his ways and returning closer to his true nature, only this time with great-er knowledge of when he is nearing the threshold of self-centeredness.

Suppose he is in the unique position of being rather low in agreeable-ness. In that case, the nice guy could make rapid and profound changes in the relationship power gradient by carefully and attentively supporting his partner's emotional experiences. Through validating her experiences, he can elicit more love and appreciation from her rather than seeking only to validate his own experiences. Understanding that she may not be able to negotiate for her needs as well as he can, he could make good use of his noble traits and negotiate for her needs when she struggles to do so. This will alleviate her frustrations caused by her unmet needs, even— perhaps especially—if she is not conscious of them. Of course, he should negotiate well for his needs, but he could also work to restore balance by teaching his partner, by example, how to negotiate for her needs. This is a meaningful way to make progress while honoring his low agreeableness.

For the nice guy who is average to high in neuroticism, restoring the relationship balance means he must not neglect to broaden this trait. He must learn to take a step back away from the threat or occurrence of pain and discomfort. This version of the nice guy finds it difficult to see the whole picture, in which he seeks to eradicate the pain and discomfort, be it through shutting down or aggression. His habit is to either overly respond to the pain and discomfort by not giving his partner space to adjust and to process, or he withdraws and freezes, believing that the predator of pain and discomfort will not detect him. He must adopt the practice of patience and learn to watch things unfold, for it is not as bad as he thinks. Lastly, he must learn to reframe events that cause him anxiety.

The Unprincipled Leader and the Relationship Power Gradient

The unprincipled leader can arise from the former alpha type or the nice guy type. It is important to understand that what breeds an unprincipled leader is an underdeveloped sense of self. It is common for men who fit these descriptions to reach a point of frustration in their relationship and resort to controlling tactics, projecting their false sense of entitlement onto the relationship. Regarding the relationship power gradient, the most challenging obstacle for this partner type is that they do not see that there is an underlying power gradient; they only see how their partner's behaviors threaten their own level of comfort and security. This kind of man sets rules that drive his partner away or drive her into a sort of unearned submission, failing to garner her true respect and love. This is the crux of the unprincipled leader.

If this is an aspect of your partner type, restoring balance to the relationship power gradient requires taking a personal inventory to identify barriers that narrow your sense of self while focusing on becoming more responsible as a leader. Of course, the unprincipled leader must first be open to the idea that there is an imbalanced power gradient and that its restoration hinges on his leadership style.

Striving toward a balanced relationship power gradient requires you practice respecting your partner's boundaries. It would be best if you practiced empathy. The unprincipled leader has either never been skillful with other people's emotional experiences or has lost touch with the true nature of that aspect within himself. Empathy will maximize your efforts more than anything you do if this is your leadership style. Improving your responses with good character is imperative to restoring a healthy balance to the relationship power gradient and eliciting genuine love and respect from your partner. Adjusting your frame to one that seeks to achieve outcomes where everyone benefits can best ensure your desires are met while genuinely supporting your partner's needs and desires. Practicing authentic confidence cultivates a newfound sense of self, one your partner will cherish. All these strategies will help you transcend your much-maligned masculinity and allow room for a magnificent connection with your partner.

To reiterate what was previously said of the unprincipled leader regarding personality, the only trait that would signify someone as this type is extremely low agreeableness. However, there are certainly many good men who are extremely low in this trait. Nonetheless, it is worthwhile to explore the faults of this trait in that case. Otherwise, the emergence of this partner type is due to ideological thinking that lay dormant for a while, and then crept into his leadership style within his relationship. He likely was not conscious of his true desires or the degree to which he was covert in his attempts to meet them. Because of his covertness, his desires were never expressed, resulting in his partner's inability to clearly see them, which prevented her from tending to them properly.

Perhaps, she thought she was responding to his needs, but if they were false needs concealing his true desires, then there is no fault to be placed upon her. Therefore, he would have assumed she couldn't meet his needs and would begin to believe she was the problem. He would have subtly coerced her into obligatory acts of care and attention, which she had no authentic desire to give. Any experience of having his needs met this way reinforced his negative behaviors, further entrenching him into an unprincipled leadership style.

Each partner type must manage character-building tests and covert comfort requests (discussed later). However, the degree to which the emphasis is placed upon managing these depends on which partner type you are and where you fall on the relationship power gradient. Understanding yourself within this context will illuminate other opportunities for improvement, which will guide you to an elevated sense of self.

Covert Contracts

Dr. Robert Glover coined the term "covert contract,"[37] which are methods discretely used by today's man to get approval or sex from his partner. In his childhood, today's man learned that he would be rewarded if he completed particular tasks. This began by performing tasks that gained his parents' approval. This is typical with childhood development. However, from an avoidance-based perspective, we can see that he learned that he would not be disapproved of as long as he did a good job. Later in childhood, he learned that he could form social relationships if he behaved in certain ways. That is, if he showed value on the surface, he would be accepted by his peers, which would alleviate his fear of being cast out and becoming too isolated. It is through these tendencies that he made friends. In adulthood, he took these deeply ingrained tendencies with him into his intimate relationships and unknowingly began forming unwritten agreements with his partner. A common pitfall for today's man is that he fails to be aware of the underlying intentions with his behaviors. The problem with covert contracts is that the other partner is clueless that there is a contract in the first place. Because of the infatuation and naive adoration for each other that occurs at the beginning of a relationship, neither partner sees that these unwritten agreements are put in place.

Rodion & Regina XI

As Rodion reflects back on his shortcomings, which have now come to light, he begins to recognize times in which he had covert contracts. These unwritten agreements gave the impression that he was not needy or lacking, hoping his partner would offer him sex or some degree of validation in return. Rodion's underlying narrative here says, "I'm doing this particular behavior for my partner on the surface so that she will meet my deeper, concealed need." As it turns out, this type of behavior has been a common occurrence in his interactions with Regina. He likens it to people who seek constructive feedback from others about a project or something they have accomplished when it is in reality a veiled attempt to get validation for their abilities to perform certain tasks. And he is deeply bothered by this.

He can hardly stomach the idea that he could have displayed such weak and cowardly behavior. He recalls times when he would do a load of laundry or bring flowers home for his partner, hoping he would get something in return, be it praise and gratitude, sex, or to get to go out with his friends. He believed that, by doing these things, he would be rewarded with having Regina fulfill his desires and fantasies. When those covert desires were not met he would become frustrated or even resentful. Covert contracts prevent the clear expression of desire because Regina only sees Rodion's behavior as meaning something else, deceptively giving the impression that he wants something other than what he truly desires. Beginning to understand the problems associated with this approach will help prevent conflicts in the future. Furthermore, doing so will make room for more effective methods of getting the sex and intimacy he wants while increasing overall relationship satisfaction.

Replacing the costly habit of covert contracts is challenging. By taking ownership of the tasks in his life and practicing overt expression of his desires, today's man begins forming his own internal validation, and he will be surprised that his desires are met more than ever. Taking responsibility for expressing his own desires and making them part of his primary focus eliminates the need for his partner to read his mind then become frustrated when she does not understand what he wants. This often leads to each of them resenting one another.

Clearly expressing his desires allows him to focus on effective methods of having his desires met, such as establishing boundaries, practicing assertiveness, and improving frame control. When his partner understands what he wants, today's man can spend less time implementing pointless strategies, and instead, spend more time building a harmonious connection and becoming an integrated man.

Everything is Open for Interpretation

Imbalances in relationships aren't always clear. The discord and conflicts that emerge from imbalances in the relationship power gradient occur due to some phenomenon unknown to us. The experience of discord and conflict often seem to come out of the blue, catching us off guard. This creates confusion and cognitive dissonance, which sends our brain into a bit of a tailspin because we need to understand what we're up against so that we may know what to do with it. If we don't understand where something is coming from, or what it is, we don't know how to prepare ourselves. As a man in a relationship, failing to see the connection between the conflict and the imbalance of sex and commitment prevents you from responding appropriately. This is where it gets precarious.

While today's man may easily identify his lack of commitment and how it can cause an imbalance—or realize a lack of sex and intimacy causes the imbalance—he will experience difficulty figuring out how to deal with it properly. The problem lies in the experiential differences between him and his partner. The troublesome part of relationship conflict is that it is usually a result of people working with different sets of facts. Due to the subjective nature of each individual's experiences and the infinite amount of information available to us, it is impossible to gather and comprehend all of it. People collect a particular set of facts that are unique from other people's particular sets of facts. That is, when two people experience the same event, it holds an incomprehensible number of facts. Therefore, a person can only take in enough facts to comprehend the event and interpret its meaning.

Because each person can only derive a small percentage of facts of the event, their understanding of it is inconclusive and incomplete. This leaves a great deal of information remaining in the event. Another person may extract very different facts, which may conflict with those of another. Much of the time, people are not even arguing about the same thing. It is challenging to get on the same page with someone without first coming to an agreement on what facts the two individuals are working with.

Therefore, when a man is confused about the origin of the discord in his relationship yet believes he is committed to his partner, he is experiencing a different set of facts than her. Failing to recognize and understand his partner's experience results in an inadvertent dismissal and invalidation of her experience, further contributing to the discord. His partner might be experiencing a set of facts that suggest his behaviors do not indicate true commitment. And this disturbs her in an alarming way.

The feminine demands total commitment from her masculine partner, not because she is selfish, but because she must hold this trait above all else so she may be free to express herself fully, which includes giving herself and her intimacy to you. The feminine experiences events from a much different perspective than the masculine. In order to connect with her, he must take her experience into account and tend to that.

Regardless of where Rodion and Regina's relationship balance is, she will judge his behaviors based on how she perceives his level of commitment to her. If he is experiencing an imbalance or a lack of sex and intimacy, and wishes that to improve, he must look first at his commitment level as well as how Regina perceives his commitment. Essentially, the natural order of relationships is that if she believes in his commitment to her, she will want to give herself to him. If she does not feel that she is getting the commitment from him that he is capable of, Regina will inherently be inclined to withhold herself from him until she feels he is committed to her.

This can be unspeakably difficult for Rodion to comprehend. Sometimes he might think he is great at giving his gifts. While Rodion should give his gifts principally for the sake of giving, he may sometimes give the wrong gift, or at least give it halfheartedly. For example, if he cooks a meal for Regina for the sake of cooking a meal for her, that is good for him. Yet, if he does not consider the potential joy of her experience of the meal, then he is giving halfheartedly, and that is not true commitment. Suppose Rodion is displaying a lack of relationship commitment but continues getting sex from Regina. In that case, he is disrupting the natural order of relationships by failing to earn her intimacy. He is getting the sex without reciprocating commitment to her. This causes a disturbance in her because, if she properly values herself, she needs to have his commitment before giving herself to him.

Rodion's lack of commitment puts into question Regina's own self-worth. At some point, she will set out to regain her self-worth, and she will turn to him for this, and not with a look of adoration, but with either a look of fury and scorn or worse, a look of a defeated and broken child. She will blame him for this disturbance, or she will make a plea for him to save her. Either way, she is right to believe the disruptive force from which the conflict was born directly reflects his commitment to her, real or imagined.

This is the kind of undeniable truth that paints us into a corner. Something deep inside tells us that this is true, but the task of positioning ourselves to transform our relationship requires us to transcend a lesser version of ourselves. And that is daunting! Suppose we have committed major transgressions in our relationship. In that case, it is even more daunting to stand in our own humanity and extend enough grace to ourselves, which is precisely what prompts us to change the way we respond in our relationships. Shame only diminishes our value as men. We therefore must answer the call to courage and face our souls. If we turn away from that call, we turn away from the very thing that helps us develop into a more wholesome and integrated version of ourselves.

Perhaps, the most heroic job is to *solve* the task of transcending lesser versions of ourselves while simultaneously sinking into our own humanity. And this is a deeply unconscious process. Carl Jung states in The *Archetypes and the Collective Unconscious,*

"But if we understand anything of the unconscious, we know that it cannot be swallowed. We also know that it is dangerous to suppress it, because the unconscious is life and this life turns against us if suppressed, as happens in neurosis. Conscious and unconscious do not make a whole when one of them is suppressed and injured by the other. If they must contend, at least let it be a fair fight with equal rights on both sides. Both are aspects of life. Consciousness should defend its reason and protect itself, and the chaotic life of the unconscious should be given the chance of having its way too - as much of it as we can stand. This means open conflict and open collaboration at once. That, evidently, is the way human life should be. It is the old game of hammer and anvil: between them the patient iron is forged into an indestructible whole, an 'individual.' This, roughly, is what I mean by the individuation process."

To rise above and sink below is to have our excellence and humanity merge into one, resulting in a more magnificent version of ourselves, opening a pathway to a harmonious connection with our partner. This pathway is created through the transformation of becoming conscious of our true potential as men and the awareness of our unconscious drives that propel us forward into a much more meaningful life—particularly one that benefits those around us. This is a difficult practice. This book aims to demonstrate how to transform ourselves as men in the context of relationships and the excellence demanded of us by our partners.

However, it is not the excellence demanded by our partner that is most difficult. The true difficulty is in demanding more of yourself than others do. Choosing to improve yourself in an environment where you demand little of yourself bears little to no fruit—choosing to improve yourself in an environment where your best is demanded positions you to bear the most fruit possible.

In a letter to Kendig B. Cully, Jung stated, "Knowing your own darkness is the best method for dealing with the darknesses of other people."[38]

Honoring masculinity requires that we engage with the chaos within us, perhaps, to prepare ourselves, as men, to engage with the destructive and creative chaos of our feminine counterpart. This is necessary for our individuation as men, for that destructive and creative feminine chaos forges us into an indestructible whole. Forgoing this procedure, knowingly or unknowingly, means we attempt to eliminate that chaos, believing we can bring order to life, to our relationships, with little to no resistance. While the masculine consciously seeks to inject a necessary order, if we fail to step into chaos, the order we inject will have nothing to resist it and will inevitably go too far. This blinds us to the answers that lie in chaos, particularly the chaos that resides in the feminine nature of our partner. Going too far, we sideswipe her feminine chaos, thinking that we have conquered. That is until the feminine chaos unleashes its fury upon you, or worse, disappears forever. Therefore, we must attempt to see that, in her feminine chaos, we discover great gifts—the gift of reflection of our masculinity, the gift of attaining our own magnificence, and the gift of giving our own gifts.

Rodion & Regina XII

Rodion is faced with this exact story. Regina's feminine dragon of chaos has emerged from its dungeon, seeking her ancient masculine counterpart. Through her worldly connection with Rodion, she hears rumors of a hero residing beyond the horizon. Hopeful—and fearful—she vacillates between patiently awaiting him and compulsively seeking him.

Occasionally, she believes she's seen a glimmer of him within Rodion, only to lose sight of her hero once again. And this tortures her. As this torture becomes more unbearable, Regina becomes fiercer and more distraught. On the surface, this appears as typical superficial frustrations women have with their men. Regina has waited too long for her hero to arrive, and she must smoke him out, so to speak—to drive him toward her with fire. She must use her greatest weapon, terrible destruction.

Rodion has no idea that the feminine dragon of chaos is about to activate a process within that will send him on a journey of transformative redemption. Yet, there is no guarantee that he will choose to embark on such a journey, let alone emerge victoriously. There is great doubt in this story, for Rodion is a reluctant and unlikely character in this story. Rodion is even more of a hopeless man because he longs for a hero outside himself to rescue him. And this is most unattractive to Regina. Rodion has an insurmountable task ahead of him if he is to transform himself and his relationship, beginning with powerful and dangerous narratives of the world.

Descent into the Dungeon of Transformation

It is important to recognize and acknowledge that in each of us resides our own Shadow. As much as Rodion laments that he has found himself at the bottom of the hierarchy, his tumble into the precarious world of chaotic threat does not have to be in vain. In fact, it is necessary for him to live out the element of redemption—an ineradicable part of all human stories. He does this by preparing to confront his dragon—in this case, Regina's feminine challenges. To do this, Rodion must learn to stand in her humanity, and it is in his courage to stand in his own humanity that he can be just another soul as he touches another soul.[39] If not, then what should have been a tender and warm touch will have been a venomous sting.

Today's man can, with relative ease, pull himself from the bottom of the hierarchy. Yet, he remains dangerously close to it if he does not use his experience of that dark and chaotic world to revolutionize himself and his relationship. If Rodion's only goal is to escape the bottom, then his only reward will be an alleviation of pain, and he will miss out on the greatest reward, which is that of what only heroes know. Something stirs in Rodion, however, and he knows he must conquer a great and formidable foe here. In his deep introspection, it occurs to him that it has been Regina who sparked the activation of the story within himself that leads him into this dungeon of transformation. Rodion is frightened by what he sees upon having had this revelation. It is not Regina whom he must conquer. Rather, it is the feminine dragon of chaos within her that he must slay. As Rodion descends further down the abyss, he comes upon the dragon's lair. He knows that to slay a dragon, he must master the fundamental principles required to do so. That is, he must gather for himself a shield and the weapons necessary for such a conquest, for they are the formula for the magnificence to do so. However, the shield and the weapon are obscured by the violent dragon, and Rodion must gather them quickly. It is in his heroic effort that he will transform. Heroic—what a terrifyingly wonderful word.

Part 2

Slaying the Dragon

Assertiveness

Most people have heard, "Communication is key to a successful relationship." Although this is true, it is imperative that it be quality communication. Striving for quality communication is best achieved when coupled with understanding the importance of speaking the truth and giving the thoughtfulness necessary for its reception by others. Talking is easy. Using the right language and thoughtfully choosing the right words requires conscious effort and open-mindedness. This is especially true in conflict when people experience attacks on their character and feel the need to defend themselves. Conflict may give rise to stonewalling—refusing to communicate. Aggression can emerge as frustrations arise out of unmet needs. A relationship's spiral into chaos can often attribute to these types of responses.

Assertiveness establishes the necessary order for relationships, which allows the relationship to function properly and thrive. Without it, chaos will ensue, boundaries become nonexistent, and conflict becomes cyclical. It is difficult to navigate a relationship that has no boundaries.

Assertiveness is an important component of successful relationships because it creates the environment necessary for positive emotional experiences and affords us the ability to practice other skills that contribute to harmonious relationships, such as intimacy and quality communication. The alternative is too much chaos and conflict.

Many people understand assertiveness as a way to manage, diffuse, and prevent conflict. Yet, conflict is a natural part of relationships and even necessary at times. Since conflict is unavoidable, having the skills to manage it is vital. Managing conflict with appropriate, healthy skills helps prevent destructive forces from disrupting the connection with our partner. Assertiveness is also about establishing boundaries and maintaining their integrity. Assertiveness enables us to grow stronger through navigating the challenges presented to us in conflict and boundary setting.

If the goal of your relationship is to have a harmonious connection with your partner, then having quality responses should be your objective. How you respond to your partner is important because they will judge you by your actions. More so, you are judged by the implications of your actions. Ideally, the implications of your behaviors will reflect a well-developed inner masculine. The more poorly you respond—passively, aggressively, and defensively—the less your partner can trust you with what is meaningful to her. The more you respond in an emotionally reliable manner—assertively and truthfully—the more room you create for intimacy. How you respond to your partner's attempts to connect with you is a direct reflection of your masculinity. The manner in which you engage with your partner's feminine nature determines the degree to which she will be receptive to you.

The biological and evolutionary drives that prompt your partner's desire to connect with you are complex, frequently causing her to employ methods to do so that can be easily misinterpreted or missed entirely. Her reasons are deeply rooted in her feminine nature and, to the untrained eye, will not be clearly understood, if at all. The obscurity of your partner's reasons for connecting with you is important to understand when practicing assertiveness in the context of long-term relationships.

Exploring the reasons behind her way of connecting with you is to help you understand that, when those reasons are misinterpreted or unrecognized, it will lead to a missed connection or even discord. For instance, sometimes, your partner may attempt to create intimacy in an effort to repair the damage of something hurtful she might have done. You must respond to such attempts in a manner that allows intimacy to flow between you and your partner, such as openly receiving her repair attempts by acting assertively, creating the orderly place for that to occur. Failing to recognize your partner's attempts to connect with you is often caused by passiveness, defensiveness, and aggressiveness, which usually restricts intimacy.

Responding in a way that restricts intimacy will likely deter your partner from giving as much effort the next time she desires to do something meaningful or attempts to repair some hurt she may have caused. Thus, the spiral into chaos will continue. Your responses to your partner, over time, condition their behaviors toward you. You can use this aspect of your relationship to create and allow intimacy to happen, or you can use it to drive your partner away.

Rodion & Regina XIII

As of late, Rodion has undeniably failed to practice assertiveness in his relationship with Regina. It is not so much the case that he was never assertive or that his temperament is not built for it. Rather, it is that he has not improved his assertiveness to the level necessary for managing conflict and setting boundaries with Regina's emerging needs—rooted in her emerging feminine. Rodion has been struggling with the relationship due largely to his frustrations toward her frequent criticisms of him.

However, his real frustrations have more to do with Regina never apologizing for her wrongdoings and not owning her part in their conflict. Rodion would confide in a close friend of his, saying, "the one thing that upsets me the most is that, sometimes after an argument, Regina would want to fix me dinner or watch one of our favorite shows together."

He told his friend that he would be ruminating over the conflict and that Regina would "just act like nothing ever happened." This is Rodion being defensive and passive. However, through processing these experiences and reading books to help him understand himself, Rodion has begun to recognize that, when Regina wants to fix his dinner or watch a show together, it was her attempting to restore intimacy. It was Regina's own way of apologizing.

More specifically, these were her attempts to repair the damage she might have caused. Because Rodion framed this as her pretending nothing happened, his responses to her attempts were preventing intimacy and, over time, conditioning her to be less intimate. Rodion is now trying to view these behaviors of Regina's as attempts to connect with him.

He is beginning to respond in a much more emotionally reliable way, acknowledging her repair attempts and allowing her to express her apologies in her own way. Rodion is improving the quality of his responses to Regina by examining his own behaviors and attitudes toward her. He is beginning to realize that he was being defensive and passive and that responding assertively injects the necessary order that makes room for more intimacy. Perhaps, unknowingly, Rodion is beginning to establish the appropriate kinds of boundaries in his relationship with Regina.

In relationships, there are three areas in which you must establish boundaries and manage conflict: you, your partner, and the relationship itself. The ability to effectively manage conflict and establish healthy boundaries is paramount. The key is to broaden your skill sets and give greater efforts to ensure that you are emotionally sound. It is frequently the case that men who need to transform themselves in the context of their relationship must first establish boundaries both with themselves as well as around the relationship.

This is often difficult for today's man because he does not understand the nuances of this concept and because he cannot comprehend standing his ground while simultaneously striving to support his partner, while also ensuring the relationship as a whole is tended to. The idea that one cannot love someone and at the same time allow them to experience consequences is a common experience, but it is a false dichotomy. This is driven by the erroneous ideas around unconditional love, which misleads people to black and white thinking. Relationships are not unconditional. For a relationship to have any hope for success, the relationship's terms and conditions must exist and be carefully and attentively addressed as needed.

Because long-term relationships span over long periods of time, these terms and conditions must be set in place as both partners grow and evolve. This is part of the natural process of relationships. Failure to grow and change is a failure to thrive. Furthermore, the terms and conditions of a relationship are subject to revision as we grow. As our wants and needs change—which they usually do—the terms and conditions often need to be refined or even amended. Some may need to be eliminated altogether. What worked for you and your partner ten years ago may no longer work today. Conversely, you both may have changed your stances on particular subjects.

On the surface, people change all the time, and it is likely the case that both you and your partner have changed a great deal. Yet, failing to modify your boundaries and refine the ways you manage conflict signals an alarm in your partner that you are not growing. And this is distressing to her. Growth and evolution signify progress and value. Your partner unconsciously judges you in this regard, and she will not value you if you are not growing because it implies you are not moving toward your potential.

Restoring harmony and intimacy in your relationship, and improving yourself as a man, requires that you shore up the foundation on which you build your life. The formula is in the types of boundaries you set and how you reinforce them.

Managing Conflict

Managing conflict means preventing it as it arises and diffusing it when it escalates. The integrated man steers conflict in a way that brings order from it. The hero sees conflict and courageously extracts from it the key to his feminine counterpart's heart. For today's man to elevate himself, he must first improve the quality of his communication skills so that he may improve his responses during conflict.

Assertive communication is foundational for quality communication and forward progress. Most people are familiar with the concept that communication is key to a successful relationship. As true as this statement is, it is an incomplete notion. Communication is key, but by all means it must be quality, truthful communication.

Assertiveness helps today's man end unnecessary attacks from others, prevents him from needlessly defending his words and actions, and sets the necessary limitations that create the space for his relationship to thrive. Most people automatically resort to offensive attacks or rely on defensive strategies when engaged in conflict. These methods of operations are used to win wars, not diffuse them. In relational conflict, offensive attacks and defensive strategies only reinforce the other's stance or, worse, drive them away defeated. Others may tend to act more passively, concealing their actual experiences, making it difficult for the other person to respond well to them. Today's man must strive to master assertiveness skills, for they are indispensable tools that manage conflict most effectively.

Establishing Boundaries

Assertiveness is not just about managing conflict; it is about standing up for what is right and taking steps to ensure the right things happen. In relationships, it means proactively doing what's best for the individuals and the relationship itself. In other words, it is about setting boundaries. In this context, boundaries are the conditions of relationships, which are based on the needs, desires, interests, and preferences of the individuals within the relationship.

All relationships come with terms and conditions. This is not to imply that we should all sign written agreements when a relationship starts. It does suggest that if we clearly set boundaries and enforce them, we will experience less damage from conflict and, perhaps, become stronger through conflict. People often narrowly think that boundaries are only about drawing a line in the sand, which expresses to the other person, "Do not cross this line. If you do, you will have violated me, and there will be consequences". They are not wrong, and it is important to establish this kind of boundary. Yet, only exercising this type of boundary is an incomplete approach to properly setting boundaries. The line in the sand creates the necessary space between the individuals in the relationship. This space is what keeps one person from impeding the other's needs. This space also allows other experiences to occur, such as individuality and personal identity, which is paramount in relationships. This kind of boundary serves to ensure that an individuals' needs have room to be met.

If the individuals in the relationship are not having their needs met, they cannot function well, and the relationship will suffer. Therefore, the health of the individuals directly influences the vitality of the relationship. The individuals' needs and desires must be attended to. Being conscious of this type of boundary in our responses to our partner reminds us to maintain self-respect and also to respect her boundaries. Our responses improve as the line in the sand becomes more meaningful.

Drawing a line in the sand is essential. However, equitable attention should be given to the relationship itself. While the line in the sand creates a necessary space between the individuals for trust and individuality, it also creates distance by default. If we only create distance, and there is nothing to buffer that space, there will be too much distance—the relationship will not be possible.

Therefore, it is important to establish the kind of boundary that surrounds the relationship to protect it and to enable the needs of the relationship to be met. This kind of boundary is called a perimeter. The perimeter aims to provide optimal limitations for the relationship to exist yet also allows enough room for exploration and growth. It is similar to fencing in the backyard for the dog to be, well, a dog. While it keeps the dog safe from wandering off too far or running onto the road and getting hit by a passing car, it also allows the dog to explore more territory outside the confines of the house. The perimeter keeps us from distancing ourselves too much or focusing on ourselves too an unhealthy degree—it also prevents us from focusing too much on the other person. More importantly, it allows trust, love, intimacy, and other factors that build harmonious connections to flourish.

Seeking to create appropriate perimeters around the relationship paves the way for us to improve our responses to our partner. As we respond to our partner and situations in the relationship, we must ask ourselves, *"How might my response create a perimeter around this relationship? How might my response promote growth and connection?"* Practicing this helps us consider alternative behaviors that might be better suited for improving the quality of the relationship. Below are some general ideas to consider as a way to improve the quality of your responses. They are the *three-second rule, ownership vs. apologies, nonverbal communication*, and *I Statements*.

The Three-Second Rule

Effective responses will increase as you master communication skills. One such skill is the *three-second rule*, which is taking three seconds to respond to a question or statement, allowing time for more thoughts to come to mind, potentially providing you with a more effective response. Let's say we have about one thought per second. If you allow yourself three seconds to reply to the other person's question or statement, you are giving yourself time to process three additional thoughts. These thoughts can spawn alternative ideas for more positive responses, enhancing conflict resolution. This might be especially true in more intense conflict. During intense conflict, or even casual, stimulating discussions, we often begin replying to the other person before they have finished speaking. This overlap might be as much as two or three seconds, which potentially means that if we wait until they finish speaking, and then apply the *three-second rule*, we could possibly process an additional five or six thoughts before responding. The number of thoughts that could spark a quality response is just that much greater.

The *three-second rule* also serves as a display of respect to the other person and can enrich the conversation overall. This might have more of a profound impact if our previous tendency is to interrupt our partner. People are often reluctant to practice this rule for fear of appearing indifferent to the conflict or appearing dumb. However, when they take an honest look at their reluctance, they might discover that it is about feeling too awkward and uncomfortable. And that is a different story. People report that three seconds feels like a long time and that it seems as if their partner will view them as being too silent. However, the opposite is true. Implementing this rule shows that you give your partner's questions and statements the thoughtful consideration they deserve. Delivering thoughtful consideration with the appropriate nonverbal communication bolsters the effectiveness of this strategy. People appreciate thoughtful consideration. At the least, it indicates that you are giving an improved effort, which is attractive.

Practicing dialogues with yourself and counting out loud to three, in order to get a feel for how long three seconds is, allows you to get more comfortable with this rule. Perhaps, the most advantageous way to practice this rule is to implement it during inconsequential interactions. When people let down their guard and are less defensive, they are likely to appreciate you waiting three seconds before responding. At most, they will be curious about this new behavior. The subtle implementation of the *three-second rule* will likely go unnoticed in these calmer, more carefree conversations.

This practice strategy has two rationales. The first rationale is about conditioning, which exposes others to this new behavior. Therefore, when you use the technique in intense conflict, your partner will be likely to be calmed by your three seconds of thoughtful consideration, which might otherwise induce an emotional reaction from your partner. The second rationale in this practice strategy in subtle conversations is proficiency built through inconsequential interactions. If a professional baseball player skips batting practice or practices with minimal effort, he risks being under prepared for the real game. When he is called to the plate, his ability to deliver will be minimal. Therefore, if we do not practice such strategies, our conflict management skills will be in question when we need them the most.

The *three-second rule* is a profound antidote to impulsivity and emotional reactions, which can be detrimental to intimate connections. Our brains operate in two modes: rational and emotional. These two modes exist on a scale: the higher the rationale, the lower the emotion; the higher the emotions, the lower the rationale. Irrational choices often translate to regrettable actions. Hence, it is imperative that we be rational enough to make sound decisions and give higher quality responses in serious conflict. Allowing three seconds to pass between her speaking and your reply provides you with an opportunity to notice better ideas. Allowing a little more time for your emotions to settle and your rationale to increase gives you an optimal chance to improve your responses in the heat of the moment.

Ownership vs. Apologies

Ownership vs. apologies is about appropriately responding to mistakes and wrongdoings. While apologies are exactly what are called for at times, they should only be issued when necessary. Your apologies should carry a lot of weight and be given only after careful consideration. Do not overuse them. When apologies are used too liberally, they lose their effectiveness and, at worst, will only fuel resentments. For instance, if you apologize in the same way every time, it will likely be perceived as simply an attempt to end an argument or conflict.

Eventually, your partner will realize that the actual problems never get better when you avoid ownership and responsibility with them. Therefore, we must be selective when choosing to apologize, opting to assume ownership instead. Oftentimes, however, apologies are prompted or even demanded by others when we say or do something hurtful, and we may feel it is the right thing to do in that moment. The problem with this is that we tend to lump together everything we said or did during the conflict and apologize for saying anything at all. For example, when Rodion and Regina are experiencing a rapidly escalating moment of conflict, the suddenness of the conflict catches him off guard as he may not be emotionally centered enough for conflict. Although he starts by practicing assertiveness, he eventually falls short of his capacity to manage conflict, and, in his attempts to get his point across, Rodion yells at Regina.

Yet, he does well to recognize he has lost his composure and sees that he needs to regain control of his frame. His solution is quickly telling

Regina, "I'm sorry for yelling at you. I should not have even brought this up. Let's just forget about it and move on". This seems like a noble action to take in this situation. While there are far worse alternative endings to this example, this is not the best response. He gave up on his capacity to be creative enough for an optimal solution. And that is not good.

Being selective with your apologies forces you to become more creative with your assertiveness. Being creative with assertiveness—without apologizing—propels you to take ownership of your behavior, assume responsibility for managing conflict, and maintain frame control. In the above scenario with Rodion and Regina, we can see a lack of assertiveness as he dismisses his own needs by telling her, "Let's just forget about it and move on." Although he attempted to take ownership of his wrongdoing (yelling), he was irresponsible with it because he sacrificed his self-respect by ultimately ignoring a legitimate issue that needed to be addressed.

Essentially, he lost frame, which is counterintuitive to the relationship's growth potential and the connection between him and Regina. As we have learned, lacking frame control can cause us to be wildly inconsistent, severely limiting the stability and longevity of relationships. By taking responsible ownership of his wrongdoing in this conflict, Rodion might have said something like, "You know, I shouldn't have yelled at you. That's not who I want to be. Yet, I stand by what I said, and I should get my point across without yelling. So, what I was trying to say is…" This type of response is important because it distinguishes exactly what Rodion did wrong and did not lump everything he said and did as wrong. There was nothing wrong with the point he wanted to get across.

Perhaps, he needed to establish a boundary with Regina or reinforce a previously established boundary with her. Maybe he needed to express a particular desire to her. Therefore, owning what we have fallen short on must be done with precision. Owning our shortcomings is highly valuable; saying we are wrong for something we did right is low value behavior.

Limiting how many apologies you allow yourself also displays high value in the sense that you are not willing to be shamed or manipulated or to simply overuse and devalue the act of apologizing. Owning your failures and shortcomings shows that, despite your flaws, you can withstand your mistakes and continue improving as a quality man. Standing up for what you do right is indicative of self-respect. Sacrificing your self-respect because you "felt bad" translates to a loss of self-control (the resulting quality of assertiveness and frame). Healthy relationships work better when the individuals within it have self-control and address conflict with a sense of ownership and self-respect.

Nonverbal Communication

Nonverbal communication includes eye contact, body language, tone of voice, timing, and content of speech. Like other animals in the animal kingdom, human beings are sensitive to subtle cues given off by particular physical behaviors of the body. Sudden bodily movements or jerky eye movements may suggest hyper-alertness or an unconscious preparedness to defend oneself or even attack. These signals indicate anxiety, which, combined with subtle defensive or aggressive behaviors, might induce distress in other people. Our physical stance may reflect strong concealed emotions, which might alarm others to anticipate an intense situation. Vocal cues can signify to others that you are concealing significant and strong thoughts and feelings. If a certain tone of voice is too aggressive, it might put others on the defensive. Maybe your tone of voice lacks authority, which exposes a lack of confidence regarding what you are attempting to convey. Appropriate and timely communication is often the difference in another's receptivity to what you are attempting to discuss. The content of speech has to do with the message itself. Having some precision with your message allows you to stay on course during conversations and conflict.

As you read through the following sections, notice what behaviors you find in yourself and experiment with modifying them. Some might resonate with you more than others. The more they resonate with you, the more profound your behavior changes will be with each respective aspect of communication as you modify them.

Eye Movement

Proper eye contact shows that you are engaged and demonstrates focused attention. This is important because your partner can see in your eyes that you are focused and present. Jerky eye movement might suggest to your partner that you are hyper-alert, and you may appear to be overly anxious. Being overly anxious during confrontation or conflict could signify distress, making it difficult to create a calm environment. This is a low-value behavior in relationships, especially when the quality of the relationship and the individuals' well-being are at risk.

To recover from, and prevent inducing, distress in those around us, we need to understand how behaviors are often modified. Just as smiling quite often induces feelings of happiness or joy, slowing down our jerky eye movement to a slower, more controlled eye movement might induce a calmer environment and more assurance in yourself, as well as your partner, particularly during conflict. Most importantly, it will help cultivate confidence in your abilities to manage conflict, increasing your value as a man.

Body Language

Body language should coincide with the nature of the message you are getting across because it strengthens your stance on what you are communicating. Being mindful of your bodily movements and posture can tip the scales of conflict by going from body language associated with non-assertive communication to a more confident posture. Look around at people throughout the day and try to guess what's going on with them emotionally. Are they confident? Anxious? Preoccupied? Angry or frustrated? Happy? Carefree? Notice their body posture and how it reflects what that person could be experiencing at that moment. Then, notice your own body posture and what possible message it conveys.

Tone of Voice

Tone of voice is often the most vital component of nonverbal communication. The volume of your voice should indicate that you are authentically passionate about your needs while conveying thoughtful consideration for your partner's needs. Your voice level should be one that is convincing yet non-threatening. Most of us have some degree of accuracy when assessing our tone of voice. Yet, when it comes to conflict, we are often too emotional.

Therefore, we might benefit from being conscious of the tone of our voice in such situations. Doing so can help us maintain composure and stay in our frame. If we sense that we are aggressive, frustrated, or angry, our voice might become elevated, and the cadence of our speech may speed up.

We could benefit from consciously calming our voice and slowing our speech. For some, however, their voices might become eerily calm and almost monotone. This could be misconstrued as cold and emotionless.

Therefore, making our voices a little livelier can make our partner feel safer with us. If we notice that we are passive, anxious, or even intimidated during confrontation or conflict, our voice might be pressured, strained, and at a low volume.

Shoring up our speech and the volume level of our voice helps convey our message more convincingly. If we detect that our voice sounds a little higher pitched than normal or our rate of speech has increased, it might suggest that we are becoming defensive. Settling our voice and decreasing our speech rate can help us shift toward a more assertive frame.

Some men may have the problem of being tone-deaf with their own voices. There may also be a tendency for such people to be in denial of this issue. It is useful to recognize if others have told you that you have this problem or that you sound annoyed or angry; there's probably some truth to this. Be open-minded to this potential issue with yourself and be willing to work on it. Ask those close to you, whose opinion you value, to be candid regarding your tone of voice. This can produce constructive feedback for you to improve yourself.

However, it may not just be angry tones you are not noticing. Maybe you are monotone or speak too softly, and people have difficulty hearing you. Perhaps this coincides with other thoughts you, or others, have about your demeanor. Alternatively, overthinking aspects of communication, such as tone of voice, could easily lead to neuroticism, which is not helpful. Therefore, only you can determine how satisfied you need to be with your efforts.

Using the Three-Second Rule is an excellent tool when we sense our mood shifting toward a negative, unhealthy frame. Taking a few seconds to gather ourselves provides insight and clarity into our mental and emotional state. It can increase our rationale, leading to a more assertive and confident version of ourselves. You might think that you have too many big problems to be worried about such unimportant things as tone of voice. However, just as the little stressors wear us down and make life complicated, it is the little improvements that make us stronger across all aspects of our lives. Part of the mastery of our skill sets is knowing them inside and out. It is learning about all the little nuances of that skill set to be the expert of our own abilities. While getting hung up on a single aspect can impede our mastery, taking it for granted can be costly.

Timing

Timing is the art of identifying when your partner is likely to be receptive. Timing is important because it can be the difference between your message "falling on deaf ears" or being heard. For example, refrain from bringing up an important and potentially emotional discussion with your partner when you two are on your way to an important business networking event or before meeting friends for dinner. This will only cause an emotional distraction, which will deepen the conflict. Carefully consider how receptive to your message your partner will be and practice patience.

On the other hand, do not procrastinate. Do not pass up a prime opportunity to deliver your message; strike while the iron is hot. It may be when she happens to bring up a related issue or is simply free of distractions and not preoccupied. Make it clear from the outset that you need to have a serious conversation, and then proceed to communicate your message.

There are, of course, social and cultural considerations with nonverbal communication. Throughout historical eras and different cultures, body language, eye contact, tone of voice, etc., hold various significant meanings. Understanding the social norms of nonverbal cues can help you improve yourself as a man. We need reference points (our peers) to more accurately gauge the significance of our body language and other modes of nonverbal communication and how others experience them. For instance, seeking to be more stoic, a man might think he should rarely smile and only do so in certain situations.

Yet, if he looks at other men in the world around him, he might realize that smiling is often associated with confidence or being satisfied, which are stoic traits. Considering the timing of a discussion may not naturally be a priority for many men. Suppose you are on the low end of the trait agreeableness (low agreeableness is self-oriented and high agreeableness is others oriented).

In that case, while you tend to negotiate well for your own needs, you might not have a proclivity for considering and understanding the emotional needs of others as well as their sensitivity to the way you carry yourself. For such individuals, learning to identify the right time for a particular discussion may take practice and conscious effort. This could be especially true if you are also low in neuroticism (sensitivity to pain and discomfort). In other words, sensitivity to others' emotional pain discomfort plays a major role in conflict, especially in the sense of being trustworthy. Therefore, considering the timing of your confrontations may help broaden the trait agreeableness.

The higher you are in the trait agreeableness, the more difficult it is for you to negotiate for your needs effectively. People high in agreeableness may find themselves with too many unmet needs. For a man who is relatively high in agreeableness and is attempting to set boundaries, confident body language and well-timed conversations can bolster your efforts to get your needs met.

Experimenting with changing the more anxious or passive aspects of your body language can help set the tone of the interactions with your partner. As confidence indicates assurance in our abilities, it can be a strong determinant of how much others believe us, which is especially true when establishing and enforcing boundaries.

If you are high in neuroticism, modifying your body language, tone of voice, and eye movement to reflect assertiveness will begin to induce feelings of confidence in the way you manage conflict and boundaries. The benefit of this is that it decreases your negative emotional experiences and creates room for more positive emotional experiences. The mindful experimentation with your nonverbal communication will also strengthen your frame, making you more consistent in getting your needs met while increasing self-control.

I Statements

I statements have two uses: to express a want or a need; or express a feeling or emotion. Expressing a need or want is done when you need someone to perform a certain activity or need specific information. Expressing a feeling or emotion is useful when the other person's behavior affects you emotionally. In relationships, clearly and explicitly expressing our desires is imperative for giving the other person a genuine chance to respond in a quality manner. I statements are often underrated and erroneously dismissed, often to the detriment of the relationship.

Using I statements allows you to focus on your needs and wants instead of focusing on your partner's shortcomings by eliminating the perception of you attacking your partner's character. For example, regarding

Regina's recent criticism of Rodion for the way he handled their last conflict, he might say to her, "You are always so critical! You never give me any credit for my hard work". Besides being an emotional reaction, this is an attack on Regina's character ("always so critical") and an emotional accusation ("You never give me any credit"). Strong words such as "always" and "never" are almost too absolute in this context and are often simply not true. They are the kinds of words that are tied to resentment.

More importantly, pointing out her undesirable behavior without expressing his needs and wants is simply a reflection of his own insecurities, and it projects the fault and blame onto her. This does not serve the relationship.

Using *I statements* positions you to express your needs and wants and how her behavior is affecting you. Moreover, it enables you to establish boundaries with her behavior based on your needs and wants. By saying to her, "I don't need your criticism" and "I feel like I don't get enough credit for what I do," it demonstrates that Rodion has a boundary indicating that he does not need her criticism and how her criticism affects him. Although this technique is designed to demonstrate ownership, it highlights the effects of Regina's behavior.

This gives her something genuine to respond to, which is beneficial to cultivating harmonious relationships. Using I statements displays self-control and aims to assert yourself properly. By doing so, you bring value to the relationship in the sense that you are emotionally reliable and can assume responsible leadership when necessary.

Assertiveness Skills

Relational conflict is unavoidable and is simply a part of relationship growth. This type of conflict is not detrimental to a relationship; what damages relationships are how people respond to such conflict. In the book, *When I Say No, I Feel Guilty*,[40] Manuel J. Smith illuminates why we are not assertive enough and why we should improve our assertiveness skills. Smith states, "Each of us is ultimately responsible for our own psychological well-being, happiness, and success in life."

Reducing your own aggressive behaviors, and removing the likelihood for your partner to act non-assertively, increases the opportunities for relationship growth and a harmonious connection. The most important aspect of assertive communication is the use of empathy.

Empathy is the ability to understand and share the feelings of another. Keep in mind that empathy is what will most enhance all of your assertiveness skills. The following assertiveness skills can radically improve your communication, boundary setting, and conflict management. These skills can be read about in greater detail in Smith's book. They are discussed here as they relate to the concepts in this book. Do not disregard these skills. Apply them holistically, for they can enhance your efforts to become an integrated man.

Broken Record

Broken record is a technique involving repeatedly saying what you need or want until you reach a workable compromise that includes having those needs or wants to be met. Practicing the assertiveness skill of *broken record* enhances your capacity to maintain frame by keeping sight of the outcome you desire and brushing off your partner's misinterpretations and deflective tactics. Utilizing the *broken record* skill increases the likelihood that your partner will honor your request or, at the very least, begin to progress toward a workable compromise. Conveying your message is your responsibility and persistence is key to having success with your message being received.

Broken record is an assertiveness skill that allows you to get your message across to your partner by overcoming distractions. Such distractions might include verbal remarks from your partner that point out her needs or your shortcomings, as well as argumentative baiting, which is a defective tactic designed to pull you from your frame of getting your need met and into her frame of not wanting to put in the effort it takes to meet you halfway.

Broken record is effective when you stay calm and incorporate positive nonverbal communication. This assertiveness skill is straightforward, which prevents the need to psych yourself out, that is, psychologically manipulating yourself to engage in a stressful situation when, in reality, you are undermining your confidence.

When you psych yourself out, there is a tendency to create a false sense of confidence, and you will undermine your efforts to manage conflict. Your false confidence will bleed through any attempts to veil your insecurities. Be direct and truthful, and there will be no need to conceal your insecurities.

Fogging

Fogging is the skill of being comfortably receptive to criticism. This skill helps diffuse accusations and verbal attacks issued to you by your partner. *Fogging* is acknowledging criticism by agreeing there is at least some degree of truth to what your partner is saying—or that it technically could be true—while refraining from making unnecessary confessions, for you are the one who validates your own behavior. Emotional accusations and verbal attacks issued to you by your partner are undesirable and aggressive. Rewarding such undesirable behavior from her only perpetuates such behavior and removes her incentive to be more assertive.

Conversely, there is no need to become aggressive and retaliate when she displays negative behavior or harshly criticizes you. An example of *fogging* could be, "I understand that you are upset, and I can see why you would be" or "You're right, I did say that, and I understand you are upset about that."

Fogging serves to diffuse accusatory statements and hostile arguments by empathizing with your partner's emotional response to the conflict and diminishing the impulse for them to aggressively defend their irrational—although understandable—stance. Remember, the *why*, or *function* of her behavior, is more important than what she is doing or saying. The function of her statements and behaviors is reflective of what the resolution to the conflict is. Everything we do we do to meet a need. Suppose you ignore the accusatory and hostile statements and behaviors from your partner. In that case, you are minimizing their emotions, which will make her resent you more or escalate her emotional responses.

Fogging is an assertiveness skill that improves the capacity to accept harsh criticism by peacefully letting your partner know she is heard and understood. It is a technique that subtly reinforces frame by practicing self-control rather than responding poorly and needlessly contributing to the chaos.

Negative Inquiry

Negative inquiry is a skill that deliberately prompts criticism, which encourages your partner to be more assertive. When using this skill, you are essentially asking clarifying questions about particular statements made about you by your partner. These statements may be accusatory in nature or assassinations of your character. Using this skill, your partner may not even realize you are maneuvering the conversation and leading her to be assertive. An example of this could be your partner making an accusatory statement such as, "You always ignore me, just like you are right now," a negative inquiry from you might be, "What is it about me that makes you feel like I'm ignoring you?"

An example of a *negative inquiry* about a character assassination statement from your partner, such as, "You think you're being funny, but your humor is offensive and upsetting," might be, "What is it about my humor that is offensive and upsetting to you?" These types of clarifying questions eliminate the need for you to defend your actions and character and allow your partner to express herself without her having to use negative or hurtful tactics. Defending such actions is arbitrarily inferred as an admission of guilt—an adamant denial of an accusation can be perceived as concealing guilt.

Using *negative inquiry* provides a degree of useful information about yourself from your partner, which can bolster your self-improvement plan. This skill can also be implemented to diminish your partner's unconscious, manipulative ploys to control the relationship arbitrarily.

Furthermore, asking for criticism puts you in the driver's seat of the conflict by removing your defensiveness while disarming your partner's unconscious, manipulative tactics. Recognize critical comments and seek to understand those criticisms; they indicate a hidden, unconscious process—everything we do, we do to meet a need. *Negative inquiry* can peel back the proverbial layers of the onion, which reveals the true nature of the distress.

Eventually, you will get to the root of the conflict and then reach a workable compromise. *Negative inquiry* looks for criticism about yourself from your partner by eliciting sincere expressions of your partner's negative emotions about her experience of you, leading to higher quality communication that will help address the deeper needs within the relationships.

Negative Assertion

Negative assertion is a skill that enables you to accept and overcome your mistakes and flaws—past and present—through the use of paraphrasing the criticism of those mistakes and flaws. *Negative assertion* allows you to exist in a more secure sense of self and emanate a calm air of stillness in the face of accusations and character assassinations without needlessly defending your behavior. This assertive skill, when properly used, diminishes the power of your partner's criticism of you by not only acknowledging her criticism of you but by exposing your mistakes and flaws.

For instance, in prior conflicts, your partner has expressed a negative experience with a particular behavioral pattern of yours that has often induced emotional distress in her. Perhaps, she has expressed to you that you have a habit of being hypercritical of the way she parents, yet, you have a legitimate concern you wish to express regarding some recent interactions between her and your child. Likely, you are not too far removed from the conflict in which your partner expressed that you are hypercritical—at least in her mind. Therefore, you might consider saying something to the effect of, "Hey. I know in the recent past I've been unfairly critical of how you raise our child, but I do have something I'd like to address with some interactions I've seen lately, when you're up for it."

One way to understand *negative assertion* is to view it as a method of preemptively acknowledging your partner's negative emotional experience with you and her attacks before she can even use them. This technique serves to disarm her criticisms and accusations, leaving her more receptive to open communication. This skill prevents unnecessary warfare, which opens room for more conflict resolution. If you fail to use *negative assertion* until after the conflict has already escalated, it is still an effective skill. Even in a delayed application of this skill, your partner will grow tired of criticizing you because it will have lost its effectiveness over you.

Free Information

Free information is the observable, subtle clues (typically verbal) given by your partner in day-to-day interactions. Your partner's *free information* gives you insight into what is interesting and important to her. Familiarize yourself with this skill, for it is essential in mastering assertive communication.

You can use subtle clues about your partner to further inquire about certain topics, or you can use them to transition into other related topics. As it pertains to resolving conflict, you can use the clues of *free information* when applying the previously discussed assertiveness skills. For example, she may have expressed subtle comments and random questions lately about missing you and what your weekly schedule looks like.

These subtle comments and random questions may not hold much significance when viewed as separate and non-related. Collectively, however, they may be representative of an unconscious emotional need. Recognizing the collective significance of the free but subtle information she expresses in your communication can help in two primary ways: enhancing conflict resolution and enhancing your efforts to connect with her. *Free information* keeps the conversation from being superficial by recognizing significant details of your partner's discussions and following up by warmly encouraging her to talk more about her interests and what is important to her. Doing so positions you in a vantage point that allows you to see her feminine behaviors as something beautiful and glorious. If attuned to, *free information* will reveal to you the dynamic and fluid nature of the feminine.

Self-Disclosure

Self-disclosure is an assertiveness skill that involves internally acknowledging your personality's defects and assets, followed by talking about how you think, feel, and react to the *free information* your partner discloses. Do not underestimate the value of *self-disclosure*, for it is an indispensable skill in your mastery of assertive communication. Your partner's *self-disclosure* of *free information* should be strategically followed up by your own *self-disclosure* to her. That is, it is useful to thoughtfully respond to her vulnerability with your own controlled vulnerability. This enhances two-way communication.

Self-disclosure prevents you from being experienced as too invasive regarding your partner's experience, causing her to withdraw when she becomes uncomfortable. In other words, if she is the only one sharing her vulnerable thoughts and feelings, and she continues to be pried open, she becomes skeptical of your intentions and puts her guard up. Be careful not to display too much questioning behavior, for it will spark suspiciousness in your partner about you because it makes you appear to be nosy or jealous.

Balancing the openness in your interactions with your partner through the use of *self-disclosure* can signify a clear effort to connect with her. It can also signify to your partner that you understand her or are seeking to understand her. People want to be understood. Your feminine partner wants you to understand her, not to be able to articulate who she is, but to connect with who truly she is.

The feminine nature is so much deeper than the vast majority of people can imagine. Ancient history's depiction of the feminine represented a much different understanding than what is portrayed in modern times. It is as though the feminine nature has evolved into a non-functioning aspect of humanity.

Similar to our understanding of the appendix, it is often thought best to extract it. From the perspectives taken throughout this book, we can see that the feminine nature's essence has been reduced into an evolutionary leftover. It is an eternal aspect that has been suppressed over millennia.

Your partner's longing to be understood and connected with is driven by a long-suppressed feminine nature aching to be actualized in the consciousness of the masculine; that is, the feminine's deepest desire is to express itself with her man's deepest presence and freely so.

Self-disclosure is an ineradicable part of the process of masculine and feminine connections. *Self-disclosure* builds self-control, increases attractiveness, stimulates progress, and opens us up to give our gifts. This personification of masculinity is made possible through embracing today's woman.

Workable Compromise

When used, all the previously mentioned assertiveness skills can give you a sense of satisfaction. However, the greater reward comes from integrating these skills and consistently utilizing them to reach a *workable compromise*, which is an agreement or settlement which allows you and your partner to have both your needs met.

However, if a compromise puts into question your self-respect, then there should be no compromise; continue using these assertiveness skills until you can reach a *workable compromise* without sacrificing your self-respect. *Workable compromises* are different from sacrifices due to the mutual understanding of—and willingness—to meet each other's needs versus giving up a need or desire without clear communication of the impact of such a sacrifice. Sacrifices leave too much room for unmet needs and resentments because of the avoidant nature of sacrifice, representing neglect of self—it is not a noble and selfless act.

Reaching a *workable compromise,* when the conflict escalates into an emotionally imbalanced conversation and you sense your partner becoming antagonistic, is made possible through certain assertive communication techniques. These techniques are as follows:

- *Fogging* — helps diffuse the antagonistic behaviors in conflict

- *Broken record* — seeks to maintain self-respect and prevents you from neglecting your needs

- *Negative inquiry* — directly and efficiently navigates through the superficial and emotional manifestations of deeper unmet needs, bringing you an understanding of what needs to be tended to.

- *Negative assertion* — affords you the ability to preemptively disarm people and quickly reach a workable compromise

- *Self-disclosure* — creates an environment of open communication that can prompt a mutual desire to connect.

Empathy

Rodion & Regina XIV

Regina came home from work late one evening. She and Rodion had already been at odds with each other for the past few days over her criticism of him—rather, his mismanagement of her criticism. Rodion expressed his desires with Regina about wanting her to be less critical of him by saying, "You are too critical of me. Do you really think that makes me want to change?"

Meanwhile, Rodion was not aware that a close friend of Regina's had been offering her suggestions about being more assertive with Rodion in the relationship (a reasonable skill to explore). Experimenting with being more assertive, she responded to Rodion's expression of wanting less criticism with as much of a serious face as she could muster, but with a slightly high-pitched voice, "I'm sorry you feel that way." Not wanting to come across in a non-assertive way, she tried not to move or change her expression as she awaited his response. Rodion searched his skill set for an appropriate response, sensing something wasn't quite normal. It was clear that she was behaving differently—the strange new facial expression (anomaly). Her facial expression was unexpected and held unspecified significance; hence, Rodion was unsure how to categorize it.[41] He was skeptical of this new behavior. Rodion had known Regina long enough to notice the subtle emotional cues in her facial expression. The expression on her face seemed to contain contempt.

Although he tried to dismiss this, he became more and more frustrated. He responded to her, saying, "I don't buy your bullshit apology." Regina, in one last attempt to be assertive, replied, "I'm just trying to let you know that I'm sorry you feel that way." Rodion took this as Regina being stubborn and became less inclined to resolve the conflict, leading to him shutting down and stonewalling her.

Assessing the Issue

The scenario above is common in many relationships. A quick analysis of this interaction might conclude that Regina was right to assert herself and that Rodion could stand to learn how to be more receptive to her assertiveness. While this is true, it only speaks to half the equation here. On the other hand, had he used a little empathy, he may have gotten a better response from her. While it is Regina's responsibility to respond well, it is Rodion's responsibility to effectively get his message across to elicit the best possible response from her. Going a little further into this analysis might reveal deeper issues.

Most people can learn what assertiveness is and how to be assertive. Assertiveness is acting firmly while standing up for yourself and for what you believe to be right. It is important to understand why a person would need to be assertive. Assertiveness is necessary to get what you need and to do so in a way that reaches a *workable compromise* by getting the other person to support a particular point of view. In other words, it is used to attempt to change another person's behavior regarding its effect on you. The challenge with assertiveness is balancing standing up for yourself and considering the other person's needs.

However, assertiveness is about getting what you need when it comes down to it. Rodion stood up for himself yet did not consider the reasons that would have supported the idea that Regina was attempting to manage the conflict more appropriately.

Why Empathy is Important

Back to the other half of the equation. The problem with the way many people use assertiveness pertains to a lack of empathy in its implementation. Empathy is the ability to understand and share the feelings and experiences of other people. When empathy is practiced, people feel understood. When people feel understood, they are more receptive to the person practicing empathy with them. If assertiveness is about getting what you need, then the other person must be receptive to you. Practicing empathy in your attempts to be assertive will cultivate your partner's willingness to change their behavior as it pertains to you. Although it would have been challenging at the moment, Rodion's attempts to practice empathy might have prompted Regina to be more flexible and understanding. Instead, he responded with defensive skepticism, resulting in an unresolved conflict and stonewalling.

Empathic Assertiveness

Here is the same scenario again, but this time it involves empathy.

Rodion & Regina XV

Regina came home from work late one evening. She and Rodion had been bickering for a few days over her criticism of him—rather, his mismanagement of her criticism. Rodion expressed his desire for Regina to be less critical of him by saying, "I know you love me, and I trust you. Yet sometimes I feel like you are too critical of me, and it rubs me the wrong way. Again, you do a lot of things well, and I appreciate that. But I also need to let you know what's going on with me" Little did Rodion know that a close friend of Regina's had been offering her some suggestions on being more assertive with her partner. Prompted by Rodion's empathy, she responded to his expression of wanting less criticism by looking at him with a facial expression that showed concern and tenderness. Then, reciprocating the empathy, she calmly said, "I'm really sorry you feel that way, and I'm glad you told me. I don't want to be critical of you" Regina calmly awaited his response.

Rodion's attitude began to change, and he wanted to respond even more empathically. It was clear to him that she was using assertiveness, yet he felt her empathy and believed her intentions were positive. Rodion had known Regina long enough to notice the subtlest of emotional cues as he processed her facial expression. There seemed to be a hint of remorse on her face. This inspired him to reassure her that she does many things wonderfully and that he appreciated her willingness to listen. As a result, Rodion and Regina were inclined to reach a *workable compromise* and experience more intimacy.

The Case against Assertiveness

There is no logical case against being assertive. Many will attempt to explain why assertiveness isn't always good. What people call "overly assertive" is another term for aggression. When someone who is aggressive practices true assertiveness, he might be considered by others as being passive. This is due to the comparison of the new assertive behaviors to the old aggressive behaviors. Another opposition to assertiveness is often found in people saying that there are times when assertiveness is not necessary because there is no conflict taking place, suggesting that tending to the other person is all that is necessary.

However, tending to someone is asserting your care. Assertiveness is also about injecting an appropriate amount of order into a situation. Even when caring for someone, a lack of order can come with unintended consequences. Boundaries, as discussed earlier in this book, are necessary. Although too many limits can be restricting regarding enjoying a relationship with someone, existence would not be possible without limitations. Therefore, limitations bring order—it is our attitude toward assertiveness that determines our opinions and experiences of them.

Successful Integration

The successful integration of assertiveness into your life takes place as conflict management and life-giving boundaries begin to occur more naturally. A good sign of such integration is when both you and your partner can maintain self-respect at the same time. Assertiveness results in an improved quality of communication when successfully utilized. Practicing assertiveness skills in insignificant situations bolsters your ability to implement them in more serious situations.

The workplace is often an optimal environment for practicing assertiveness skills. Relationships at work are not as complex as our relationships at home, for they come with a different set of consequences. Therefore, there isn't as much to lose if you don't hit the mark with your attempts to be assertive. Successful integration of assertiveness skills also breeds confidence. Confidence drives behaviors that are indicative of achieving goals. This is victory, and victory is sweeter than defeat.

Although assertiveness is defined as being forceful, it is more about being confident and willing to do what needs to be done. Sometimes this means fighting the urge to say something. You may be conflicted with two ideas or values, and you must be assertive within yourself to arrive at a workable compromise. For instance, in a meeting, or group of people, you might find yourself wanting to assert your opinion about an undesirable behavior taking place or some bad information being conveyed within the group. You may, in part, want to assert yourself by speaking up.

However, the other part of you may realize that the people discussing the issue know much more than you and they have their own style of arriving at a solution. If you speak up, you might provide helpful insight and be appreciated. Alternatively, you might provide insight yet be viewed as egotistical. Either way, you would be asserting yourself in the situation.

On the other hand, you might choose to sit back and say nothing. Although this is not indicative of being assertive, choosing your actions requires practicing assertiveness within yourself. The decision itself does not hinge on assertiveness; yet assertiveness enables you to act upon that decision.

Wrongful Implementation

Wrongful implementation of assertiveness is not utilizing it, or not using the skills correctly, especially in serious conflict. Assertiveness, like many skills, can be viewed as amoral. Morality should be emphasized on the boundaries you assert and the environment in which you assert them. Directing your assertiveness at someone about a serious concern of yours during lighthearted moments will prove ineffective and push your partner into resenting you for it—remember the importance of timing. You can have the strongest assertiveness skills, yet, how, when, and where you use them is vital to achieving workable compromises that maintain self-respect.

Most importantly, the mistiming of particular assertiveness skills creates confusion, which further obscures your path to arriving at an agreement on which you and your partner can settle. If you are inconsiderate with your assertiveness, you could fail to be a safe place for your partner to express herself. This is why it is imperative to consider all the assertiveness skills when practicing any of them; they enable you to be more thoughtful. Lastly, assertiveness that is self-seeking diminishes your ability to achieve intimacy in your relationship. In other words, if a lack of empathy defines your pattern of assertiveness, you will find yourself unable to connect with those who are most important to you. If you are the only one who benefits from your assertiveness, it is quite unlikely that you will be able to discover a deepened sense of purpose.

Corrective Actions

As with any process of mastering a practice, you will encounter various failures to some degree or another. You will miss the mark. How you respond to failures defines your character. Responding to your own failed attempts at assertiveness with more attempts to be assertive is admirable. As admirable and effective as such a response can be, it is your responsibility to assess your failures with the intention of correcting only the subtlest nuances of your skill set when possible. This is because it is not the assertiveness itself that is the problem. Rather, it is the subtle ways in which we implement them.

Gradual changes are best when correcting your mistakes with assertiveness, if you can get by with it. Focusing on your skill set's subtle nuances allows you to make gradual, more sustainable changes to your behavioral responses. Slow and steady wins the race. Gradual changes allow time and space to develop useful habits and to become familiar with them. However, there may be times when you need to make radical adjustments to your delivery of assertiveness, yet this is symptomatic of a complete failure to implement any assertiveness whatsoever.

If you inappropriately utilize assertiveness and cause more harm than good (such as asserting yourself in an untimely manner), own your mistakes by acknowledging them and course correct. Begin to reassert yourself based on your skill set's reevaluation, determine the necessary adjustments, and become more consistent with them.

Negative assertion can be a powerful skill when correcting your unsuccessful implementation of assertiveness skills. This shows you are willing to expose your own flaws in a confident, relaxed manner. Whatever you do, correct what needs to be corrected, yet assert your previous stance when you believe it is right to do so.

Keys to Improvement

Maintaining self-respect is one of the most important principles to keep in mind while mastering assertiveness. Do not give up your self-respect when striving toward a workable compromise. When faced with conflict, responding with nearly anything other than assertiveness puts you at risk of losing self-respect, at least temporarily. There are many ways in which you can sacrifice self-respect. The most common of these ways comes in the form of poor responses to conflict, such as being aggressive and attacking your partner's character; becoming defensive and rationalizing or justifying your behavior; becoming submissive and overly apologetic; or distancing yourself from your partner and giving her the cold shoulder. These are low-value responses that cost you your self-respect. If you do not display self-respect, others will be less inclined to respect you.

Strive to become consistent in the integration of assertiveness in your life. Consistently practicing assertiveness will lower your partner's guard, which opens her up to your communication. If she is accustomed to you communicating assertively in less consequential interactions, she will not think much of it when you are assertive with her in the midst of conflict. This is representative of your emotional reliability and allows your partner to trust you with her vulnerability. As you create an environment of safety and security in your relationship, your partner will experience her own unique opportunity for growth and evolution.

Make gradual changes. Radical changes are rarely sustainable, although for many men, practicing assertiveness is a drastic change. It is important to improve your assertiveness while displaying emotional reliability. Consider your partner's potential point of view. If you are normally aggressive, she may see your assertive behaviors are passive. They will lead her to misjudge you as too submissive. If you are naturally more passive in nature, she may view your assertive behavior as too aggressive, and this will repulse her and lead her to be defensive with you. She will see you as unstable and too domineering, which may cause her to either take her own aggressive stance or force her into compliance. Being mindful of the impact your changes have on your partner will help you spend more time in the zone of proximal development,[42] that is, the process of developing a mastery of assertiveness. The integrated man recognizes all of the components of assertiveness as the need for them are presented to him. He is steadfast, always standing "at the edge of the world, with the abyss of the future before him."[43]

Slaying the Dragon

Rodion's willingness to make a searching and courageous inventory of his resistance to the dark and shadowy aspects of himself has led to a painful awareness that he has been failing to move toward his potential and thereby failing to meet Regina's needs. The growing discord in his relationship had been evidence of this, as Regina seemed to be angrier and more upset with him than ever, and that it is the result of an underdeveloped masculine nature. This insight was terrifying for Rodion, for it meant that he had to look at what he wanted and needed in his relationship with Regina—to develop and honor his masculinity, which meant that he discovered what constitutes failure. This is frightening to Rodion if he's truly looking at it. It is easy to see failure as the most probable outcome when you are at the bottom of the hierarchy, or at least too uncomfortably close to the bottom. This is a pivotal point for today's man, for he must practice faith in a process that scares him and is full of uncertainty. Fortunately, for Rodion, he musters enough courage to swallow this hard pill, so to speak, and makes a decision to transform himself. This courage, coupled with a decision to become a more magnificent version of himself, sparks an unconscious revolution within him. For all that he can comprehend, Rodion is determined to find self-worth once again and restore harmony in his relationship with Regina. This decision is followed by a realization of the immensity of the task before him. He will encounter the feminine challenges of Regina. This time, he carries with him something different: courage and hope. This is a good thing, for he will need it.

Little does Rodion know he is beginning to answer the call of his ancient feminine counterpart by activating within himself the masculine development necessary for connecting with the ancient feminine within Regina. When a man answers the call to the feminine, she must know for sure if he is real. Hence, she will test him. As Rodion explores what masculinity is, he sees a meaning behind the stories he reads and hears. The stories of other men living deeply and fully in their masculine evoke familiar feelings within, but it seems as though he has never experienced them in the real world, so to speak. It is as if they are the feelings of men who lived before him—the heroes of old. Encoded in the language of the ancient heroes is a message for Rodion: *the feminine dragon of chaos despises imposters, and she will engulf her man in a fiery blaze intended to burn off any disguises that conceal an unworthy man.* But with assertiveness, Rodion realizes what he has discovered; it is the shield. It is not everything he needs to cut his ancient feminine counterpart from the belly of the beast, but without it, he does not stand a chance. The shield of assertiveness protects what is true and steady with Rodion from Regina's fiery blaze, leaving what is false and useless exposed and burned away. And this is painful! Nevertheless, Rodion is able to fend off the fire of the feminine dragon of chaos while he gathers the other weapons.

The ancient masculine within has awakened, exciting the feminine within Regina. Rodion is happy about his discovery, but Regina—or the dragon within—has much more to her gauntlet for Rodion than he is yet aware of. She must make sure that this new assertive version of her man is legitimate. Something inside Rodion tells him that he is on the right path. He cannot articulate it, but he knows his way is true. He has begun to establish the first pillar, yet he must establish the others. There is much more to slaying a dragon, but Rodion is off to a good start. Now, he has to look within to discover his gifts. However, Regina will not receive Rodion's gifts, for she must ensure that he can, in fact, provide that optimal place for him, to give his gift—if he has the character for it.

Chapter Seven

Character

The second of the four pillars is character. Character is an important part of the integrated man. It represents a deepened sense of purpose with an explorative dynamic, which serves to develop a more wholesome sense of self. To become a more magnificent version of ourselves, we must thoughtfully choose to respond with virtuous aspects of our character.

When formulating our responses to others, we must consciously choose which of our character assets to display. This means asking ourselves, "Who do I want to be in this response?" By displaying our assets, we increase the quality of our responses, while acting on character defects leads to poor quality responses.

Conscious efforts put forth with others increase our value and attractiveness to others. What we bring to others is a reflection of our character, so it's important to exhibit the appropriate character assets in our responses, given the current environment.

While assets are positive traits of our character, not all character assets are best suited for every situation. Assets and defects lie at the opposing ends of the spectrum of our character. Carelessly displaying certain assets can become defects if misguided.

For example, responding with stoicism to a partner's attempt at humor could be seen as inappropriate, indicating being too serious. In contrast, playfulness and humor can be great assets, but misusing them can backfire, such as being playful when your partner is in emotional distress.

Therefore, we must be conscientious of the character we display in our interactions with others. By asking ourselves, "Who do I want to be in this response?" we can exhibit the appropriate character assets and increase our value to others.

Women want their men to be supportive and understanding and to provide them with an optimal degree of safety and security. Your partner needs to know you are capable of this and that you have the character it takes to meet these needs. Furthermore, she wants nothing more than to express her feminine energy as a gift to the world and, more specifically, to you. How you respond to your partner's emotions, distress, or criticism, as well as any of her other feminine expressions, are a direct reflection of your character—you are judged by the implications of your behaviors. Your responses to her are cataloged in her memory bank.[44][45] There are subtle skills with which your feminine partner assesses your character by gauging your worth and credibility, particularly regarding your perceived level of commitment to her, as well as your "fitness" level (the capacity to provide for particular needs of hers). This speaks to an evolved psychological mechanism that is unconsciously used by women to ensure that their partner can and will support certain needs.[46][47] It is her way of understanding facets of your character to ensure her needs are met, which happens to serve as tremendous opportunities for growth for you.

Character-Building Tests

The concept of character-building tests in your relationship and understanding why you should respond in the ways discussed in this book is, with absolute certainty, the most essential concept you need to grasp regarding your relationship. Although assertiveness must be the foundation on which you transform, character-building tests are the doorway to your partner's soul. They are gifts from her that reveal to you her true nature and what she wants—more importantly, what she is capable of creating. When you can understand character-building tests, you will see that they are the most evident and plain-to-see pathways to her heart. They are an open invitation for you to connect with her deepest and most sacred sense of self. The integrated man is one who can see that the fiery blaze of his feminine partner's emotional distress she projects onto him is intended to throw off impostors. Today's man will see that his feminine partner is irrational and that being irrational is wrong. The problem for today's man is that his biases and current understanding of this—or the lack thereof—severely obscures the intent—or function—of his partner's behaviors. Instead of seeing these tests as gifts, he usually sees such behavior as willful defiance, unnatural and uncalled for. Simply put, today's man interprets character-building tests as unreasonable and unnecessary. This bias thwarts his efforts to cultivate a harmonious connection with his partner. The irony is that there is no way around it. He must walk through the fire of the feminine.

To best understand character-building tests, we must look into what they are, how they work, and why they occur. Research has shown that women err on the side of caution when assessing their partner's level of commitment to them. Women err on the side of underestimating prospective mates' commitment so that they may avoid the high costs of pregnancy without support or harassment, hostility, or even sexual coercion.[48] [49] They do this by unconsciously evaluating their mate's behaviors as a way to avoid mating with someone who might fail to support their safety and needs. Because women are typically the physically weaker gender and, biologically, are more vulnerable when pregnant and when nursing a child, it behooves them to have a mate who will stay with them, especially after procreating. This theory is known as commitment-skepticism bias. Commitment-skepticism bias:

- Is a theory that arose from error management theory

- Hypothesizes that humans inherently possess an evolutionarily derived mechanism for making decisions based on risks (cite research).

- Approaches these types of decisions in one of two ways: assessing for false positives or assessing for false negatives.

This theory is predicated on whether it is to be "better safe than sorry" or to "live with no regrets." Biologically, when it comes to securing a mate, a woman's error management system takes the approach of assessing for false positives. At a basic level, this suggests that a woman seeks a man who gives her the lowest risk of being abandoned, leaving her to raise a child on her own. Her approach is "better safe than sorry."

Mating rituals and mate selection processes are chaotic in nature due to the uncertainty of people's intentions and qualities as well as the significance of the probability of long-term relationship success. Chaos—the unknown—holds both promise and threat. Chaos, in this context, is the uncertainty of relationship success. Experiencing the complex world of romantic relationships highlights the difficulty of determining not only what promise and threat are but how to navigate ourselves through the unknown that contains them—committing to and acting on the expressed commitment of others. If we misidentify something as a promise or a threat, we risk taking on a burden or risk missing out on potential benefits, respectively. Haselton and Buss proposed that error management mechanisms are designed to be predictably biased when the costs of false-positive and false-negative errors were asymmetrical over evolutionary history—if the potential errors are symmetrical, we then go down the next level in the hierarchy of decision making.[50] There is sort of a cost-benefit hierarchy. Predicting asymmetrical errors protects us from making too costly of an error based on the potential risks of our choices with a given situation. Our error management system can lead to systematic cognitive errors whenever costs of false-positive and false-negative decisions are present. When people make decisions in conditions that hold uncertainty, they must assess for two possible errors: false positives (Type I error) and false negatives (Type II error). Conditions that call upon our error management system to assess for Type I errors involve a person feeling compelled to act upon a need or desire, but examining how doing so may increase the risk of personal loss or rejection. In these conditions, Type I errors are assessed. Assessing for false positives involves looking for pitfalls in what appears to hold potential benefits of a choice; that is, if something appears to be promising, one looks deeper to find potential evidence that it, in fact, is not promising. In conditions in which one assesses for Type II errors, a person takes the approach of making sure they don't overlook an opportunity to fulfill a need or desire, particularly when the alternative is more costly. Since there is a tendency to interpret a situation as not having benefits when it does, these conditions call for one to assume there is an opportunity. In other words, if something seems threatening, or at least perceived as not having potential, one must persist long enough to determine if it is not threatening and has potential.

This type of error management occurs when people interact with the opposite sex regarding interest in sex and pair bonding. In a courtship context, sex differences in selecting a potential partner rely on this evolved psychological mechanism. In these situations, we can observe two possible outcomes: 1) a person may judge correctly about the other person's interest, or 2) a person may commit an inference error with such. When referring to judgments of relationship interest, a false positive occurs when a woman incorrectly assumes that a man is interested in a committed relationship with her. This is a Type I error—she committed an inference error by assuming the potential mate was committed when he was not. This could be a costly error. Therefore, women are biologically geared to assess for Type I errors when it comes to courtship. This is commitment-skepticism bias in a nutshell. It involves a "better safe than sorry" approach, which assumes an underestimation of actual commitment interest from a potential male partner. It is safer for a woman to assume that her male counterpart has no interest in a committed relationship when he does (type II error) than for her to assume he does have such interest when he doesn't (type I error). This bias reduces the probability of making a type I error, which helps her avoid the high costs of pregnancy and single motherhood without support. Yes, she may lose out on a good man, but it is not as costly as the alternative. Commitment-skepticism bias influences a woman's judgment of her mate. Even after entering into a long-term relationship, she continues to assess for those false positives to ensure her mate will continue to provide safety and security. She needs to be well-informed about the potential sustainability of her mate's commitment and fitness for the job of providing for her deepest needs.

This type of error management occurs when people interact with the opposite sex regarding interest in sex and pair bonding. In a courtship context, sex differences in selecting a potential partner rely on this evolved psychological mechanism. In these situations, we can observe two possible outcomes: 1) a person may judge correctly about the other person's interest, or 2) a person may commit an inference error with such. Women are biologically geared to assess for Type I errors when it comes to courtship. This is commitment-skepticism bias in a nutshell. It involves a "better safe than sorry" approach, which assumes an underestimation of actual commitment interest from a potential male partner. It is safer for a woman to assume that her male counterpart has no interest in a committed relationship when he does (type II error) than for her to assume he does have such interest when he doesn't (type I error). This bias reduces the probability of making a type I error, which helps her avoid the high costs of pregnancy and single motherhood without support. Yes, she may lose out on a potentially good man, per se, but it is not as costly as the alternative.

From an evolutionary perspective, in the early, more primitive days, it may have been rather apparent as to whether or not a man was committed to his woman and fit enough to protect her. The environment in which they lived may have served to demonstrate a man's capacity to fulfill his role in relationships. If he was fit for the job, it showed. His worth and value were evident as long as he fought off the lions, tigers, and bears. If he also fought off other men from taking his woman, his dominance assured her she would be safe. If he demonstrated an ability to teach their children to thrive in the world, he clearly exhibited the potential to serve as a high-quality father. Now, if after she committed to him and began having his children he was eaten by a bear, clubbed to death by another caveman, or neglected their children, she would have paid dearly because of her false assumption that he had been fit for the job. So, even in those days, there was a reason for females to begin developing a commitment-skepticism bias.

Times have changed, and we don't live in caves anymore. However, commitment-skepticism bias drives many of the behaviors women display in relationships. Modern society does not provide the same situational tests that show a man's worth and commitment as it did in ancient times. Yet, men and women interact in courtship—commitment matters, even though we are not fighting off lions and cavemen. And although more modern social constructs normalize many human behaviors, we must understand that many of the behaviors around mating rituals and relationships represent a deeper, more ancient psychological process. This process is symbolic of something intrinsically and ineradicably spiritual in the oldest sense of the word. It is a deeply human experience to bond with a life partner, which cannot be uprooted by social constructs that have only been around for a few centuries or even decades.

Evolutionarily speaking, women are hardwired to assess a man's level of commitment. Her challenge in modern society is that there is not a need for men to fend off vicious animals and cavemen. She doesn't have the apparent day-to-day evidence to inform her of his commitment to her and if he is fit for the job. We typically don't have to fight off other men from "taking our women." Nonetheless, her need to assess her man's capacity to do so is strong. Women have developed methods of determining your commitment to her. Since women no longer have the same types of overt demonstrations of a man's capacity to provide these relationship needs, they have had to adapt to modern times, coming with up clever and creative ways to ensure they are not making Type I errors (false positives) in choosing a partner. Today's man displays his qualities that provide a woman with the information to accurately determine his potential. It is, however, covert, and today's woman has become attuned to the implications of her man's behaviors.

Safety and security have been basic human needs. Women must have their needs met in the context of relationships, even in modern times, and they have evolved ways of ensuring these needs are met. A man's failure to meet these needs may come in the form of being absent or in the form of poorly responding to her needs and emotional distress, all of which are symptomatic of him neglecting the relationship. A man who neglects the relationship is what she has sought to avoid. A man's neglectful behaviors fuel a woman's skepticism of his ability to commit to her.

Therefore, women avoid bad prospects for mates. As a woman searches for a competent mate, she will utilize this psychological mechanism to filter through various men to find a partner who seems to meet her standards. This skepticism is an important aspect of her feminine nature that allows her to advocate for her needs to be met with the lowest possible risk.

However, getting into a long-term relationship with a partner does not mean she discards this psychological mechanism. After gaining a man's commitment—and even after having children with him—a woman will assess her partner's commitment to her. She will use this evolutionary tool in a much more elaborate manner than she did in ancient times, ensuring she made the right choice in a partner, assessing whether he is able to meet her needs. The fulcrum in this context is a man's character; for it is his assets and defects that shift the relationship toward discord or harmony. It is the deliberate nature of his character that engages with his feminine partner on which the relationship pivots.

The better your character and the more positively you can respond to your partner, the higher she will perceive your value. This can be an exhaustive process for men, for the tests she administers are fluid and dynamic. Yet, his partner's constant evaluation of his commitment and fitness necessarily provides the character-defining moments that either drive him into anxiety and obsession or propels him to greatness. Either way, his true sense of self is revealed in his responses to her.

The behavior and communication style of your partner serves a purpose. Essentially, women test their partners. This notion has often carried a negative connotation, yet we are beginning to understand the contextual value of a woman's behaviors regarding her interactions with her partner. A woman tests her partner by observing his behaviors and analyzing their implications within the rest of the relationship—what he does in one insignificant interaction implies how he might act in a more significant situation.

Today's woman utilizes common, everyday interactions as methods of determining her partner's commitment to her and his ability to provide for her needs. These tests are most often unconscious in nature, which conceals the deeper meaning of her behavior behind her actions and what she verbalizes. That is, she does or says something that has an overt, superficial meaning, yet her behaviors principally serve as a way to expose your true nature, revealing to her the implications of your behaviors. These revelations are then stored into her perception of you[51,52], which manifests in her emotional responses to you—appreciation or challenges.

Hidden in her interactions with you are ways of categorizing your behaviors in the sense of your intrinsic value and the degree of your commitment to her. She is unconscious of her testing of you. This is perhaps to protect herself from her positive biases and partiality to you, which would otherwise weaken the integrity and effectiveness of her tests. If she does not prevent her partiality to you from interfering with the testing process, she will make it too easy for you to know what she is up to, and she will not be able to gauge your character accurately. She must conceal these tests so that you cannot respond in the way you know she wants you to. She unconsciously safeguards herself against your pretenses. Therefore, she is almost never aware that she is testing you. She may tell you one thing and mean it, yet what she says also serves to elicit a response from you in a way that reveals your character. On the surface, she may question your current abilities, hold your past transgressions against you, and demand things of you. She might do this by verbalizing doubt with your decision-making skills, bringing up a mistake you made long ago, or aggressively demanding that you explain your actions to her. This is part of the test; it is not the primary focus.

However, she will usually believe it is the primary focus. This aids in preventing her from giving herself away, making it too easy for you to fool her. She is skillful with her tests and often does so in ways that trigger your emotions, for it is in our emotional states that our capacity to respond in a quality manner is revealed. She knows how to push your buttons and stir up your resentments. Once she gets you into an emotional state, she can expose your true nature with her subtle tactics of using your words and actions against you or by ferociously targeting your weak spots. It is these emotional moments in which your character is vulnerable and exposed. As men, we must look at our partner's skepticism-driven behavior as character-building tests.

Rodion & Regina XVI

In a poor attempt to act on his newfound assertiveness, Rodion bought himself a new laptop—he needed one powerful enough to keep up with his work demands. He saw it as a justifiable purchase, and it made reasonable sense, business-wise. However, Regina became rather upset about it when he told her and overreacted to it. The catch here is that her laptop is much more outdated and is slower than his old one—although she only uses hers for personal reasons. Nonetheless, she is upset about it. Rodion has once again found himself in a conflict that he stumbled into.

However, he is making a conscious effort to improve his assertiveness. Regina's emotional distress alerts him to the need to practice assertiveness, yet the unanticipated situation somewhat confuses him as to how to be assertive in this particular circumstance. The two of them begin to fall into the pattern of argument they used to before Rodion started learning about assertiveness. This feels like a setback for him. After the argument becomes somewhat heated, Regina expresses to him that she's upset because he did not think to consider her previous mentioning of wanting a new laptop when he bought his new laptop.

Ordinarily, Rodion would become quite defensive and resort to justifying himself and minimizing Regina's needs in the process. Yet, this time he detects the direction this conflict is going and considers how to steer it, based on assertiveness and wanting to respond well. Should he use assertive communication techniques? Should he take ownership? Is it the right time for any of these? Rodion's deepened understanding of assertiveness makes him ask questions he would never ask during conflict in the past. He knows he should be assertive, and it seems to him that taking ownership is probably best in this situation. With noble intentions,

Rodion assumes ownership of his shortcomings by saying to Regina, "You know I should not have acted so inconsiderately. That's not who I want to be. I will work to be more considerate." This is a magnificent response, especially for him, for he has a notable history of rationalizing his behaviors with Regina.

Rodion feels accomplished in his use of assertiveness. Yet, as he begins to find peace with this, Regina fires at him once more by demanding that he explain himself for the way he handled the situation, and with a furrowed brow, aggressively says, "Well, why did you not talk about that in the first place?!" With a continued determination to respond well and take ownership, he calmly explained to her that, "I felt I was simply making a business decision that had to be made regardless, and I thought you would be supportive." After all, he thought, I am the one who hurt her; the least I could do is help her understand what factored into my behaviors. He followed this by reiterating his commitment to being more considerate in the future. Rodion walked away from this conflict feeling successful. He was proud that he managed the conflict well and took ownership. He had never been so assertive with her. It was a victory.

However, for the rest of the evening and into the night, Regina was visibly upset but had said what she wanted to say and no longer confronted Rodion. As bedtime came, something did not feel quite right to Rodion. He had hoped she would show some affection, especially since he had taken ownership of his behaviors. He was frustrated but believed that the reason the rest of the evening and night unfolded the way it did was understandable, that it was simply due to the gravity of the situation that she was upset.

Today's man might respond by explaining himself in an attempt to right his wrongs. He might, in fact, attempt to avoid the confrontation altogether. These are passive responses. Or he might get defensive and start asking, "Why do I need to explain myself?" Alternatively, he might become aggressive and retaliate with anger. All these responses show poor character. Perhaps, if Rodion was not just assertive in his response but also aware of the character-building test, he would respond differently to Regina by saying, "No. I'm not going to give in to your demands. When we calm down, and I feel like it, I might help you understand why I did what I did". This would be a radically different response than what

Rodion is comfortable with, and even considered extreme relative to his responses historically. He may view this as being aggressive or self-centered (passive people feel—and even are perceived as—aggressive when they start practicing assertiveness). However, he must see the test, which was the demand of him to do something. On the surface, Regina wanted an explanation, but more deeply—unconsciously—she wanted to see what character he would show in the face of an aggressive demand. The content does not matter in the test as much as the context. The test was not about the explanation; it was about how he would respond to the aggressive demand. Rodion must remember, the feminine is concerned with the implications of her man's behavior. He thought he was doing right by giving her an explanation, and she got what she wanted—on the surface. However, Rodion failed the deeper meaning of the demand by responding poorly. She did not respect him for it due to the implications of him easily giving in to someone's demands, even if it is her demands. The unconscious feminine narrative says, *if he gave in to my simple demands so easily, he would certainly give in to the demands of someone strong and powerful, and who wishes harm upon us*. Regina may have been upset initially that Rodion didn't give her the explanation. Perhaps, she would have been furious, but as her emotions settled down, she would have respected him for being assertive and showing good character, perceiving the implications of his behaviors, and understanding that he must respond assertively to anyone's demands or aggression in general. She may have even begun to show affection.

Your partner, over time, will infer critical information about your character based on your responses. Understanding the differences in what constitute responses being right or wrong will equip you with pertinent information in becoming an integrated man. Learning how to pass these tests improves your responses and, in turn, the quality of your relationship. The commitment-skepticism bias that drives your partner's character-building tests fundamentally categorizes your behavior into two ways: behaviors that are indicative of committing to the relationship and behaviors that are indicative of neglecting the relationship. If you respond poorly (passively, defensively, or aggressively) to your partner's character-building tests, your partner will interpret such responses as negative traits of your character. Too many poor responses to these tests and you develop pervasive patterns of negative responses, indicating that you are neglecting the relationship. You will appear more and more low value to your partner, and as your value decreases, you become unattractive to her, making it harder to cultivate a harmonious connection with her.

Although your partner will overlook many of your shortcomings, she will become acutely aware of your continued streak of poor responses, making it more difficult for her to notice your positive traits. Beware. Overlooking your shortcomings can serve as a character-building test in itself. She might be giving you room to fail. If you take for granted that she is willing to overlook some of your mistakes and flaws, she will also see this as a negative trait. Consistently striving to respond in a quality manner is a simple antidote for failing to recognize these particular kinds of tests. If you respond thoughtfully yet confidently to your partner's character-building tests, she will infer positive information about your character. By developing clear patterns of assertive and confident responses to character-building tests, your partner will find you more and more attractive, creating more room for intimacy as well as a stronger faith in you. As you replace poor responses with quality responses, more space will be created for you to display high value.

The more your partner loves you, the more she will test you. Because of her need for you to provide certain things for her, as well as her commitment-skepticism bias, she expects your best. She is attuned to your potential, and because of this, she is well aware of your weaknesses. She knows your shortcomings, where you stop giving effort, and where you stop being creative. She knows your minimal standards, as well as what you are capable of. Your feminine partner's character-building tests provide her with a clear view of your character, which allows her to assess your capacity to respond from your masculine nature. Responding confidently and thoughtfully to your partner's emotional distress displays high value and a well-developed inner masculine. Indifference and intolerance toward her emotional distress will prove detrimental to the intimacy between you and your partner, for it indicates an underdeveloped inner masculine. When you respond to character-building tests in an unflappable yet empathic manner, your partner will experience your fearlessness and tenderness, which will diminish her skepticism of your commitment to her. As her skepticism diminishes and you provide a space conducive to her feminine expression, she will reciprocate that with love and intimacy. This will not be because she is obligated to do so; it will be because she desires to do so. David Deida writes about this in *The Way of the Superior Man*:

She wants you to be your fullest, most magnificent self. She won›t settle for anything less…Her gift, if she is a good woman, is to test you with her darkest moods, over and over and over, until your consciousness is unperturbed by feminine challenge, and you are able to pervade her with your love…In response to your fearless consciousness, she will drench your world in love and light.[53]

Life is full of tests and celebrations. These experiences manifest through your partner's feminine nature. She is designed to be skeptical of you, and she is eager to test your character. Your strength excites her, though, and she wants to celebrate it. Therefore, although asserting yourself in response to her test may appear to upset her, she knows deep down that she is getting the strongest version of you—that is, if you are responding with good character and not withholding your gifts. When you stay on your path, despite your partner's emotional distress, it arouses her, for she is then willing and able to experience more intimacy with you. Intimacy is needed for a harmonious connection to be possible with your partner. She will know without a doubt that you are a quality man when you give your best efforts. However, if you display anything less than that, she will let you know. If you display little to no effort, she will persecute you with her destructive feminine chaos, and rightfully so. As you may well know, she is a master at it.

Poor Responses

Responding poorly to your partner's character-building tests gives her reasons to believe you are emotionally unreliable and incapable of providing for her needs. Remember, she categorizes your behavior as either committing to the relationship or neglecting the relationship. Regarding behaviors that she perceives as neglecting the relationship, a rule of thumb is that they are passive, defensive, and aggressive responses. The more neglectful your behaviors, the less her needs will be met. As a result, she will take it upon herself to get her needs met, either by herself or by another person. When this happens, your partner will become even more critical of you, and she will become resentful of your incapacity to respond to her in a positive, respectable manner. When negative responses develop into pervasive patterns, they will diminish other valuable aspects of your character, making it difficult to implement other self-improvement strategies. Showing poor character too often will obscure any other pillar you possess. It also makes it more difficult to cultivate a harmonious connection with her, for your feminine partner cannot afford to feel scared when you withhold your gifts.

Your partner's emotions, distress, and criticisms of you may induce distress in you. This action and reaction are a phenomenon that occurs in infancy. In infancy, one infant's emotional distress can affect another infant's responses, even without understanding the other's emotional state.[54][55] If you have ever been in a room with two babies and one of the infants begins to cry, you likely observed the other baby starting to cry, too. For example, two infants named Ricky and Jay are in the same room lying on the floor. Suddenly, Jay starts crying. Typically, this would indicate that he is hungry, sleepy, scared, or hurting. Nonetheless, he is experiencing emotional distress. Ricky recognizes Jay's cries as emotional distress, which signifies potential danger, and being the helpless infant that he is, Ricky wants nothing more than to be safe. Ricky only knows that the safest place is in his mother's arms, so he cries out for her. Jay experienced emotional distress, which induced emotional distress in Ricky. As you grew out of infancy, you began to develop pro-social skills, which enabled you to assess other people's emotional distress more accurately. You were less frequently distressed by your peers' emotional distress as you could more easily determine whether or not there was a real threat. This allowed you to behave positively in the context of gaining social acceptance and forming peer relationships. These skills continued to improve as you grew and came into play with dating and pursuing romantic relationships. By early adulthood, you had your own unique set of pro-social skills (Toddlers' Responses to Infants' Negative Emotions). These skills fell within the normal range of those your peers possessed. Even if you were somewhat of an outlier, you were able to get into a long-term relationship. Here, your pro-social skills were put to the test in ways that would challenge you. These challenges caused you to question, and even doubt, your skills and abilities as a man.

Long-term relationships have a way of challenging people. One of the most difficult of these challenges for today's man is recognizing that the pro-social skills—rules— that served him well in the past may no longer be sufficient enough to help him positively respond to his partner's present emotional distress. That is, it has not occurred to him that his skill level at the beginning of the relationship would turn out to be detrimental if he did not continue to evolve. This is important to understand, for one of the more costly faults of an underdeveloped masculine is the uncompromising adherence to established methods—rules—when they longer serve the original purpose of the rules. The masculine seeks to bring order from chaos, to bring things to consciousness, understanding—even establishing—the order of how things are and should be. The underdeveloped masculine believes solely in basic rules and the adherence to them. However, today's man must consider the rules about the rules. At some point, following the previously determined set of rules he set for himself undermines the purpose of the rules. He must, perhaps for the first time, consider what has been rather imperceptible up to this point, and that is what supersedes the rules. "It is necessary to conform, to be disciplined, and to follow the rules—to do humbly what others do; but it is also necessary to use judgment, vision, and the truth that guides conscience to tell what is right when the rules suggest otherwise. It is the ability to manage this combination that characterizes the fully developed personality: the true hero."[56]

In relationships, it means taking into consideration the reasons for the rules, or pro-social skills, in the first place. They were implemented in the relationship to serve the good of the relationship, but the challenges of relationships can become too great for your previous skill level. Responding positively to difficult challenges in an evolving relationship entails developing a more refined set of skills that maintain the integrity of the rules—the spirit of rules. This includes understanding your partner's emotional condition, managing your own induced distress, implementing particular strategies, and developing new methods for addressing her distress when necessary. Following the spirit of the rules allows you to recognize when the rules themselves need to be modified so that the original intent of the rules can be adhered to. In other words, you have to know when to break the rules.

Rodion & Regina XVII

Rodion is beginning to recognize that Regina's character-building tests require him to look beyond her criticizing demands, character assassinations, and emotionally driven accusations. Recently, she came home from a stressful day at work and started cleaning a few dishes that were left in the kitchen sink while at the same time venting to Rodion about her day. Amid her distress, Regina made an indirect, emotional accusation toward him, saying, "I do most of the chores around here!" Rodion sensed her emotional distress and thought to himself, '*Here we go again*!'

Perhaps, in her mind, she relates this to another stressor of hers and says to him, "You never help with planning our trips and vacations either. You just take me for granted." Rodion could easily construe this as an indirect accusation that he never helps with household chores and that he takes advantage of her. This could also be an indirect attack on his character, implying that he does not care about Regina enough to help her with household chores or planning trips. With this narrative, it is easy for Rodion to see nothing but Regina's emotional distress, which begins to induce emotional distress in him. There are a few different ways he might respond poorly to this kind of interaction. If he focuses on what is being said on the surface—the content—he might defend himself by explaining to Regina that he does, in fact, help with the chores. If he reacts to how she's interacting with him—accusations and character assassinations— he might act aggressively by reciprocating the accusatory behavior and assassinating her character. Or he might act passively by cowering down and becoming overly apologetic. This is avoidance, and avoidance is not a good solution. Even an assertive response can be poor if it is untimely or directed at the content— the *what*—rather than the context—the *why*. When the *what* drives the narrative, assertiveness would be an incomplete response due to the failure to respond to the true reason for her behavior. None of these responses are indicative of Rodion being an integrated man, and they also prevent intimacy. No workable compromise will be possible if these types of responses occur. The fact that these responses cost him his self-respect can be most detrimental to his goal of becoming an integrated man.

Masculine Responses

Responding in a masculine manner to character-building tests requires you to respond in a way that connects with your partner's feminine nature with tremendous emotional reliability and integrity. Responding assertively and confidently while maintaining self-respect lets your partner know that she can freely express her femininity. Identifying your and your partner's sensitivity and reactivity to emotional experiences goes a long way with understanding when your partner simply needs to immerse herself in the emotional gravity of the events of her life. Consciously reacting to this, in the context of a long-term relationship, means having the capacity to understand and regulate your emotions while responding to your partner's emotional experiences. It also means being able to manage relational conflict with a judicious, thoughtful, and confident approach. When you respond in this way, your partner's criticisms, emotional accusations, and character assassinations of you will have far less of a negative impact on your behavior. In fact, such responses will excite your masculine spirit, which will elicit qualities such as competitiveness, fierceness, and dialed-in focus. Capitalizing on this energy during her feminine challenge puts you in a position to act on outcomes from which you both will benefit. Furthermore, operating from a stable sense of self will open your eyes to the free information she gives you during these tests, which will illuminate aspects of the relational conflict and expose barriers to intimacy. Once awareness of this grows, you can begin managing those barriers, improving the connection between you two, and creating more harmony.

When these insightful masculine responses develop into consistent patterns, they will reveal other valuable aspects of your character to your partner, making it easier to use other self-improvement methods and cultivating a harmonious connection. Acting on your character assets will reinforce other assets. Acting out on your character defects will reinforce other defects of character. Consciously choosing to respond in ways that exhibit your character assets increases your value as a man. Conversely, minimizing the frequency of shortcomings prevents a vast amount of unnecessary suffering for both you and your partner. It prevents the subjugation of her creative feminine expression. Removing your shortcomings clears the way to emotional reliability and trustworthiness regarding her vulnerability. When you arrive at this echelon, so to speak, your partner will be grateful to have a place to experience her emotions safely. Instead of becoming overly critical of you and resentful of your inability to respond well, her trust in your commitment to her will grow, and her desire for you will begin to flourish. Assertively advocating for your needs and desires, setting boundaries and calmly enforcing them, and reaching workable compromises with your partner without losing your self-respect must take place before you can master other relationship skills. Employing assertiveness skills positions you to experience much more of your partner than her flaws and her shortcomings. You will see that responding to her behaviors with poor character obscures the resolutions for the discord. If you maintain the development of your inner masculine, you will better manage these distractions without losing sight of the outcome you desire. As you work to become an integrated man, you will see her behaviors you once deemed as unattractive and repulsive as something quite impressive and amazing.

Rodion & Regina XVIII

Consider the scenario discussed earlier in which Regina comes home from a stressful day at work and starts cleaning a few dishes while venting to Rodion, saying, "I do most of the household chores around here" and "You never help with planning our trips and vacations either. You just take me for granted." It would bode well for him if he began responding from a deeper place in his masculine nature by practicing assertive communication skills and by consciously exhibiting his character assets. This is one of the more arduous tasks for him as he strives to improve himself in his relationship. Depending on how far along Rodion has come in his masculine development, he will experience a certain degree of difficulty mastering responses to the feminine challenges of his partner. As he attempts to change how he responds to Regina's emotional distress, it would be helpful for him to err on the side of caution and say as little as possible without sacrificing his self-respect and becoming passive. When today's man has limited experience with managing relationship conflict, saying less is useful because it keeps him from having to recover from slips of the tongue. However mature in his masculine, there is usually room for improvement in Rodion's connection with Regina.

Although in this scenario, Regina is indirectly making an emotional accusation about Rodion and attacking his character by implying that he does not care enough about her, he might begin his response by using assertive body language. Perhaps, he holds his hands in a low, non-threatening position, quietly and attentively nodding his head. Then, he might begin using affirmative interjections, such as "mmhm," "oh," or "okay," to show that he can be calm and fearless. Concerning any character assassination from her, he could respond by saying, "Hmm. I can see how you feel that way" (fogging). This matches what his body language conveys. He could also maintain steady eye movement while regulating his speech in a caring yet controlled tone. Rodion will have to implement several assertiveness skills if he is to bring the conflict to a place of harmony. Although he could implement advanced stage responses, Rodion must crawl before he walks. Timing is everything. Therefore, an appropriate response could be something like, "I know you do a lot around here, and maybe I could show more appreciation. It sounds like you've had a bad day. Is there anything I can do right now?" From Regina's perspective, this may be a novel response from Rodion, and she may be skeptical of it. However, by consciously trying to implement such skills, he regulates his responses better and therefore regulates his emotional distress better. And this is a victory, for Rodion has managed to prevent the discord and Regina's emotional distress from pulling them down into more severe discord.

Catering to Your Partner's Individuality

You know your partner better than most people, if not everyone. You will want to use words and terms your partner will be most receptive to. Although you have a particular outcome in mind as you assert yourself, keep in mind that your partner will not automatically understand and agree with your vision. She will naturally be skeptical of this new behavior. Therefore, give her time to adjust and relax into this new version of you. If you aim to get what you want and to achieve a harmonious connection with her, you must get her to buy into your vision on her own accord. Connections are much more sustainable when partners willingly engage in meeting each other's needs. If your partner feels too obligated to meet your needs due to your forceful coercion, she will do so with no sense of self-respect and will resent you in the long run. Do not force her behavior; instead, elicit behavior from her that is most conducive to your relationship. Love her enough to reward her behavior you find desirable, which leads to intimacy; do not reward her behaviors that do not respect who you are as a quality man. In the end, pursue outcomes that are beneficial for both you and your partner.

Managing Extreme Situations and Abusive Behavior

In the case that your partner is a little more extreme with her accusations and character assassination of you by saying something like, "You're going to start doing the dishes before I get home and stop being so worthless!" At this point, your partner is directly challenging your ability to respond well. If your body of work shows that you are, in fact, not lazy and that you do your part around the house, then this is clearly an irrational challenge from your partner. However, a direct character assassination such as this indicates something more disturbing. It is important to recognize when your feminine partner's behaviors seem rather extreme and even abusive in nature. Typically, such behavior appears to be an anomaly, particularly when contrasted against the backdrop of the overall health of the relationship over the span of its existence, as well as her collective history of behaviors. It is likely that this sort of behavior is the manifestation of suppressed—and repressed—needs, feelings, and thoughts. Between consciously holding back her thoughts and feelings and unconsciously denying that particular needs exist, today's woman will often experience the emergence of deep pain and sadness cloaked in anger and frustration, appearing as unwarranted aggression and abuse toward you. To put it simply, when too many needs have gone unmet, coupled with her denial of this, interactions with you will devolve into projecting her shadowy anger onto you. Depending on your personality and partner type, there are a few ways you can effectively respond to aggressive projections of pain and sadness onto you. Furthermore, your overall body of work will determine the nature of your responses to such behavior. The key is intuiting the proper approach, be it stoic warmth or detachment from the drama. Sometimes, these kinds of situations are simply the case that things have gotten too serious, and it is best to respond with amusement.

Imagine, if you will, that your body of work is good, and while you may not have an abundance of care and attention, you give plenty, and it is adequate. Your partner would be justified in demanding your most magnificent self. However, this does not necessarily equate to a shortage of your gifts. When acting irrationally on unfounded beliefs that you do not support her—and you see that she is taking this too seriously at this point—it may be the case that her behavior should be amusing to you in the way a father finds his child's irrational sadness about a dropped spoon. This sounds absurd and cold, but do not be naive. Such amusement comes in the form of noticing that this deeply upsetting problem is a relatively good problem to have. Due to your overall body of good work, there should be no remarkable concerns regarding the implications of her projected emotions onto you. In this case, she is acting purely from her feminine chaos, yet does not know how to express her feminine creatively, rather than only destructively. At the least, she needs to be counterbalanced. If she is acting from an extremely dark and serious place, counterbalancing her experience with lightheartedness could be the answer. By showing amusement in your response, you show your partner that you think her aggressive attacks and demands are cute and amusing. You might introduce levity into the situation, saying, "Aye, Captain" or "Um, try again, but this time in a nicer way." Such an alpha display of confidence will signify to your partner that you are unperturbed by the darkest moods of her feminine nature. Although she may not be emotionally ready to see the value of your response at the moment, once she has had time to process her emotions, she will be more apt to see the value of your masculine response. Following up this kind of response with warmth and assurance that she can safely experience all of her emotions with you is conducive to maintaining and increasing the overall health of the relationship. Remember, your body of work must be able to support these kinds of responses. Understand, if you are trying to improve yourself, this type of response will make character-building tests much more difficult. Bear in mind that a masterfully amusing response is an intense response to a highly serious situation. These types of responses only work well if there is an established history of comic relief during emotional conflict.

If your body of work in the relationship is adequate, yet there are gaps in your capacity to give your gifts to your partner—character—then a response to her aggressive attacks and demands should indicate an appropriate amount of seriousness while simultaneously reinforcing boundaries and tending to the issue. In other words, show good character without sacrificing your self-respect. Emotional distress activated by the dirty dishes may signify a potential gap in your skills to meet her particular needs. This may be a difficult association to make. This is understandable. Oftentimes, she may not even realize what unconscious needs have long been neglected. The effect from those unmet needs may manifest only after she has reached a tipping point with her frustration and anger. This can catch you off guard. From an assertive communication techniques perspective, *negative inquiry* might be best suited for managing this kind of anomalous behavior of hers. However, regarding character, stoicism and warmth must also be integrated into your response. For instance, if your partner begins to raise her voice and it escalates into yelling or screaming, you could say, "I want to hear what you are saying, but I am not going to engage with you if you are yelling. Help me understand what I can do to tend to you." This is establishing a boundary with stoicism and warmth. You made it known that you are emotionally sound enough to hear her emotional expression, yet you reminded her of a boundary that prohibits yelling. You also followed up with a second expression of warmth by reiterating your desire to comfort her. Furthermore, it shows a willingness to fill in the gaps of your relationship skills. However, suppose she does not stop yelling. In that case, you may attempt to calmly reinforce that boundary using assertive communication skills, such as *fogging* and *broken record*, saying, "I understand you are upset, but I am not having this discussion if you are yelling." This works well to diffuse such behavior while keeping everyone's self-respect. However, in more extreme cases in which your partner continues to yell despite your best efforts to be assertive, it might be time to disengage with her and walk away. If she follows you, continuing to yell, you might consider leaving—detaching from the drama.

In some cases, your partner might behave in an overtly disrespectful manner. This type of drama takes the form of a persecutor. To take the earlier scenario to an extreme, imagine you and your partner have friends over for dinner and drinks. Sometime after dinner, she mentions that the kitchen needs to be cleaned, followed by saying to you, "Why don't you make yourself useful and go clean the kitchen?" There are several ways to respond effectively based on a given set of factors. Such factors may include her emotional state, history of disrespect, as well as your body of work. Responding in a basic masculine way is most effective. Simply looking at her with a calm, serious expression and saying, "No" will suffice. After the uncomfortable silence, she will either realize what she has done and adjust her behavior or escalate the situation with more tests. Unless your body of work is strong enough to respond this way, be prepared for her to escalate the situation, and be ready to use the skills you learned up to this point. As you master assertiveness skills in relational conflict, you can become more playful with your responses to her character-building tests.

If such actions of aggression and disrespect persist, detaching from the drama may be a necessary last resort. Although it is possible for today's woman to respond this way to her male partner, who has historically done well in his relationship, it is likely that she will never treat him that way. Rather, it is likely to be the case that she only treats today's man this way if his body of work is severely lacking—he can be the former alpha or the nice guy. Nonetheless, detaching from the drama is often the best antidote for the drama, at least at the moment. Here, drama must be understood in the context of relationships and the severity of the drama. Drama becomes severe when it is pervasive and fundamentally oppositional to healthy and appropriate behaviors and interactions with each other. While drama is an ineradicable part of life and relationships, operating solely from the position drama triangle[57]—persecutor, victim, and rescuer—is highly dysfunctional. Having grown frustrated and angry over conscious and unconscious unmet needs, the feminine will often take the form of persecutor. As with any persecution from the feminine dragon of chaos, today's man faces a test in which he must respond with his deepest inner masculine. The true masculine man will not be perturbed by the drama and will respond only to what needs to be tended to. By default, this means he does not respond to the drama. Rather, he responds to the underlying issue, which usually centers on the need for an optimal place to contain his feminine partner's destructive and creative chaos.

The antidote to the pervasive and dysfunctional drama itself is detachment. Any response to this kind of drama only reinforces the drama. Conceptually, it is much like when a child flails around on the floor in the middle of the aisle in the grocery store in response to his parent refusing to get the cheap toy he wanted. The parent may squat down and try talking calmly to the boy, but that will not work well. Now, if the parent pushes the grocery cart further down the aisle and turns the corner, the child will realize they are being left alone. Suddenly, the cheap toy does not seem so important to him. The removal of the parent's attention is brought to his acute awareness. At this point, he then reprioritizes his wishes, which will reorient his behaviors. This reorientation is predicated by the desire for attention from his parent, which is ultimately greater than his desire for a random toy. Behaviors surrounding the desire for a parent's attention are determined by the success of past efforts to gain the attention and approval of his parent—this goes for both positive and negative behaviors. Behaviors have a function, and when the function of the boy's behaviors is to gain attention from his parent, any attention given to his behaviors positively reinforces his behaviors—for better or worse. Any parent who is aware of this will easily set boundaries with their child regarding positive attention-seeking behaviors or negative attention-seeking behaviors. Adult relationships involve a more complicated dynamic regarding how we reinforce positive and negative behaviors. Conceptually, however, they are the same. Therefore, when it comes to the kind of drama discussed here, it is important to understand that it is a regression into childish behaviors in an attempt to gain attention and approval. When today's man encounters such drama from his partner, it is often best if he simply turns the proverbial corner of the grocery store aisle. The idea behind detaching from the drama is about letting the negative, unhealthy attention-seeking behaviors fall flat. Allowing the other person's dramatic attempt to gain attention or approval to fall flat opens the door to other types of behaviors with which we are more inclined to respond more positively.

In the rare event that your partner might become physical, hard boundaries should be enforced, and consequences should ensue if they are within ethical and legal parameters. Physical retaliation should never occur, although you may have to practice your legal right to defend yourself from physical harm. Furthermore, your word must have integrity. If your partner is physically aggressive with you and you tell her you will call law enforcement on her if she does not stop any violent behavior, you must follow through. This is true of any expressed potential consequence for her. If you do not follow through, you show your partner that it is acceptable to violate your boundaries and even be violent toward you. Unnecessary violence is about as close as one can come to an irreversible barrier to intimacy. However, if this type of situation occurs for today's man, he must realize how far down he's gone. Finding oneself in this kind of predicament is indicative of a severe need to make radical changes in one's life.

Transforming Tests

Once you are skilled enough with assertiveness and character, you will transform character-building tests into covert comfort requests. The active pursuit of responding with assertiveness and character contributes to the development of your inner masculine. Hone your assertiveness skills and practice good character so that you may steer your partner's behavior from that of targeting you and your actions to that of expressing her feelings and desires. Tilt the scale from criticism of you to that of trust in you. We will later examine covert comfort requests, how they differ from character-building tests, and how to respond to them. For now, you have begun to understand the function of character-building tests and how to recognize them. As you implement the insights you have gained into your relationship challenges, seek first to respond to character-building tests in a warm yet powerful manner. Typically, today's man must build a leg to stand on before he can elevate himself to advanced levels of masculine responses. To do so, he must learn to see the pitfalls that lie before him in his quest to improve himself. He must be ready to hear the case against this concept, how to correct himself if he falls short with character-building tests, the key points of improving his responses to them, and integrating these insights into his sense of self.

The Case against Character-Building Tests

The notion of character-building tests rests upon the idea that, in relationships, each partner brings unique biological and evolutionary differences that present contrasting experiences for the other. Women carry a different set of vulnerabilities and strengths than men. The idea of character-building tests is based on the theory of commitment-skepticism bias, which drives many behaviors in women engaging in relationships with men. This, and other biological considerations, such as the size difference in the female amygdala—the part of the brain involved in experiencing emotions—compared to males,[58][59] accounts for much of the basis for the concept of character-building tests. This leads to criticism of this concept from two different perspectives. One perspective is that of analytic psychology, which finds the notion of commitment-skepticism bias incomplete. Based on the theory of the anima and animus—the inner masculine and inner feminine, this perspective might seek to better explain the function of male and female relationship behaviors through the psychology of the unconscious, which would present a much deeper and broader understanding of this type of experience. This perspective would look to understanding the ancient aspects of the unconscious, which illuminate the development—or the lack thereof—of the anima and animus, rather than the more recently developed theory of commitment-skepticism bias. While this perspective would, in fact, provide an all-encompassing abstraction of the concepts of this book as a collective whole that the degree of abstraction would be too vast to be of any use at this point in the developmental stage of male self-improvement in the context of relationships. We must crawl before we walk, so to speak. For now, this book expounds on concepts appropriate for a precise stage of masculine development. The developmental stages of the masculine addressed in this section are explained by the precise experiential and behavioral factors that directly contribute—or impede—such development. By its nature, the analytical psychology perspective makes it difficult for today's man—lacking the necessary integration with the self at this point—to extricate himself from the binds of his underdeveloped masculine.

By adopting the concepts examined in this book, today's man can finally begin to position himself and arrange his environment to resume this development, which had previously stalled. Just as we observe the dramatization of "grownup" behaviors in children, which position them to become conscious of their individuality,[60] today's man must go through the dramatization of the individuation process.[61] That is the process in which the individual self develops out of the unconscious and integrates, over time, into a well-functioning whole. The strategies in this book intend to prompt a particular aspect of individuation that is acted out in romantic relationships. By embracing today's woman through the use of the concepts in this book—which seeks to modify the experience of their relationship in a way that opens both the man's and his feminine partner's souls—today's man can revive the maturation process of his inner masculine. This stage sufficiently equips men for a better experience with themselves and their relationships. If he completes this process, today's man will discover that this particular stage activates the deeper unconscious process necessary for integration that analytical psychology emphasizes.

The other perspective that criticizes the notion of character-building tests is that of egalitarianism, whose good intentions often overextend its morality into areas in which asymmetrical dispositions between men and women serve a unique and ineradicable function. When left uncontested, the egalitarian perspective can interfere with the natural developmental and psychological processes that underlie the achievement of compatibility in long-term relationships, such as those that serve to differentiate the unconscious process of the masculine and feminine. The "testing" that female partners administer to their male counterparts serves to ensure both biological and psychological needs are met. This applies to needs that can only be met within a relationship—some needs only exist when engaged in a relationship, such as the need for commitment from a partner. Commitment-skepticism bias—the basis of character-building tests—suggests that some needs are based on the notion that some aspects of a person cannot exist without a place for them to exist, such as the boundaries set in a relationship. The evolutionary biology perspective highlights particular vulnerabilities specific to women—physical strength, pregnancy, nursing a child, and being a single mother.

However, some may argue that this concept places women in a social construct intended to make them inferior to men and as if they are incapable of taking care of themselves. It also can be argued that this stereotypes women as "overly emotional, nagging, and needy partners." While there might be narratives in society that create and perpetuate the oppression and misguided stereotypes of women, the concept of character-building tests proposes that women's behaviors toward their male partners are marked by strengths and vulnerabilities unique to women. Within this concept, vulnerability means being capable of being wounded, which holds a positive connotation rather than a negative one. This denotes value and particular kinds of strength unique to women. Character-building tests, rather than holding implications for women bringing less value than men, hold implications that women bring a kind of feminine judgment and truth that deepens her partner's inner masculine and feminine development (integration). She serves as a barometer for his progression toward a more well-functioning self. The dramatization of conflict in relationships necessarily engages the man with today's woman in an experience that activates—or even revives—the individuation process not just for him but also for his feminine partner.

Successful Integration

Successfully integrating the concept of character-building tests requires today's man to consider the function of his feminine partner's behavior toward him. This involves a conscientious, exploratory effort to not only modify his behavioral responses to his partner but to become profoundly aware of the implications of his responses to her. His malignant beliefs about life and relationships have found their way into the far corners of his mind. Therefore, his beliefs must undergo reconstruction to become a deepened, transformative power that will awaken him and his feminine partner to be fully conscious of the present and in touch with the unconscious, respectively. In other words, he must learn to see his feminine partner's behaviors in relation to him as an opportunity that serves to both elevate himself from a lesser version of himself and bring the necessary masculine order to her feminine chaos, for the container in which she can optimally express herself is established by the masculine. The feminine chaos is both destructive and creative. It is in her relationship with her man that the significance and implications of his behaviors—and the degree to which his purpose drives them—determines whether her feminine chaos is destructive or creative. If he elevates himself as a man in relation to her, he will be met with love and appreciation (creative chaos). If he displays regressive traits as a man, he will be met with the feminine challenge and tension (destructive chaos) with her. Today's man will only become an integrated man once he begins to see beyond the superficial aspects of today's woman's behaviors and peers into the depths of her creative forces, which are waiting for him to put into order a place for those deeply important aspects of her feminine nature to thrive.

The successful integration of this concept into his relationship leads him to embrace his feminine partner, which, in turn, allows her to lead him to a more integrated sense of self. This requires acts of effortful revaluation, which Dr. Jordan Peterson, in *Maps of Meaning: The Architecture of Belief*, states as a "thorough, exploratory reconsideration of what has been judged previously to be appropriate or important."[62] When understood through the lenses of evolutionary biology and behavioral economics, character-building tests provide opportunities for a man to formulate useful and meaningful responses within his relationship that pave the way for more intimacy and harmony. And this is a much different thought for today's man. By responding to her feminine nature with an effort to better understand it, he will begin to develop his masculine nature more fully. He must take control of the trajectory of his life in a manner that no longer produces paradoxical implications—sets of behaviors of which some indicate to his feminine partner a commitment while others indicate neglect of the relationship. These diametrically opposed implications conflict with each other, which deems a man's potential as indeterminate, causing a great deal of uncertainty for his feminine partner. In other words, based on his volatile, erratic responses to today's woman, she cannot accurately predict whether or not he is fit for the job. Through effortful reevaluation, today's man can modify his behaviors with more precision and reframe his environment—and his experience of it—as a way of solving the dilemma of contradictory, simultaneous meanings of his behaviors—and the confusing discord it causes. At the same time, he will begin to consciously live according to his purpose, with which his feminine partner will be the beneficiary.

Wrongful Implementation

Wrongful implementation of the skills surrounding the concept of character-building tests occurs through multiple errors. One of the most common and costly errors through which this concept is improperly managed is experiential avoidance in the form of self-saving escapism, the pervasively destructive pattern of avoiding unpleasant realities. Today's man can often be observed loosely applying the concepts discussed in this book in a manner that seeks to simply silence the superficiality of the emotional distress of his feminine partner. To illuminate the potentially dangerous pitfalls of wrongfully implementing this concept, we will look at the misguided use of empathy often identified in those diagnosed with Antisocial Personality Disorder, or APD. It has long been said that those with APD, often identified as sociopaths, lack empathy or comprehension of others' emotions. However, some experts believe these criteria for APD are wrong—at best, incomplete. This is because the lens through which clinicians have viewed the area of empathy with these people leaves it undifferentiated. Those few experts who see it differently have differentiated this area. They suggest that, while the person with APD may not hold others in the space of authentic empathy, they understand it. This possibly explains, to a large degree, why they can be so proficient with their manipulation tactics. Their ability to sense other people's emotions while not letting their own emotions interfere gives them a diabolical edge in their efforts to take advantage of an otherwise intact human being. This rather extreme example of misguided use of empathy seeks to illustrate that silencing the superficial aspects of today's woman's behaviors— your feminine partner's emotional distress—steers the relationship in the wrong direction. And this is not good character. This type of implementation represents the self-seeking, irresponsible man of today who neglects to use an important concept in a way that benefits those around him. The man who is unaware of or ignores the implications of his actions, particularly when he cherry-picks certain aspects of a useful concept, can only implement an incomplete strategy. In the case of self-saving escapism, he uses his undeveloped understanding of it to avoid the fear and discomfort of the problem rather than seeking to reconcile it. Responding to character-building tests for the sole reason of quieting his partner's distress is to respond with a feigned empathy, which is, in truth, a veiled disdain for her feminine chaos. It is an empty response. Nancy Qualls-Corbett states, in The Sacred Prostitute: The Eternal Aspect of the Feminine,

"The stage of anima development in a man is concretely reflected in his external relationships with women. When he views the female as a sinister threat, someone to distrust, or as an inferior species which must be kept in its place, it is a sign that his inner feminine nature is at a juvenile stage, ready to tease and taunt the male. Such a man steels himself against emotions lest they manifest in over-sentimentality or inappropriate aggression. The inner feminine and relationships with women develop reciprocally when he is able consciously to value the feminine. Both the inner and outer woman may then be recognized as the embodiment of joy, passion, inspiration, creativity, spirituality and, in the highest order, wisdom."[63]

The concealed disgust behind the superficial, empty responses to his feminine partner will not alleviate any suffering within the relationship. Today's man, left unchecked, will avoid the difficult challenges brought by relationships—particularly the chaotic nature of the feminine—by responding as an adolescent boy would to his female peer. It is in this familiar adolescent stage of male-female relationships that he has a proclivity to reside. He must move beyond this juvenile stage of the anima before experiencing true harmony with his partner's creative feminine chaos. To do this, he must implement the insights that accompany this concept.

Corrective Actions

It is easy to stall in one's development of the inner masculine and inner feminine. Today's man has been faced with oppressive ideologies that not only tell him that he needs to step up and be a man but also ridiculed when he attempts to do so, being told he is displaying toxic male behaviors. He was not shown how to develop his understanding of himself as a man, nor was he guided to a deeper understanding of the feminine nature. In other words, at some point his parents and the community missed the mark with development of these fundamental aspects. This is not to criticize his parents and the community; it is intended to help him accept his position in the world as it stands and encourage him to take responsibility for his own development. In this context, responsibility is about taking the necessary corrective actions toward filling in the developmental gaps left by the shortcomings of his parents and community with his adolescent development. Alternatively, he assumes responsibility for his current development by reactivating the exploratory aspect of his psyche with a questioning attitude and heroic, conscientious effort.

Regarding character-building tests, the corrective actions required of today's man consist of practicing assertiveness within the context of his relationship, which means managing the boundaries of his relationship with his partner and managing the conflict between them. Suppose there is a default place to begin looking for corrective opportunities. In that case, it is within the area of assertiveness, for this is the singular point from which order is necessarily injected into the chaos of his relationship. There must be an appropriate, orderly environment for the relationship to function in a way that produces harmony and intimacy. In other words, you can have a remarkable character, but it will be obscured by the haze of too much chaos. If you find yourself struggling to act out of good character, consider revisiting the foundation of your assertiveness skills to begin a course correction. Oftentimes, simply practicing some fundamental assertive communication techniques steers the relationship back to its optimal path.

Remember, today's woman has a way of masterfully pinning her man against himself in the sense that her tests of him will result in one of two sets of behaviors. First, he might respond poorly, representing a lesser, regressive version of himself. This, of course, will worsen her emotional distress, for what she sees is both the manifestation of character defects and the implications of his shortcomings. Alternatively, he might respond with qualities of a higher order, representing an elevated, more magnificent version of himself. This not only dissipates her skepticism of his commitment to her, but it also satisfies a deeper, more meaningful need to connect with her man so that she may express her feminine nature, giving him the gift of the discovery of his Self. Moreover, the act of connecting with his feminine partner with a more magnificent version of himself primes him to re-engage in the development of his anima, bringing him closer to integration. By embracing today's woman—and his partner's true feminine nature—with reverence, today's man can learn to honor his masculinity in a way that considerably benefits those around him.

Keys to Improvement

Improving yourself in the context of relationships means subjecting yourself to a deeply uncomfortable and wonderfully arduous process in which your partner's destructive and creative chaotic feminine nature leads you through a necessary psychological transformation from adolescence to manhood. This is a process that took place more naturally in ancient times. Unfortunately, the occurrence of several significant historical changes in ancient times has trivialized this process by reducing humanity to meaningless parts and erroneously discarding aspects of the human experience necessary for deep psychological development. The diminution of this process took it from a deeply symbolic and transformative relationship between the inner masculine and inner feminine—played out in both the outer physical world and the inner psychic world—to a watered-down, superficial experience that no longer serves as a place for men and women to each meet the particular developmental needs of the other. In those ancient times, a man and woman would bring their respective masculine and feminine strengths to each other. In those days, the feminine strength, or destructive and creative chaos, would bring the man closer to his true self by bringing him out of his orderly and homeostatic—sometimes violent and predatory—existence and into a more complete, yet dynamic, existence as a man, one in which he could control his violent and predatory tendencies without losing sight of his capacity for them. For the woman, the man's masculine strength, or orderly and stable nature, would bring her out of her cold, dark, emotionally tormented world, which held an incomplete sense of self, and into a warmer, more secure, and exalted existence, one in which she could be the embodiment of joy, passion, inspiration, creativity, spirituality and, in the highest order, wisdom.[64]

There is good news, however. The dissolution of this process is not irreversible. With a course correction that sparks improvement, today's man can revive this ancient process in the modern world by engaging in his feminine partner's challenges and viewing them as character-building tests rather than something strange and inadmissible. Today's man often sees his woman's challenges as negative and as if they simply should not occur. On the other hand, the integrated man sees his woman's behavior as beautiful; at the least, he sees her as amusing and high-spirited. The keys to improvement with character-building tests require a man to elevate his responses to his partner's challenging behaviors as if they are creative and not just destructive. This means he must accept chaos for what it truly is, which is the place he grows and transforms. Additionally, this means he must, through an exploratory quest within himself, consciously choose to exhibit a true and good character—or at least do something other than escaping from her challenges. He also improves himself with character-building tests by capitalizing on the opportunity to showcase his masculine qualities in a way that serves to create a space for his partner to express her feminine nature more fully. When properly done, he will transform her character-building tests into requests to be comforted, revealing to him the proverbial keys to her heart, which she holds in her outstretched hand as an offering to him. At this point, however, this is not clear to him. The keys to her heart are veiled and have to be earned, for it is in a certain obscurity that her gauntlet lies for him. This gauntlet will reveal to her any false pretenses that linger in him. If he successfully navigates these tests, her skepticisms and doubt of him will vanish, and he will then hold the keys to her heart. When character-building tests transform into this, they are called *covert comfort requests*.

Covert Comfort Requests

Covert comfort requests are similar to character-building tests in the general sense that your partner displays emotional distress to you through her behavior toward you. Another similarity is in the importance of your response to her emotional distress. However, unlike character-building tests, in which your partner can come across as accusatory, assassinating your character, or projecting her fear and skepticism of you, covert comfort requests have more to do with an unconscious projection of her unmet needs for comfort and general desires to connect with you. On the surface, she may need your comfort and assurance. Covert comfort requests are underlying assessments of your ability to support these needs, gauging your level of commitment to her. Whereas character-building tests deliberately provoke you by focusing on and targeting you and your shortcomings, covert comfort requests focus more on her and her feelings. It is literally the difference between focusing on you or her. Character-building tests might be directed toward your alpha traits, from which the ability to provide safety and security emerge.

From a psychological perspective, the aspects of you geared toward meeting your partner's safety and security are driven by your inner masculine. Alternatively, covert comfort requests are, perhaps, most often directed at your beta traits. Psychologically, the aspects of you geared toward meeting her comfort and connection needs are driven by the anima—or the inner feminine. The anima allows you to recognize and cater to more sensitive needs, such as romance and intimacy. One might sum up the difference in these two types of tests as one type seeks to elicit your most magnificent self by way of stealth and fire while the other type seeks to appeal to the warm and charming aspects of your character through subtle expressions and requests. This might explain the dichotomous nature of character-building tests and covert comfort requests. Both represent emotional distress, obscure intentions, and potential positive and negative consequences. Character-building tests tend to engage with the aspect of the masculine man driven by order and resolution, which seeks more to get rid of chaos (emotional distress). Covert comfort requests tend to engage with the aspects of the masculine man driven by her creative, imaginative, and regenerative inner feminine, which seeks to spawn growth, emotion, and adventure.

Since character-building tests and covert comfort requests are both emotionally driven phenomena, they are often misidentified—today's man is more likely to mistake covert comfort requests for character-building tests. This is because his autonomic, involuntary responses to his partner's emotional distress do not position him to differentiate such information.[65][66] Left undifferentiated, the tests he gets from his feminine partner will usually appear as unbearable and undesirable. Without understanding the reasons for her tests—and the difference in them—today's man will struggle to move beyond the frame of mind that finds these behaviors intolerable. If he learns to differentiate these subtle yet fundamental differences, he will achieve more success in improving his responses to his partner. The ability to detect these subtleties allows him to move past his initial involuntary responses to her emotional distress, which enables him to sense the distress in the first place. With his newfound ability to differentiate this phenomenon, his unconscious narrative poses questions such as "Is she targeting my character, or is she in need of comfort and assurance?" Your brain detects, at least initially, the emotional distress, then your psychological mechanisms engage.[67][68][69]

The integrated man is one who can more quickly move beyond the superficiality of the distressful experience (principally driven by the involuntary response to it) and into the deeper, more unconscious meaning for it (driven more so by the active pursuit to understand why it is happening).[70][71][72] When he can do this, time seems to slow down for him, enabling him to finesse his way to her heart. Covert comfort requests artfully conceal their true meaning, for the man who solves the algorithm of this maze is worthy of entering the sacred vulnerability of her feminine. That is, once you pass through the gauntlet of her emotional distress—more or less a smokescreen—you will experience the creative and fertile aspect of her chaotic feminine nature. If you are going to master this phenomenon, you must first develop healthier habits for responding to her emotional distress. Mastery of this phenomenon cannot happen without enhancing your pro-social skills, which help you determine whether your partner is critical of your actions or is expressing her feelings of distress and covertly wants you to comfort her. By clearly identifying the differences between the two, you will be able to respond more appropriately.

Rodion & Regina XIX

Recall the scenario discussed in the Character-Building Test section in which Regina is experiencing the same emotional distress (work stress, dirty kitchen, event planning, etc.). In this scenario, she says, "I feel like I do most of the household chores. It's exhausting. I also feel like you take me for granted when it comes to planning vacations and weekend trips."

It is important to notice the differences in this scenario. She is using I statements and impact statements (how she feels), which is a positive way of managing conflict and expressing her thoughts and feelings to Rodion. Although she is directing her emotional distress toward him, she is not targeting him; she is expressing her emotions and desires, secretly wanting him to provide her with comfort. Perhaps, Rodion would begin providing such comfort by saying something to the effect of, "I can see how you feel that way. I'm willing to look at myself and change whatever I need to." If his body of work is strong enough, he might say, "You're right. I need to help you more. You do a wonderful job around here, and I appreciate that! I say let me treat you tonight and go out to eat. How does Mexican sound?" This type of response gives Regina the comfort she covertly seeks while simultaneously maintaining his self-respect. It validates her emotional distress while showing her that he is confident enough to manage her emotions, solidifying her trust and confidence in him. Of course, Rodion must follow through with this commitment, or his word will mean nothing.

Masculine responses to character-building tests and covert comfort requests address Rodion's and Regina's behavior. Engaging with her distress without discouraging her from expressing her emotional experience indicates Rodion is attentive to Regina's thoughts and feelings without telling her how to feel or think. He must not challenge her thoughts or risk addressing superficial concerns and missing the mark with Regina's deeper needs. It is important to understand that our thoughts are the product of our experiences and that changing our behaviors changes our experiences and subsequently changes our thoughts. The dismissal of this notion is detrimental in relationships. For example, saying, "You have to realize that I do help you with household chores" may seem helpful, but he has to remember it's not about the content—what is observed on the surface—but about the deeper meaning of her emotional distress. If he does, in fact, help with the household chores, she will then come to her senses and realize this on her own, but only once the situation plays out appropriately. Furthermore, he must not challenge her feelings by saying things such as, "You don't have to worry, baby" or "It's not that stressful; you'll be fine." Asking your partner not to feel a particular way asks her to be someone other than the woman she is. She has her own process; let her have it. Reassure her of your commitment to her by addressing behaviors, but do not tell her how to think and feel. Addressing the behaviors properly gives her the optimal space to experience her emotions fully. This is the way she will be brought to a more fulfilled version of herself.

Today's woman will test her masculine partner with an array of challenges and demands. Some of these challenges and tests are more intense than others. Today's man fails to see the true meaning behind his partner's behaviors toward him. He tends to experience them as an annoying distraction or even immoral. At the least, he simply finds them undesirable. Regardless of how he views them, the problem lies in the fact that he finds them inadmissible. And that is not good. Such a lopsided view usually results in a view that is justified strictly through a moral lens. The moral interpretation of her behaviors distorts his perception of her, which, in turn, alters his responses to her. In other words, if he sees her as annoying, overly emotional, and, worse, evil, he will respond accordingly. The image we hold of a person determines the place from which we respond to them. That is, the degree of reverence—or the lack thereof—in which we hold a person determines the degree of grace—or contempt—with which we treat them. While it may be necessary to treat people accordingly, we usually fall heavy to one side or the other on the spectrum of grace and contempt. This is made pronounced by our confirmation biases and outlooks on life. That is, we are prone to miss the mark on our judgments of people and how those judgments should determine our responses to them. The key to Rodion improving his character is in his willingness to make a conscientious effort to respond in a way that considers the implications of his actions. That is, to bear in mind the action that moves him toward a more magnificent version of himself or a lesser version of himself. The integrated man elevates himself above the temporary satisfaction of his ego, and he settles into a more virtuous nature, one that benefits everyone involved. He seeks to respond with the utmost value.

Take, for example, a scenario in which two people have committed the same transgression upon you. Imagine you know both of these people, and one is notoriously self-seeking, rude, and obnoxious. At the same time, the other is revered by many as caring, compassionate, and all-around good-natured (yet, still human). Although the transgressions against you by these two very different people are, in essence, identical, the response to them will, in all likelihood, be different. Your best response to the jerk will differ from your response to the pleasant person. Most would agree that the response to the pleasant person would be the higher quality of the two different responses. Yet, although of less value, the response to the jerk is justified by most people. This approach is faulty, for it leads to an incomplete sense of self. This is because one cannot fully live out a more complete version of himself if he allows external forces to determine both his actions and his reasons for them. This can be difficult to comprehend, but effort and open-mindedness can take you a long way. People have a proclivity to be willfully naive when declaring their own moral interpretations of someone's behaviors, which leads them to unconsciously treat people based on the other person's judged morality rather than on their own principles. This does not necessarily mean that his response will carry the utmost value if he treats others based on his principles. If today's man generally treated others based solely on his principles, his response to these two contrasting people would be similar in nature, for better or worse. He needs something else integrated into his sense of self that determines if the treatment of others, although similar and consistent, is for the greater good or for the detriment of them. This is where character comes in.

By allowing his principles to guide him while simultaneously choosing to display his character assets, Rodion positions himself to develop the Self further. In other words, by improving his responses to his partner's challenges and needs, he opens himself up to a pathway that leads to a deepened sense of self. The feminine is most concerned with creative expression and exists fully and wholly in that creative process. However, she cannot carry out her purpose without a place to contain the process. This place must be optimally matched for her in a way that only her ancient masculine counterpart can provide, and she does not want to settle for anything less. Therefore, Regina will test Rodion in her quest to find the most optimal place for her to express her feminine nature. Hence, he must solidify his understanding of covert comfort requests by being mindful of the pitfalls and managing his mistakes. Of course, he must be prepared to overcome the narratives that oppose these concepts while remaining steadfast in his willingness to see the faults of his character.

The Case against Covert Comfort Requests

The notion of covert comfort requests presents problems in and of itself. One might argue that the "covert" aspect is a pleasant way to describe the true nature of their feminine partner's behavior, claiming that it is manipulative, cunning, and even malicious. Today's man tends to view his partner's behavior from a place of defensiveness, frustration, and, quite frankly, too much seriousness. The case against covert comfort requests takes on a moral interpretation of today's woman's behavior, tending to arbitrarily declare her intentions as evil, or, at least, malicious. Today's man has not developed a mature understanding of the feminine—or the biological makeup of women. Therefore, he is prone to perceive his feminine partner's covert comfort requests as an inefficient, unnecessary way to get what she needs. Men have often expressed, "I wish she would just say what she wants and stop trying to drop hints or manipulate me to get it," and that it's a "complete waste of time; just get to the point." Today's man finds fault with this process because of the unnecessary manipulation she uses to meet her needs. This can often lead to a starker outlook, declaring she is "too needy." The man who fails to mature his understanding of the feminine nature—and the fundamental biological and evolutionary differences in men and women—stunts his relationships with his woman.

As the psychological development of his woman's own inner feminine continues to progress, she will, at times, outgrow him. During these times, she is settling into her feminine, which, in turn, means her behaviors come from a more feminine place. Hence, her behaviors become representative of the polar opposite of the masculine nature—although immature and underdeveloped—that dominates today's man. Herein lies the problem. A man who is dominated by his underdeveloped masculine nature thereby suppresses his inner feminine, the anima, which, by default, neglects the aspect, whose function at this stage of development is to lead him to his true self. The arrival to his true self, or the progress toward his true self, opens his eyes to a deeper and more meaningful interpretation of his feminine partner's covert comfort requests.

With a better understanding of his partner's behaviors, today's man can become further integrated. Rather than seeing a woman's behavior as manipulative and malicious, it can be seen as a deeply creative and wonderful process of connecting with him and his masculinity. In other words, within the context of relationships, her behaviors are phenomena that, in and of themselves, hold no inherent morality or value. Instead, it is the interpretations of them that hold value regarding whether promise or threat is derived from them. The challenges and tests—including covert comfort requests—that today's man receives from today's woman position him to develop himself psychologically or remain underdeveloped. It is in this type of interaction that today's man is given a platform to grow. The qualities and character assets required of him to traverse her emotional, unpredictable chaos are the things that will land him in the center of her heart. Accomplishing this teaches him a lot about himself, and it brings to consciousness aspects of himself he did not know existed.

Successful Integration

Successful integration with character regarding covert comfort requests is best achieved when slowing down and taking the time to consider why your partner is behaving the way she is. Here, the three-second rule is quite useful, especially for the man who has begun transforming himself in his relationship. The three-second rule:

- Gives you more time to consider other alternatives for understanding what is driving the current interaction

- Gives you a chance to witness the true meaning of her actions toward you.

- Helps prevents unnecessary pain and discomfort by waiting to respond

The three-second rule helps to refrain from habitually acting on emotional reasoning—a cognitive distortion that causes a person to conclude that their internal emotional experience proves a particular notion is true, regardless of evidence that supports the alternative. There is an aphorism in 12-step recovery programs that says, "Don't give up five minutes before the miracle happens." This means that recovering addicts often relapse just as they were about to reach a point in their recovery in which they would experience newfound freedom from addiction. Similarly, today's man is often moments away from gaining clarity into his partner's feminine nature, yet he frequently acts upon his underdeveloped understanding of the feminine. Success with covert comfort requests comes as a result of patience; oftentimes, that need only be practiced for a few moments longer.

Another useful step in successfully integrating character concerning covert comfort requests is the active use of reframing (covered in the next chapter in more technical detail). In the context of relationships, reframing is consciously revisiting your original interpretation of your partner's behaviors. If you see her covert comfort requests as manipulative and malicious, commit to looking for an alternative explanation. This will open doors for you to find out the true meaning behind her interactions with you. Today's man often falls victim to emotional reasoning, often causing him to see his partner's behavior in a negative light. Friedrich Nietzsche once said, "There is no such thing as moral phenomena, but only a moral interpretation of phenomena."[73] It is easier to attribute complex behaviors that we don't understand as wrong and immoral. Today's man is susceptible to experiencing his partner's complex behaviors as immoral or nonsensical. Therefore, due to his proclivity to undervalue the feminine, he cannot fathom her behaviors as anything more than irrational. This is especially true when he perceives the cause of such behavior as somehow a result of his own inadequacies, leading to him deflecting and attributing the problem to her. In short, it is easier to deal with a problem when it is someone else's fault or when it is the other person's burden to carry. The integrated man sees this type of behavior in his feminine partner as an invitation to her heart, which holds a vast amount of treasures that necessarily play a role in him arriving at a more integrated version of himself. Therefore, today's man must endure the chaos and volatility of his partner's tests, moving beyond them and into her creative force. He must willingly and gratefully carry his burdens of the relationship, leading by example to show her that she too can carry hers.

Wrongful Implementation

As with character-building tests, today's man must base the use of the skills presented in this book on outcomes that benefit both him and his partner. It is ultimately counterproductive to master covert comfort requests for the sake of escaping the frustrating and unnecessary use of them by his partner. By default, using the skills from this book to eliminate the chaos of your partner's feminine nature prevents the aspect of her that promotes your growth as a man. Men grow through challenges.

The challenges that come with the feminine nature's drive to lead men to a more integrated version of themselves present some of the most turbulent periods of psychological development. When the experience of such turbulence becomes volatile for men, they are tempted to seek a way out, desiring to escape the restrictive limitations his partner's challenging behavior places on him. The active avoidance of what seems to be an array of circumstances too impossible to deal with drives today's man further away from the development of his masculinity. In other words, when he perceives his woman's behaviors as unsolvable, he is compelled to disengage.

This frame of mind is problematic, and perhaps, this is a two-stage problem. The first-stage problem perceives his woman's behavior as impossible, placing a meaning upon her behaviors that imply she is impossible to satisfy. At this stage, he incorrectly assumes two things: 1) that she is unable to be satisfied, and 2) that she will not accept his help. Today's man must understand that his feminine partner can be satisfied. However, because the feminine lives in the moment and moves fluidly from moment to moment, she seeks satisfaction—and fulfillment—for each independent moment. For her, each moment has a life of its own, wanting to fulfill itself for the sake of fulfilling itself—it serves no other purpose. On the other hand, the masculine seeks completion of all things, seeing all things as interconnected in the sense that they all serve a purpose for something else rather than for the expression of itself. As for believing that she will not accept his help with this, the truth is that she does wants his help. Yet, it is not to help her satisfy one need for the sake of bringing her to a different place. For instance, today's man may see his partner experiencing negative emotions, such as anger or sadness, and will tend to her in an attempt to alleviate her anger or sadness for the sake of bringing her to an experience of joy and happiness. While she desires joy and happiness, her experience of fear or sadness must be tended to in order to help her experience those emotions fully, giving her space to express the emotions occurring at that moment.

The second-stage problem of this frame of mind is that he believes himself incapable of supporting her needs. Today's man experiences frustration day in and day out in his relationship when it comes to satisfying his partner's needs. His woman believes he has the capacity to satisfy her—otherwise, she would not expect so much from him. However, when his experience of her expectations of him becomes overwhelming, he begins to question whether he can satisfy her. This turns into doubt, causing him to develop insecurities concerning his abilities as a man—a result of an underdeveloped, undifferentiated anima. Without an awareness of such insecurities, he will project them onto his partner, attributing her expectations of him to a manufactured aspect of her that implies she is impossible to please. Even if he becomes conscious of these insecurities, it is painful and too daunting to overcome. This frame of mind leads him to place the responsibility on her, implying that she must modify her behavior for the relationship's sake. Asking her to modify behaviors that are grounded in her feminine diminishes her femininity. This leads to the further detriment of the relationship.

Corrective Actions

Mismanaged responses to covert comfort requests are easy to correct due to the softer, gentler approach women have with them, unlike the more volatile, unpredictable approach that comes with character-building tests. The focal point of such corrections is how you subjectively look at her behaviors. The subjective nature of experience leaves room for cognitive errors in one's judgment, particularly in stressful situations. The goal is to change the subjective meaning of your experience, which is not a simple task—although it is quite doable. Changing the subjective meaning of one's experience regarding his feminine partner presents a unique challenge in that it calls into question many deeply, long-held beliefs about women. Making this change is a true paradigm shift. Paradigms are underlying views and patterns of one's understanding and experience of the world. They are constructed of sets of ideas about the particulars of one's life. Shifting your paradigm becomes necessary when you encounter a typical situation where your previous methods—or rules—no longer serve you. For instance, if you were struggling with addiction, and the negative consequences that can come with it (such as damaged relationships, unstable employment, and getting arrested), committing to getting and staying clean comes with a paradigm of avoidance-based motivation (i.e., not damaging relationships, not losing a job, and not getting arrested). This paradigm may be necessary while learning to stay clean and keep out of trouble.

Yet, once you establish yourself enough to where these consequences are not so imminent, you will stall in your development. This is because, while the avoidance of something can propel you away from it and into safer territory, it does not move you toward something pleasurable and rewarding. Moving toward something pleasurable requires a different paradigm than the paradigm that moves you away from trouble. In other words, the same avoidance-based motivation that got you out of harm's way is not the same kind of motivation that creates a joyful experience beyond the sensation of alleviating pain. Assuming a paradigm of rewards-based motivation is what brings about such an experience. While avoidance-based motivation and rewards-based motivation are both paradigms that move you in the right direction, the underlying views and patterns of viewing the world and your behaviors differ in the sense that the former serves to get you out of trouble. The latter serves to bring you to a more fulfilling life. By shifting the paradigm of the experience with your partner's needs, a new light is cast upon the true nature of her femininity, illuminating the beauty behind her behaviors. This revelation can be quite profound, for it changes how you respond to a deepened, more purposeful motivation. This, in turn, unlocks the creative force within her, and you will perhaps experience a new level of love and appreciation of her.

Keys to Improvement

Improving your character requires broadening your personality to create a more adaptable version of yourself. The ability to shift your behaviors is paramount. The personality trait of agreeableness is the optimal place to begin. Although the assertiveness aspect of the trait of extraversion is important regarding building character, it focuses on creating the necessary order for relationships to function rather than cultivating character assets. If you are high in agreeableness, you will be more of a natural with covert comfort requests than the man who is low in agreeableness. However, the primary fault of being high in agreeableness concerning covert comfort requests is that you tend to project onto your partner the insecurities with your abilities to meet her needs. This is no small matter. Although you might notice some of the subtleties of her emotional experiences, you are not nuanced enough with meeting needs to support hers effectively. While it is your nurturing nature that makes you well-suited for meeting her needs, your confidence to meet them comes by first learning to negotiate for your own needs. The better you become at negotiating for yourself, the more nuanced you will become in meeting her needs. Broadening your personality in this way affords you the ability to differentiate her tests. The ability to identify covert comfort requests and character-building tests will help you declare which response is best suited for the situation.

If you are low in agreeableness, the primary fault lies in your inability to recognize the nuances of her emotional experiences altogether. You also tend to see her covert comfort requests as needy or unnecessary, leading to the belief that she is impossible to please. The best thing you can do in these situations is to practice nurturance. For the disagreeable man, this is perhaps the most difficult aspect to cultivate within himself, and he often experiences many failures doing so. It is an awkward process, but it is in the mistakes and errors that truth is found. Becoming nuanced in your partner's emotional experiences will optimize your ability to connect with her because, once combined with your ability to negotiate for your needs, you will negotiate for her needs superbly.

For the man who falls in the middle of the spectrum with the trait of agreeableness, acting decisively yet thoughtfully is the best way to improve himself concerning covert comfort requests. If you are of average agreeableness, you come by the virtues of the high and low ends of this trait more naturally. Yet, you embody the faults of both ends of this trait. Having skills of each end makes you more naturally adaptable. However, this also means you are not nuanced in the extreme ends of this trait. Lacking this makes you more indecisive as the challenges of your relationship become more complex. The key to improving yourself here is to be bolder in your responses to your partner's tests, particularly with your overall effort. This will be noticed and appreciated by her, inspiring you to understand her emotional experiences more fully.

Slaying the Dragon

Having previously acquired the shield of assertiveness, Rodion possesses an understanding of his character and has begun sharpening his skills for managing character-building tests and covert comfort requests. He is beginning to notice Regina's behaviors decreasing in intensity at times and even experiencing more pleasant interactions with her. He is rather clumsy at times, but he responds to his mistakes much better than before.

However, there is still progress to be made. As he faces the feminine dragon of chaos, he sees that she is relentless with the fiery tests she projects onto him. It is frightening at times, yet he seems to catch glimpses of the ancient and wonderful feminine, deep within the dragon of chaos. Rodion predicts her moves, making it harder for the dragon to corner him.

The feminine dragon of chaos is beginning to develop an appreciation for her adversary's strength and skill. As Regina sees glimpses of Rodion's deep, ancient masculine, she grows hopeful. But she's clever, and her feminine nature knows better than to be lulled by him. She must amp up her assessments of him to see if he can be consistent. Although she is beginning to see his gifts, she does not yet trust that he will give them consistently. Her frame is strong, and she will see how strong Rodion's frame is. The feminine dragon of chaos will elevate her skepticism of him once more so that she may find a chink in his armor. Rodion is unaware of the challenges he will face next. The dragon of chaos will challenge him in ways he cannot anticipate. This is purposeful, for Rodion will never retrieve the glorious ancient feminine from the belly of the beast if he cannot sustain his courage and strength. He will have to survive the gauntlet designed to test his capacity to be unflappable and unwavering in his ability to hold frame and keep the feminine dragon of chaos in his element.

Chapter Eight

Frame

The more we understand what we are dealing with, the better we can contend with it. When it comes to navigating the world and relationships, we are perhaps driven by our personality more than most anything else. Each of us has a personality with complexities that make us quite unique. In relationships, we are constantly navigating a barrage of complexities of another's personality that is not wholly compatible with our own. People perceive the world and think differently than we do. Of course, that is not an earth-shattering statement, but it is worth unpacking. What does it mean to think differently than someone else? What does perceiving the world differently have to do with incompatibility? In the context of relationships, such differences shed light on the underpinnings of conflict and discord. First, we must understand that the world is incomprehensibly complex. As remarkable as the human brain is, it is no match for the incalculable amount of information the world holds, be it the amount of individual pieces of information or the infinite possibilities of countless combinations of information. No one person can even begin to comprehend every possible combination of data. This is an interesting thought because part of what makes human beings the dominant species is our ability to problem-solve. Yet, our superior brain power has its limitations, and it is at the edge of our limitations where incompatibility occurs. In part, this is because humans have a tendency to get the minimum amount of information possible that allows them to navigate this complex world. In other words, once we have enough information, we then shift our focus to reserving as much energy as possible for other tasks. As the limited knowledge of two people diverges, so too does their compatibility.

What does this mean for relationships? To answer this question, let us consider the law of probabilities. Imagine that we generally only understand 10% of each event we experience. Depending on how well that information matches our personality—interests and preferences—our experience will be either more positive or more negative. In other words, if the 10% of the information we extracted happens to fit well with our interests and preferences, we are likely to have a positive experience of the event. On the other hand, if we happen to detect a 10% that is incongruent with our personality, our experience of the event will be negative. However, despite the small percentage of information we can comprehend, we navigate our experiences with relative success. Yet, suppose we achieve success while only understanding such a small percentage of the information contained in any given event—what then lies at the root of conflict and discord in relationships? The answer can be understood by looking at the times when we have the unlucky draw of a bad 10% of information—when our environment is not well-suited for our personality. When this phenomenon occurs in relationships, that individual experiences discord with the other person. When both individuals extract a bad 10%, they experience incongruence with the other, and the conflict is exacerbated.

Imagine a board on a wall with 100 buttons. With your partner in another room, you select ten buttons, and this data is unknown to her. Next, you leave the room, and your partner enters the room without you and also selects ten buttons. What are the odds that the two of you will select the same exact ten buttons? The odds are extremely low. In fact, the odds are that she will pick one of the ten you selected are still quite low. Conflict in relationships usually stems not only from the limited amount of information we extract from an event but from having a different set of facts than the other person. Experiences are subjective, but part of what makes them subjective is the limited information we extract from an event. Furthermore, if we extract as much as 10% of the information contained in an event, there is another 90% of that information we do not know. That is no small matter. Now, couple that with the low probability that you and your partner will extract the same 10% of information from the event, and what you get are two different sets of facts. This is significant. If two people are arguing two different sets of facts, they cannot come to a workable solution. To have a chance to do so, they must first come to an understanding of the set of facts the other is working with.

Left unreconciled, their experiential differences will become exacerbated, further obscuring each other's unmet needs. This is a recipe for disaster, for the intensity of the negative experience and the degree of disparity of information of the event determine the severity of conflict. In other words, the more serious and painful the situation, the more the different sets of facts become problematic.

From a clinical standpoint, this notion is perhaps best conceptualized by looking through the lens of psychotherapy and change. Given that conflict is rooted in disparate sets of facts each person holds, it is imperative that they each be willing to broaden their perceptions enough to get on the same page. This is change, and to expect someone to blindly adopt a different set of facts than the one they currently hold is to threaten their understanding of reality. Therefore, people are more apt to change when they are accepted and understood. When people are accepted and understood, they no longer fear losing their grip on reality and can then begin to see a more complete truth of their circumstances. This opens them up to see the error of their ways as well as the potential truth contained in the set of facts the other holds, which empowers them to change—to climb the hierarchy in a functional manner. Otherwise, people will dig in their heels and fight for position to have their needs met without seeing the equal importance of the other person's needs—to climb the hierarchy in a corrupt manner. In the sense of achieving outcomes, resolving relational conflict is to look for more information that could possibly change us for the better. The brilliance of Carl Rogers best sums up the notion of changing when we are constrained by a limited set of facts. In his book, On Becoming a Person, Rogers stated, "If I let myself really understand another person, I might be changed by that understanding. And we all fear change. So as I say, it is not an easy thing to permit oneself to understand an individual, to enter thoroughly and completely and empathically into his frame of reference."[74] This process opens a person up to receive more information than they have so they are better equipped to make decisions that are beneficial in as many ways as possible and to everyone involved. As an individual, today's man has to strive to understand the other person thoroughly, completely, and empathically, for the more information he has, the better his understanding of the context of the situation. This, in turn, helps him infer the meaning of an experience more accurately.

What is Frame?

The capacity to infer the meaning of an experience with precision—and to identify the contextual values both within and outside of it—determines the degree of success in achieving outcomes. That is, we need to know what we are looking at—to see the different dimensions of it—so that we may know what to do with it. Such experiences include those of other people's behaviors as well as situations in which we find ourselves, be it of our own accord or due to another's actions. The capacity to infer the meaning of an experience and identify its contextual value is influenced by our prior experiences of achieving outcomes—or not—and the paradigms through which we perceive the world. Such capacity determines how we attribute particular behaviors to particular functions or motivations—that is, the framework through which we make the associations between the observable behavior of others and the reasons behind them. We utilize our capacity to understand people's actions and motivations so that we can navigate our way to the outcomes we want with as much precision as possible. This is frame. Essentially, it determines whether or not we get the outcome we want.

We can have a weak frame or a strong frame. A weak frame may cause today's man to arbitrarily infer another's reasons for behaving a particular way through emotional reasoning, which usually results in a negative emotional experience. A strong frame enables the integrated man to detect the reasons behind his partner's behaviors and how to best address them. For the sake of having a consistent aim within the concept of frame, we will default to explaining it from the viewpoint of a strong, robust frame, unless otherwise stated. Emotionally, a robust and healthy frame feels like confidence and composure—a sort of stick-to-itiveness. Psychologically, a robust and healthy frame is experienced as having a clear vision of the outcome you want and using your resources to obtain those outcomes. Perhaps, the best way to describe frame is that it is the mental structure that enables us to overcome obstacles in our quest to achieve an outcome. Of all the resources and skills that factor into a strong, healthy frame, assertiveness is the foundation that affords us the ability to execute any and all subsequent strategies for reaching our outcomes.

Due to the abstract nature of frame, it is helpful to illustrate this concept by appealing to the visual senses. Let us turn our direction toward the cosmos. The Hubble Space Telescope has given us spectacular images of the cosmos. Through this technology, we can get beautiful views of planets, galaxies, stars, and nebulae. Yet, it is how Hubble shows us what the universe looks like that is important. When Hubble sends images back to Earth, astronomers make many adjustments to produce the images we (the public) see. Hubble does not capture the color of the incoming light in the way that a traditional telescope does. Instead, it uses various filters, or special electronic detectors, that let in specific ranges of wavelengths of light, including ultraviolet and infrared light, invisible to the human eye. These detectors produce images of the cosmos not in color but in shades of black and white. Finished color images are combinations of two or more black-and-white exposures to which color has been added during image processing. Astronomers use color as a tool to enhance the detail of the image or make visible what—under normal circumstances—could never be seen. Essentially, multiple images are captured using these filters, which create individual layers, so to speak. These layers themselves are nothing spectacular, for they only capture specific wavelengths of light. These particular images are rather dull and do not give a complete picture of the object in space on which the Hubble Space Telescope is focused. It is much like taking a scenic photo that only captures one of the three primary colors—red, blue, or yellow. While it could perhaps be used artistically, the image would be incomplete.

To have a complete image is to understand and appreciate what we are seeing and experiencing. We must enhance our frame with filters—or special detectors, so to speak. Human behavior has many layers, yet we may only see one, maybe two layers. The quality of our frame is determined by the filters through which we interpret other people's behaviors. Suppose our current frame uses the filters of defensiveness and insecurity. In that case, we might only detect what could be considered an attack on our character or an unjustified accusation. This frame lacks detectors that capture what would otherwise be helpful information from other people's behaviors. This process produces a particular experience—or image—which is then interpreted and categorized. Since the frame's primary detectors filtered the experience through defensiveness and insecurity, the image is incomplete, creating dull, unappealing layers. This produces a disturbing image, which does not give us a chance to respond well. If all we see are attacks and threats, we will respond accordingly. By skillfully adding a complete set of special detectors, we can capture a broader range of the "behavioral wavelengths." This process would then produce a more complete and, perhaps, beautiful image of other people's behaviors, allowing us an optimal chance to respond well. The installation of detectors of character, assertiveness, confidence, patience, and stoicism—to name a few—can produce a much more well-rounded image of which a more accurate interpretation can be inferred. A strong, robust frame gathers more data from our partner's behaviors, giving them more color. The more data we collect, the better we can respond.

Rodion & Regina XX

Rodion has become courageous in his efforts to improve himself as a man in his relationship. He understands, at least fundamentally, the significance of setting boundaries, managing conflict, and responding to Regina's tests with good character. He has experienced moments of glory in which he managed numerous conflicts that would have otherwise been mismanaged in the past. He even notices, by the reduction in the frequency of conflict, an improvement in her mood overall. He is trying to give his gift. Yet, he has not proven to himself that he can remain consistent with this newfound ability to recognize the *why* behind Regina's behaviors (to utilize a full range of filters and special detectors). Rodion finds himself going along with plans he did not want to go along with. He thinks to himself in these times, *"Why did I agree to this? What am I doing this for? I just wanted to stay home and work on my project."* While he does his best to remain in good spirits—even though he wishes he would have spoken up earlier—Rodion feels ashamed of himself for doing what he does not want to do. Now, this does not seem like a big deal, but this is the initial point in which Rodion's capacity to infer the meaning of his experience with Regina's behaviors comes into play. It is also his ability to recognize when the contextual value of the situation reaches its limit. Although trivial, Regina subtly and skillfully pulls Rodion into her frame with little effort. Only after the fact does he realize he is not where he would like to be.

Frame is an unconscious way of perceiving things. Hence, Rodion is unaware of his frame—much less that such a concept exists. Yet, suppose he becomes aware of his frame. In that case, he can modify it in a way that gets him where he wants to be by increasing his ability to manage familiar obstacles in healthier ways and navigate difficult challenges as they arise. Rodion's capacity to manage such challenges hinges on the strength of his frame. In a structural sense, frame is what holds up a house; it holds up a canvas; it supports a mineshaft. Of course, this requires a solid foundation, one he has been working on up to this point by becoming more assertive and building character, which can serve as useful filters in his frame. However, Rodion lacks some important special detectors in his frame, and he is too blind to see that he does not honor his own desires.

This is especially the case when he wants to do things Regina objects to with an emotional yet convincing stance. For instance, Rodion has grown quite disgusted with the clutter in their home office, which has become more of a disorganized storage room than a functioning office space. Rodion assertively tells Regina he would like to declutter the office and make it into a pleasant room to do his work in. However, she becomes overwhelmed when assessing the situation of the clutter. As she and Rodion begin looking through the piles of boxes so that they can figure out where to start, she starts experiencing emotional distress as the task becomes emotionally daunting for her. She tells Rodion that she cannot handle this. Rodion, attempting to show good character, tells her that he will begin organizing by himself and that she can go do something else instead. Regina responds by expressing to him that she wants to be involved in the decision-making process regarding how it should be organized. Now, Rodion faces a conundrum. He is beginning to experience a dilemma within himself: How can one be assertive and show good character in this situation? Suppose he further asserts his desire to organize the room. In that case, it will make it difficult to show good character regarding her emotional distress with the situation due to her desire to be involved. If he agrees to put off organizing the office in an attempt to tend to her emotional distress, he will not have his desires met, potentially sacrificing his self-respect. While this may seem like an impossible situation, Rodion must first ask himself if this assessment is a false dichotomy—erroneously concluding there are only two possible diametrically opposed outcomes. This would be an incomplete image of the situation. Rodion needs to be able to see more layers to Regina's behaviors so that he may more accurately assess the situation and reach a successful outcome.

Rodion suddenly remembers the art of timing when it comes to assertiveness, and it occurs to him that he must seek a workable compromise.

Hence, he proposes to Regina that they revisit the office clutter situation when she feels emotionally ready to do so. She seems grateful for this gesture; yet it takes her some time to move past the distress. Nonetheless, Rodion feels good about the way he asserted himself while simultaneously showing good character. A week goes by, and things are going well. He has gained some acceptance with working in a cluttered office because he rests on the compromise with Regina to organize it as soon as she's ready. Another week goes by, and Rodion's acceptance is growing thin. He calmly brings up the situation again to Regina, asking her how she feels about it. "I don't want to talk about it right now. I just have too much going on," she says. Thinking this is fair and reasonable, Rodion continues practicing patience. Another week passes, and by now, Rodion is quite unsettled with the lack of progress. Through his frustration and growing intolerance of the clutter, Rodion begins acting out old behaviors of defensiveness and starts making indirect, aggressive comments to Regina. Things are not going as well as they were, and the home office is still a mess. Rodion has found himself feeling as if his progress has stalled, and the relationship seems to be regressing.

Rodion's mistake here is resting on his laurels of achieving some success with assertiveness and character. Rodion has encountered an anomaly. *"How could this be?"* he thinks to himself. He assumed that if he acted assertively and practiced good character, he would get what he wanted, and that Regina would be receptive to him without hesitation (covert contract). Yet, his plans failed as they met Regina's objection. As a result of this derailment of his plans—his incomplete plans—Rodion's involuntary fear responses begin to take over. Recall that a man's involuntary responses to his partner's emotional distress make it difficult to differentiate the behaviors of his feminine partner. Failing to make this discernment prevents him from moving beyond the frame of mind that finds her behaviors intolerable. Rodion's frame lacks a full set of filters, which produces a specific—and incomplete—image of Regina's behaviors. As a result, the meaning he placed on this experience with Regina is such that he pins the blame on her for his desires not being met. Or worse, he blames the notions of assertiveness and character, seeking to find fault in their effectiveness rather than a poor implementation of such concepts. In other words, he risks believing those pillars are not helpful. In terms of human interactions, frame refers to the meaning you place on those interactions as well as how you define them. Rodion's failure to exhibit a strong frame is costing him the outcome he wants (organized office). Rather, he falls into Regina's frame (stress-induced avoidance of the task and unwillingness to get into a solution).

Some people have little to no frame. These people are quite passive and rarely get what they want. When they do get what they want, it is through randomness and happenstance. Although many people do have some degree of frame, most people's frames are not particularly strong. These people have an average frame, and they do more than get by, yet when faced with any real resistance, they give up, too. People who have a strong frame tend to get the outcomes they want the majority of the time. The following scenario features three examples, based on a person with a weak frame, a person with an average frame, and a person with a strong frame.

A man with a weak frame goes into a home improvement store and purchases a new lawnmower. When he tries out his new mower, he discovers that the mower is not functioning properly due to some defective parts. He decides he is going to take it back to the home improvement store to get a refund. When he brings the mower to the customer service desk and requests a refund, the cashier asks the man for his receipt. The man says, "I do not have my receipt." The cashier says, "We have to have a receipt to give a refund." So, the man returns home, frustrated. He gave up at the slightest resistance.

A man with an average frame, in the same scenario, returns the mower and requests a refund. The cashier asks the man for his receipt. The man says, "I do not have my receipt." The cashier says, "We have to have a receipt to give a refund." The man says, "Well, is there anything else I can do?" The cashier says, "We can exchange it or give you a store credit." The man accepts the offer and, although he may not be as frustrated as the man with a weak frame, he still settled and did not give any real effort to achieve the outcome he wanted.

A man with a strong frame returns the mower and requests a refund. The cashier asks the man for his receipt. The man says, "I do not have my receipt." The cashier says, "We have to have a receipt to give a refund." The man replies, "I understand that, but I want my money back." The cashier says, "Sir, our policy says that we have to have a receipt to give a refund." The man replies again, "I understand that's what your policy says, but I want a refund." The cashier replies, "I don't have the authority to override the policy." The man says, "Then I would like to speak with someone who does." The manager comes over and reiterates what the cashier told the man about the refund policy. The man repeats himself, "I understand what your policy says, but I want my money back. You guys sold me a defective lawnmower, and that is unacceptable. I want my money back, and I will escalate this up the chain of command if I have to." The manager replies, "I guess I can do this one time," and refunds the man. The man with the strong frame outlasted the cashier and the manager. He used assertiveness skills and remained calm and patient. He held his frame, even against the strong resistance of a store policy and two employees. He was even willing to go further.

The frame you create for yourself should not be determined by the events you experience. Rather, it should be determined by the goals and outcomes you deem important and meaningful. Anything that is not congruent with these outcomes and goals is a distraction. Resiliency to such distractions enables you to stay on track. Staying on track prevents you from depending too much on others. Perhaps, the most common of these distractions is other people's frames. You have a frame, and you must contend with other people's frames. You may find that you are often pulled into interactions that leave you defending your behavior or rationalizing your desired outcome—taking the bait, so to speak. It is crucial to objectively look at your thought process and utilize your skills to maintain your frame when this happens. Recognize the behaviors of others that create distractions to getting what you want.

Frame Types

While it is imperative to maintain frame control so that we may achieve the outcomes we want, it is equally important to consider who is impacted by it and how much, if at all. Knowing when to implement the appropriate type of frame control helps direct our actions toward moral outcomes rather than selfishly motivated outcomes. Frame falls into three different categories. The first category is the *Ecology Frame*; the second is the *Safe Frame*; and the third is the *Self-Preservation Frame*. To understand the significance of the three types of frame, one must differentiate morals from principles. There is often much confusion about the differences between morals and principles, yet many people generally agree that morals are a subset of principles. Morals serve a much more limited role than principles—they are subservient to principles. Principles are fundamental truths or propositions that serve as the foundation for beliefs and the behaviors driven by them. Morals are derived from principles and serve to discern right from wrong. Yet, what constitutes right and wrong in one situation does not translate to all situations. However, since principles are fundamental truths, they apply to all situations.

When faced with difficult or challenging situations and how they should behave, many people arrive at their conclusion through a moral lens rather than a perspective based on principles. For instance, you have in mind the goal of getting a promotion. To reach this goal, you must do certain things, such as producing quality results that showcase your talents. With this new inspiration and potential incentive, you begin making strides, producing promising work, and you seem to be on your way to that promotion. However, due to your tendency to view your actions through a moral lens, you resist the impulse to showcase your work for fear of coming across as boastful and arrogant. Your morals may have taught you that no one likes a bragger, that it is off-putting at the least and, at worst, self-sabotaging. When the time comes to find out if you are getting this hard-won promotion, you are met with a profoundly disappointing rejection. With much difficulty, you do your best to honor your nobility but struggle to find solace in it. In the end, you failed to showcase your talents by downplaying your work and placing your morals above all else without consideration for the principles the situation called for.

While your moral lens provides you with knowledge of right and wrong, its restrictive nature limits you from seeing the potential of how principles can drive your behaviors toward different and better outcomes. The principle of positive reinforcement, for example, would have led to actions that showcase your talents. Showcasing your talents would have gotten you exposure and recognition. That recognition might have weighed heavily on your superior's biases and, in turn, inclined them to give you the promotion. It is also worth mentioning that the intuitive choice of your superior would favor a version of you that gave a stronger, more positive impression. To further illustrate the function principles can serve, consider the personality trait extraversion, which has to do with positive emotional experiences. The two aspects of this trait are enthusiasm and assertiveness. By showcasing your work, you are likely to be acting more enthusiastically and assertively than normal. This stands out, but it stands out in a positive way. Those who are interested or have skin in the game will experience positive emotions regarding your behaviors surrounding your work. And that is good.

Positive reinforcement aims to reward behaviors that lead to desired outcomes. By celebrating your productivity and giving yourself praise for your excellent work, you would have rewarded yourself for such behavior. This behavior would have activated your brain's reward center, releasing dopamine into your system, which produces positive emotions. This process would have motivated you toward desired outcomes. In turn, it would have created positive behavior patterns. Those patterns would have then solidified as a result of repetition or practice. Practice advances your skill set, which would have made your promotion goals more attainable. Therefore, by patting yourself on the back for your good work, you would have demonstrated the precise behaviors that bring you to your desired outcome. Your positive reinforcement would have ultimately positioned you for the promotion by progressing your behaviors such that you make your work known to your supervisors and other pivotal employees in a positive emotional way.

While morality may play an important role in deciding for ourselves the outcomes we want—and our overall success in life—it is of little use elsewhere. Morality lies in the outcomes and goals we choose; principles lead the way to them. Therefore, the principles that strengthen your frame are true, regardless of the outcome you set for yourself. Frame, or frame control, has moral implications, yet is driven by principles. The moral implications of your frame represent the likelihood of achieving and maintaining harmonious relationships. In other words, morality's function is to give us something high and righteous to aim for. Principles are not fixed on each action you take, as if in a vacuum; rather, they guide you with the big picture in mind, allowing you to see how each behavior is connected to the grand scheme of things, to the highest aim. This differentiation is important to understand as you master frame control. The significance of the three types of frames differs in the moral implications of their outcomes rather than the moral implications of frame, in and of itself. In other words, the impact of the moral implications on ourselves and others determines the type of frame we implement.

Ecology Frame

Achieving outcomes within the context of your relationship comes with great responsibility. Your actions will usually impact your partner. Considering how the path to your outcomes affects your partner will help create a harmonious connection with her. Your efforts to ensure she benefits from your goals will be meaningful to her. It also cultivates a strong sense of leadership within you, for it is in the spirit of unity that a man's accomplishments bring those around him closer. The ecology frame is about getting the outcomes you want in a way that everyone wins. It is about practicing good character and creating situations that benefit everyone involved. Everyone involved may include your partner, children, community, country, or the world. This type of frame should be the one most striven for if we want successful interpersonal relationships whatsoever. The ecology frame requires the most conscientious effort from a man. He must figure out how to get the outcome he wants while making it a win-win situation for others who are significantly affected by his outcomes. The conscientiousness required with the ecology frame focuses on the implications of your outcomes concerning the well-being of those around you. The level of complexity of the implications of a given goal determines the level of consideration you should have for such people. That is, the more significant the impact your outcomes have on others, the greater the amount of mental energy will be required of you.

One of the most challenging aspects of the ecology frame is the need to practice belief in your frame and outcomes when your partner does not see how the outcomes will benefit her. Even though you may see the bigger picture, there will be times when she does not. This can be difficult, for people will put up their greatest resistance when they cannot see the benefit of what they are asked to do. Difficulty can arise because of the obscure nature of your goals. Generally speaking, hard-to-achieve goals have a more complicated path. Couple that with the responsibility of tending to a significant other, and achieving your desired outcomes becomes more complicated. The most troublesome dynamic to this experience is managing the distractions and objections these complicated paths present. The more these distractions and objections misdirect you, the less likely you will achieve your goal. Otherwise, leading your partner to harmonious outcomes is a more attainable conquest when goals are less obscure. These less obscure goals have more apparent paths set before you.

Be grateful for these easier-to-navigate goals and utilize them to strengthen your frame for when the more obscure goals present uncertainty regarding the most optimal way to lead your partner. The easier conquests serve as opportunities to become nuanced with the abstract nature of frame control. Although the paths to the more impactful outcomes present a greater degree of complication, do not fret. It is in these experiences that today's man expands his capacity to establish his trustworthiness and effectiveness as a leader. His partner may experience emotional distress regarding the impactful outcomes he strives for. However, if he succeeds, she will grow to trust him more fully. If he neglects to achieve outcomes that do not benefit anyone else, he will find himself alone and lacking respect from others. The ecology frame seeks to consider the needs of himself and everyone involved, creating the most optimal chance to build and sustain meaningful relationships. It is through this type of frame that he honors his pursuit of discovering purpose.

Safe Frame

The safe frame is about getting the outcomes you want as long as you do not harm anyone in the process. It is likely your most used frame because the majority of our daily activities have little to no direct impact on others. It also does not require much creativity. This type of frame is appropriate in many situations, especially those that only affect you, have little to no long-term effect on you, and do not put you at risk of needless consequences. The safe frame is necessary for satisfying your interests, particularly the interests that your partner does not share with you. This serves to establish and maintain your sense of individuality and promote a self-directed life. This is paramount in relationships for today's man because it shows him how to be a man who seeks to live according to what's meaningful and purposeful to him. Perhaps, he enjoys woodworking as a hobby and derives nostalgia and pleasure from it. Perhaps, his father had a woodworking business during his childhood, and it is a way to connect with his earlier life, serving as a way of grounding himself. Maybe it challenges him by figuring out how to create a piece of work that is his most complicated project yet. It may also be a reprieve from the daily grind of life, creating a space for him to decompress.

Sometimes it may be difficult to tell if you are acting within the safe frame. People will try to convince you that what you are doing is impacting them. Even though this is their experience of such matters, it does not necessarily make it true. Even a single hobby can provide a tremendous amount of restoration and growth for today's man, making him a more magnificent version of himself—one from which those around him benefit. While this does not directly impact his partner, she may not see it that way. She might experience his time spent on his hobby one evening as time she is not getting with him. She may not understand the depth of meaning he derives from it; rather, she experiences the coldness from his absence. Perhaps, this experience prompts her to challenge him on why he is in the woodshop instead of spending time with her. This test is tricky, for it appeals to her need for comfort and security, which prompts him to stop what he is doing to be with her. While this would be a compassionate act, it does not mean that his time in the shop harms her in any way. It may indirectly affect her, yet her insecurities and loneliness were not caused by his time in the woodshop; they result from her experiences in and of themselves. Likewise, if he fails to pursue what is meaningful to him, he cannot be a superior version of himself. This does not advance him. By practicing the safe frame, he subjects himself to an experience that brings important aspects of himself to life. Whether these aspects are beneficial to his partner is irrelevant regarding the function of the safe frame. Satisfying personal interests (that do not harm others) brings a personal fulfillment that cannot be found elsewhere. It promotes independence and self-sufficiency. As a byproduct, his partner will enjoy a more wholesome version of him once he has satisfied such a personal and meaningful interest. But this is only a bonus. We must realize that practicing the safe frame is vital if we strive toward our most magnificent self, even if others try to convince us otherwise.

Distance makes the heart grow fonder. This axiom applies to the safe frame in the sense that tending to your needs sometimes requires solitude or perhaps time with people other than your significant other. Experiences need contrast to be appreciated. To know joy, one must know sorrow. If even for a little while, the absence of someone dear to us makes us more grateful when they are present with us. It is human nature to take the people and things we have for granted and at our beck and call. When we desire to be in their presence, that feeling can sometimes take precedence over all other rational thoughts. If your partner experiences this, it will come across as emotional distress in the form and a character-building test or a covert comfort request. On the surface, the safe frame looks like the obvious choice if the emotional distress comes in the form of a character-building test. Here, the unconscious feminine challenge is meant to evaluate your ability to stand your ground and take care of what needs to be taken care of. However, suppose in this kind of situation, her emotional distress comes in the form of a covert comfort request. In that case, the safe frame is appropriate if the outcome you have determined for yourself contains positive moral implications. As long as your goal is to do what is meaningful for you in a way that doesn't harm her, it is imperative that you maintain frame control. The key to success with this is to respond with your best. You can show empathic understanding while sticking to your plans. This is not to say that you must never be flexible with your frame, but it does suggest that you must consider the full implications of each direction your choices present.

Self-preservation Frame

The self-preservation frame is about getting the outcome you want, even if it's at the expense of someone else. In the context of a relationship, the self-preservation frame should rarely be used and should be taken seriously before implementing it. Acting within a self-preservation frame is akin to acting in self-defense. For example, if the goal is to be alive, and someone is choking you to death, gouging their eyes might cause them to stop choking you. You would get the outcome you want, even though it was at the expense of their eyes. Although sometimes necessary, the self-preservation frame is never ideal in long-term relationships. The reason for this is because a harmonious and balanced relationship never experiences the kind of character-building tests that would cause a man to resort to achieving his goal at the expense of his partner. It would be a dramatic overreaction. On the other hand, there might be situations in an extremely imbalanced and unhealthy relationship whereby a man could implement the self-preservation frame, either by verbal force or physical force. For example, if a relationship has spiraled out of control to the point where his partner is abusing him verbally, today's man, experiencing one too many defeats, might not have it in him to respond with the assertiveness and confidence needed to diffuse the situation more masterfully. Therefore, he does whatever is necessary without overreacting. Perhaps, with a stern conviction in his voice, he verbalizes to her the detestable aspects of her character to get her to cease the abuse. While this kind of response in and of itself is frowned upon, it is not as if it happened in a vacuum. Such a response is not indicative of a pleasant situation. However, the actions required to elevate yourself from the bottom of the hierarchy differ from those that propel your ascent when near the top. Although it is unfortunate to be in a spiraling relationship in the first place, the situation itself does not negate the necessary aggression that comes with acting in the self-preservation frame. In other words, sometimes, a man needs to bark back.

Regarding the implications of the outcomes, self-preservation is the most obscure type of frame due to the degree of abstraction required to implement it. With the ecology frame and safe frame, it is easier to abstract the implementable actions (or specific behaviors) necessary to attain the more obscure outcomes. The safe frame is about achieving desired outcomes without harming anyone in the process. Two criteria drive the implementable actions required for the safe frame. The first is the sole desired outcome. The second is to do no harm. As a man chooses his actions, he asks himself if those actions meet those criteria. If they do, then he proceeds; if not, he reevaluates the implications of his desired outcome and the path to its attainment. This is rather simple. Concerning the ecology frame, the criterion for the appropriate implementable actions becomes more complex because of others' needs. Based on achieving outcomes that benefit everyone, the criteria are the sole desired outcome itself, the mutual benefits of the desired outcomes, and the consideration of everyone involved. While the outcome is more complex, the implementable actions required to achieve the outcomes are straightforward. The ultimate question a man must ask himself when choosing his actions within the ecology frame is, "Will these actions benefit everyone involved?" If yes, he will proceed; if not, he must reconsider his options. The self-preservation frame is complicated exponentially by the number of variables the situation entails and the degree to which those variables negatively impact those around you. The self-preservation frame is about getting the outcome you want, even if it's at the expense of someone else.

Here, there is one criterion: getting what you want. This means there might be times when getting what you want costs other people. Placing morality on the implications of a given outcome helps us to make principled decisions with our actions. Survival, be it emotionally or physically, is not—should not—be driven by morals. If things have regressed to a level on which death (which could mean the death of a goal) is imminent, survival is then primary. Once at this primal, animalistic level, things are not only bad, but they have been bad for a while. The things people do on this level of the hierarchy are done so within a different nature than higher functioning levels. Down here, people's predatory nature thrives. He must not tolerate abuse if he is to elevate himself and his relationship. Implementing the self-preservation frame may provide the necessary jarring experience for the other person to begin working toward harmony, too. Regarding the feminine partner, the bottom of the hierarchy is where the Terrible Mother—the *destructive* feminine dragon of chaos—reigns supreme. This version of the feminine must be conquered and reconstructed into the Great Mother, the *creative* feminine dragon of chaos.

Frame Control

Frame control is your ability to strengthen and modify your frame, as well as your ability to remain in your frame rather than be drawn into someone else's frame—or to be subjugated to external forces of circumstance, real or imagined. Frame control is an important aspect of navigating relationships because it affords you the capacity to maintain logic and reason while tending to the emotional distress during emotional, chaotic situations. It plays a significant role in your ability to steer behaviors in your relationships with people.

Rodion & Regina XXI

While he is building a leg to stand on, so to speak, there are many things with which Rodion rarely confronts Regina. Although a good many of these things are unimportant in and of themselves—yet carrying significant weight as they span over time—some of these things are rather troubling to Rodion. For the past few days, he has contemplated the issue of the cluttered office that has exposed his lack of frame control with Regina. It has occurred to him that he cannot in good conscience sacrifice his self-respect by allowing the office to remain cluttered. Rodion realizes he must have faith, for Regina will resist and become distressed about him organizing the office despite her objections and procrastination. His aim is moral, for he knows a clean and organized office will be a much more pleasant place to work, leading to greater productivity. Even though she may not yet see it, he can see that Regina will benefit from his good and moral aim. This affords Rodion new filters through which he can view Regina's behaviors. He is beginning to detect layers to her that he has never seen before, which gives him the confidence to discern what type of frame he must implement and how to carry himself while doing so.

Strengthening, sustaining, and properly modifying his frame is the essence of frame control because it provides Rodion with the ability to be logical and sensible when situations are emotional and chaotic. When he is pulled into interactions that leave him defending his actions, he must take an objective view of his thought process and his skills with assertiveness and character-building. It would be best to identify how others interact with him when he is practicing frame control. He can recall experiences in which he confronted his partner about a boundary he needed to establish or a boundary he needed to reinforce. Perhaps, he has had the experience of this type of confrontation being turned around on him. If he is a nice guy, maybe he ended up apologizing for his behavior and walking away in frustration because she never acknowledged his boundary. If he is a former alpha, he might have defended his reasons for the boundary when she became resistant, resulting in the two of them falling into an argument. She may have refused to acknowledge his boundary, distracting him through deflection and misdirection, steering him away from the outcome he had for himself. She may have outright objected to his attempts to establish a boundary by calling out other unrelated shortcomings of his. These are examples of losing frame because his partner brought him into her frame.

Now that Rodion is beginning to reframe the way he perceives his circumstances and the behaviors within them—both his and Regina's—he can act on more effective behaviors that lead to better outcomes. He is acquiring more detectors that help him produce images of Regina with more detail, which aids in making better conclusions as to what he should do to get the outcomes he wants. Something tells him that Regina's resistance to the office situation is not about the office. He is starting to understand that he is enabling Regina to remain superficial about deeper problems by giving in to her frame and not de-cluttering the office. His reasons for putting off organizing the office have been reduced to groundless excuses. If he does not organize the office, Regina will remain as she is. If he does organize it, the threat of her being upset is equally likely. If he does not clean the office, he will remain frustrated. He holds the view that the first meaningful thing that can take place is his feeling of a clean office. More importantly, he has faith that Regina will be grateful for it, which will lead to more harmony in their relationship. Rodion has made his decision and commits to organizing the office. This is good. Rodion has settled upon an outcome based on morality. Now, however, he must contend with the force that is Regina's frame. In this case, it is akin to a game of chess. The catch is Regina is more like a chess player while Rodion is more like a checkers player, so to speak.

As with practicing assertiveness, practicing frame control can seem awkward at first, making a man susceptible to swaying in the direction his efforts take him, be they directed from weakness or strength. Therefore, gradual changes in behavior modification are better, for they are usually more sustainable than radical changes. Ideally, it is best to begin your practice of frame control on subtle, less significant interactions. This way, overshooting the mark will be less consequential. Perhaps, for example, you meet another driver at an intersection, and it is a toss-up as to who has the right-of-way. You can practice holding your frame by not proceeding through the intersection until the other driver has done so, even if he insists you go first. In another scenario, you might open the door to the first set of double doors at a restaurant while it so happens that another man is holding the second set of doors for you. You can practice maintaining frame by insisting that he let you hold the door for him to pass through. These scenarios may seem trivial, but, as with all behaviors, there are implications to them. That is, if you cannot hold frame in less consequential situations, you will be unable to do so in more impactful scenarios. Therefore, it is wise to shift the implications of your behaviors to healthier, more positive outcomes. This is done by practicing frame control in daily situations, which helps you understand the concept of frame better, strengthening your frame as a whole.

Re-framing Her Experience

If you see your partner's behaviors as anything less than beautiful, she has you in her frame. At the very least, perhaps, you should find her joyfully amusing. Today's man often sees his woman as irrational and aggressive, and he detests her, fears her; at best, he finds her to be an annoying distraction—he does not recognize the ancient feminine language. This is what happens when he encounters an anomaly, something unknown and unexpected, which derails him from the path to his desired outcome. This experience of the unknown—chaos—activates a process of involuntary attention to events that occur despite his predictions regarding desires he expected to manifest. Jordan Peterson deconstructs this process in his book, *Maps of Meaning*:

Enough has been learned in the last half-century of inquiry into intellectual and emotional function to enable the development of a provisional general theory of emotional regulation. Description of the role that reaction to novelty or anomaly plays in human information processing is clearly central to such a theory. A compelling body of evidence suggests that our affective, cognitive and behavioral responses to the unknown or unpredictable are "hardwired"; suggests that these responses constitute inborn structural elements of the processes of consciousness itself. We attend, involuntarily, to those things that occur contrary to our predictions-that occur despite our desires, as expressed in expectation. That involuntary attention comprises a large part of what we refer to when we say "consciousness." Our initial attention constitutes the first step in the process by which we come to adjust our behavior and our interpretive schemas to the world of experience-assuming that we do so; constitutes as well the first step we take when we modify the world to make it what we desire, instead of what it is currently.[75]

When this process occurs in long-term relationships, today's man is susceptible to experiencing a series of hierarchical defeats. That is, when he experiences a number of challenging interactions with his partner in which he loses frame control, he will fall toward the bottom of the hierarchy of his life goals. The involuntary attention to these challenging interactions is a naturally occurring phenomenon hardwired into his "human information processing." However, this does not suggest that he cannot control the subsequent behaviors regarding the emergence of the unexpected anomaly. This is where frame control comes in. Although there is no declarable threshold that signifies when his responses go from involuntary to voluntary, he does know when he has crossed that threshold and moved onto the level of voluntary control of his behavior.

Yet, the threshold where he crosses over may become a point of fixation, for he believes that if he can masterfully identify the point where he does and does not have control, he can bypass the guessing game. However, such a fixed and absolute belief will prove disastrous. The Sorites Paradox, also known as the "heap of grains fallacy," presents the absurdity of declaring absolute thresholds with things that are vague in nature and have unclear boundaries. For example, it is agreed that one grain does not make a heap, nor does two grains, or three. Yet, it is agreed upon that 1,000,000 grains make a heap, as does 999,999, 999,998…and so on. Yet, at what point can we declare that it is no longer a heap? The Stanford Encyclopedia of Philosophy states, "Because the predicate 'heap' has unclear boundaries, it seems that no single grain of wheat can make the difference between a number of grains that does and a number that does not make a heap. Therefore, since one grain of wheat does not make a heap, it follows that two grains do not; and if two do not, then three do not; and so on. This reasoning leads to the absurd conclusion that no number of grains of wheat makes a heap."[76] This inflexibility that comes with deriving such a definitive conclusion from something vague in nature will prevent him from modifying and adapting his behaviors when he encounters his partner's chaotic feminine nature. To remove the guessing game is to remove one of the most important aspects of mastering frame control. Without uncertainty, today's man cannot master the rules of the game and will not be able to revolutionize his life or his relationship.

At its core, frame control positions you to consciously elevate your perspective to revolutionize the world around you. That is, it allows you to see deeper into the events in your life to bring about changes in a more meaningful way. In long-term relationships, elevating your perspective puts you at a vantage point, which gives you direct access to what is happening deep within your partner's unconscious experience. Your partner's veil of superficial emotional distress is a manifestation of a deeper, more ancient process of the chaotic feminine nature trying to actualize herself into a more wholesome and purposeful existence. When she is met with anything other than an order that aims to bring her into this wholesome and purposeful existence, she becomes impatient and irritable.

Today's man erroneously declares this—silently or vocally—as an annoyance and a frustrating distraction to the life he believes is right for them. The integrated man knows that, behind the facade of emotional distress, his feminine partner is longing to be brought into the present more fully. He also knows that, while order will alleviate chaos, the proper masculine order must be injected into the situation to evoke the whole feminine experience in a manner that leads the creative aspect of the chaotic feminine dragon to glory. The chaos of the feminine is, by nature, unknowable and unpredictable. Therefore, the occurrence of involuntary responses of humans toward the feminine is inevitable. However, when we become conscious of the anomaly of unexpected feminine challenges, we can and must assume control of our aims. That is, as soon as we become aware of our ability to respond to the anomaly voluntarily, we must establish—or reestablish—frame control.

The Case Against Frame

Morality often emerges as an area of concern regarding frame. Some argue that the concept of frame is disturbing because it comes across as amoral. Those people are not wrong. Frame is quite amoral in and of itself. However, frame is a tool. So is a hammer. A hammer has no morals. A hammer can be used to drive nails. It can also be used to assault someone. Morality lies in the outcomes people choose. Frame is the conduit through which outcomes are achieved.

Adolf Hitler had a strong frame. So did Winston Churchill. Hitler was determined. He created a strong frame to achieve something globally immoral. The rest of the world had other plans, and their frame would outlast Hitler's frame. Hitler also operated in the self-preservation frame, and everything he did to reach his atrocious mission came at the expense of others. The United States and its allies had to operate in the self-preservation frame to stop Hitler's mission. One could argue that the difference between these two sides was the morality of their desired outcomes.

Today's man, particularly the nice guy, often struggles with difficulty practicing frame control. This is especially the case with the self-preservation frame, although the safe frame can challenge the nice guy, too.

His experience of these types of frames seems to call into question his morality and nobility. As for the former alpha, he, too, struggles with the amorality of frame. His reluctance lies in his efforts to avoid returning to a former version of himself that he views as self-seeking. Frame, by nature, is amoral. It is a tool. He must make good use of his frame, seeking to do good in the world, even if there are times when it is necessary to do so at the expense of someone else and even if it is only for himself, as long as it is not harmful to others.

Successful Implementation

The successful implementation of frame hinges on the ease with which you can abstract the necessary implementable actions from the broader, vaguer outcomes you set for yourself. In other words, your ability to appropriately choose your actions within a given situation or interaction based on your goal determines the efficacy of your frame. The better your ability to pull a detailed and precise idea from the obscure composition of your desired outcomes through the chaotic, unpredictable, and equifinal pathways, the more successful you will be with your outcomes.

To understand this notion, it is helpful to consider how a GPS map works. When you input a starting point and a destination, you are provided with a general overview. This general overview gives you a vague idea of where you are going and which direction you are heading. This is a low-resolution map at this point because, when looking at the general picture, the details would overload us with too much information, making it impossible to navigate the map with ease. Once we activate the turn-by-turn mode, the GPS map brings us to a higher resolution of the directions. When we are near the next turn, the map brings us in close to show us the precise action we must take. However, when we are several miles from our next turn, the GPS view will zoom out to a more moderate resolution until we are near the next turn or our exact destination.

As we formulate an outcome for ourselves, we have a vague idea of what it is. As we bring our goals into focus, we begin to see the many choices we must make regarding our actions. We must follow the path of our actions all the way up to the goal we have set before us. Our goals serve as the North Star, to point us toward true north, so to speak. As we take actionable steps, moment to moment, we look up to see if we are headed in the right direction. If we fail to look up, we are likely to get lost. If we only look up, we are likely to stumble.

Wrongful Implementation

Allowing your circumstances to determine your conscious experience is irresponsible and detrimental to your emotional experiences. All too often, today's man blindly submits to external forces, real or imagined. This willful naivety sacrifices the most precious freedom, which Viktor Frankl states in *Man's Search for Meaning*, "Everything can be taken from a man but one thing: the last of the human freedoms—to choose one's attitude in any given set of circumstances, to choose one's own way."[77] You can most likely recall experiences in which you surrendered your dignity when you encountered too much resistance from your partner. It is not a pleasant experience to be dominated so easily.

The failure to implement a strong, healthy frame is usually due to a lack of assertiveness. Assertiveness is the primary skill regarding frame, and neglecting to utilize assertiveness causes today's man to be inconsistent with the other positive aspects of himself. His boundaries lack integrity if they are sometimes enforced and sometimes not. Such erraticism makes him unreliable. The masculine order necessary for bringing stability and reliability is what the feminine needs to express herself fully. Even when the feminine dragon of chaos brings her destructive forces upon him, she does so with the intent of bringing forth his truest, deepest Self. Her unconscious feminine nature knows that if she is to be made whole, she must destroy the version of him that encases a more magnificent version of him. Failing to respond to her challenges with a strong, healthy frame further suppresses the hero within, leaving the feminine dragon of chaos in the unknown world—detested by the immature masculinity of today's man. He detests what he does not understand, and what he detests he wishes to eradicate. This ideological motivation is dangerous for the relationship, for even though he has yet to recognize it, there is truth to be found in chaos. If he rids his world of the chaos, he rids himself of a truth that will set him free. He will unwittingly imprison himself in his own orderliness and madness.

Corrective Actions

Truth is often found through error and shortcomings—mistakes are the foundation of truth. Success comes in the form of extracting truth from chaos. Man, masculine in nature—orderly and conscious—will inevitably commit errors when engaging with his partner's chaotic feminine nature. However, it is in his redemption that a hero emerges from within. Having descended to the depths of Hell, the integrated man knows what he is capable of, which empowers him with knowledge of what lies beyond the edge of what lesser men cannot see. It takes a certain combination of qualities to get something right the first time. Yet, when we make a mistake, we not only have to exhibit the qualities it would have taken to get it right the first time, but we must also exhibit the qualities it takes to overcome our mistake. These are redemptive qualities. Objectively, we can see that the degree of qualities exhibited in overcoming mistakes is greater than getting it right the first time. When overcoming our mistakes happens openly to those around us—particularly those impacted by them—they witness a greater display of qualities in us. When people experience our qualities, they tend to benefit from them.

It is inspiring to watch someone do what it takes to overcome their mistakes. This is why people love a good comeback story; it is the redemptive narrative, triumph over failure. People often prefer this story over a love story in which everything goes well. Therefore, we inherently know that mistakes can serve as an opportunity to provide ourselves—and those around us—with an adventurous story. Others should know that you are capable of making mistakes *and* correcting them rather than believing that you do not make mistakes.

Correcting the mistake of losing frame control requires a reevaluation of your assertiveness. Regarding frame control, your mistake is due to a failure to respond to chaos with the necessary order it calls for; that is, you responded poorly, which spurred more destructive chaos. The more you respond poorly to such chaos, the more destructive things will become. Reestablishing order by tending to boundaries and diffusing conflict is critical when correcting the actions within your frame that led to the current regression in your relationship. Additionally, it is worthwhile to consider the character you must exhibit within a given situation in which you have committed mistakes. Reactivating the pillars of assertiveness and character illuminates the way out of the darkness of the destructive feminine chaos, but not without teasing you with a glimpse of the gift that can only be found in darkness. At this point in the journey, you cannot yet resist leaving that dark place and the gift it holds, but you also cannot un-see it. The knowledge of the existence of this gift, and the curiosity of its contents, will not let go of you. Yet, your drive for predictability pulls you back to the surface. And although you find yourself back on stable ground, you know you must one day revisit the dungeon and retrieve your gift.

Keys to Improvement

When attempting to reach your desired outcomes, you will be met with objections and distractions. Practicing the skills for dealing with such will enable you to stay on track. Assuming responsibility for everything in your life will begin to optimize your environment to make achieving goals more attainable. Being mindful of another person's frame is paramount when you begin to experience frustration with them and will broaden your perspective on the situation, allowing you to be several moves ahead of them. Additionally, settling into your humanity by acknowledging the aspects of both involuntary and voluntary responses—and the sensitivity of the area in which you have the freedom to choose them—optimizes yourself for success in your relationship, regardless of the environment.

Elevating yourself in the hierarchy of your life is about positioning yourself for more victories. This means leaning into the chaotic, unknown world with more curiosity and courage. Doing so brings you to a more complete truth, albeit a frightening truth. It is a truth that weeds out those incapable of honoring it and fulfilling the role of the revolutionary hero. The feminine dragon of chaos that resides in your partner cannot be set free by cowards or the irresponsible. The one who sets her free will be the one who has withstood the destructive force of her feminine challenge and is prepared to descend into the dungeon to slay the destructive dragon of feminine chaos, allowing the emergence of the beautiful and creative feminine that resides deep within the belly of the beast.

Slaying the Dragon

Rodion is gaining a command of his shield of assertiveness as well as the quick insight that his character provides, helping him predict what moves the feminine dragon of chaos will make. As he improves his frame and increases control of it, he learns to be steadfast in the dragon's chaotic onslaught. His frame gives him the ability to detect when her moves are decoys and misdirection and when they are openings to her heart, the ancient feminine deep within. A new determination has arisen in Rodion to forge his way into the belly of the beast. His aim is true, and his heart is virtuous. He is committed to retrieving the ancient feminine from this chaotic and destructive beast. His developing consistency keeps him upright as the dragon of chaos mounts her attacks.

His aim is true. But can he rise to the occasion? Can he be trusted by the ancient feminine as he moves into the heart of the dragon? His feet are sure yet swift. His insight is keen to her next move. However, Rodion must gain Regina's trust before she will receive him fully.

Rodion's confidence must be tested; it must be built. And true confidence is built in chaos. Rodion's task is great, for if he is to bring forth the great and creative feminine within Regina, he must achieve victory over the terrible and destructive dragon of chaos. Rodion has developed assertiveness skills, built character, and established a robust frame. While this is proving to be effective against the dragon, the ancient feminine is equally skeptical as she is hopeful.

Rodion will be tested like never before. Only this time, it will not appear as it has before. The dragon of chaos will no longer conceal her motives and her weapons. She will invite him closer, even letting her guard down. As Rodion thinks he has her, she will strike with a force so cunning that it will seem like she has masterminded his downfall from within him. This will shake him to the core, and Rodion will face his greatest Hell: his own Shadow. His fate—the relationship's fate—rests on the direction of Rodion's confidence.

Chapter Nine

Confidence

Confidence is a feeling of self-assurance of one's own abilities or qualities. To become assured of our abilities and qualities, we must practice behaviors indicative of the abilities we want to possess and the qualities we wish to exhibit. If we want to be good at something, we must practice that thing. For instance, if we desire to be a good basketball player, we practice doing what it takes to be a good basketball player, such as the fundamentals of handling the ball, passing, shooting, rebounding, etc. We begin learning these fundamentals awkwardly and clumsily. We would have played against other, more experienced players whose abilities were far better than ours. In these times, we often faced frustration. That frustration resulted from having reached the limits of our abilities and knowledge of the game. This, in turn, made us better players. Once we became proficient, we could look back with laughter at how silly we looked in the beginning—but only because we are now assured of ourselves. Frustration and awkwardness are ineradicable parts of the process of building confidence.

Today's man who falls short of his potential to take his relationship to the next level is a man whose confidence is either restrained or altogether lacking. He either has confidence yet fails to practice character, or he has good character yet lacks confidence. The former is rigid with his character, grounded in fear of losing his place in the hierarchy. This inflexibility indicates inauthentic confidence, which means he has deep insecurities concealed beneath his persona. The latter places too much emphasis on character and nobility, covertly hoping it will carry him to success. In truth, he is a few hierarchical defeats from landing himself at the bottom of the hierarchy. This notion is often quite difficult for today's man to acknowledge, let alone explore.

Realizing their less-than-stellar attributes is a hard pill to swallow for many men. Both versions of today's man must take a searching and courageous inventory of their resistance to the dark and shadowy aspects of themselves. Rather than continuing to project his insecurities and homeostatic tendencies onto his partner—disguised as nobility, indifference, or overconfidence—today's man must ask himself what gift awaits him in those places he least wants to look. Searching in difficult areas of our lives yields useful and essential lessons that propel us upward in life. However, humans have the disposition to choose the easier, softer way, experiencing fewer rewards than had they opted for more strenuous pathways that take them higher. This is understandable, for we have many reasons to abdicate responsibility for difficult things when they come with so much suffering. For today's man, the proclivity to seek the path of least resistance is about making as few mistakes as possible to avoid embarrassment, shame, and most notably, the conscientious effort that otherwise pushes his capacity to master himself.

Hierarchies • Mastery • Chaos

The awkwardness and clumsiness of learning new skills are unavoidable aspects of mastery. We achieve mastery by learning all the subtleties of our craft, all the subject matter's particulars. It is about knowing what to do as well as what not to do. In long-term relationships, we learn what not to do by making mistakes and failing along the way. It could be said that we learn by making mistakes, although many have little to no harmful consequences. The hard-won experience of learning from our relationship mistakes equips us with the wisdom to differentiate between our capacity to bring order to a balanced state or shift the relationship from one extreme to another. That is, with mastery, we can identify when we are steering our lives and those within them toward harmony or destruction.

Mastery takes time and commitment, allowing us to gradually become more proficient with our relationship skills. When this occurs, the world seems to slow down for us. We begin to see things as they unfold. Sometimes we can predict how and when things will unfold. We become assured in our abilities and our knowledge. As we learn to predict pitfalls and manage the unpredictable, we spend less time with our heads on a swivel and more time enjoying a more remarkable life. However, it is useful to understand the function and reasons why confidence is vital. It is helpful to understand what the opposite of confidence is.

Confidence is the opposite of distrust, skepticism, doubt, and uncertainty. From a personality perspective, these antonyms describe the trait neuroticism, particularly the aspect of withdrawal, which has to do with anticipatory anxiety. Generally speaking, neuroticism is the sensitivity and reactivity to pain and discomfort or the potential for it. It is the experience of negative emotions. From this viewpoint, negative emotions serve as an indication that we are experiencing pain and discomfort or that the experience of pain and discomfort is potentially imminent. While unpleasant, neuroticism, at the root of human processing, alerts us to situations that are derailing or could derail us from the outcomes we desire. In other words, they help us escape danger or avoid pitfalls altogether. The more we experience negative emotions, the more precarious our lives are. Therefore, negative emotional experiences help us infer our position in life and the direction we are heading. This experience is perhaps best explained in the context of hierarchies.

Hierarchies

In the hierarchy of our lives, we find one of the more basic human experiences of aspiring to better life outcomes. From a personality perspective, hierarchies can be understood from the context of extraversion (enthusiasm and assertiveness), which is associated with positive emotional experiences, and neuroticism (withdrawal and volatility), which is associated with negative emotional experiences. Some life outcomes are rooted in basic human needs. How we achieve those outcomes is based on our individual and collective interests and preferences. Hierarchies emerge from the desire and drive for better life outcomes—and the interests that drive them—because we need reference points to know if we are progressing toward those outcomes. And what better reference points than other people striving for life outcomes similar in nature to yours? To desire better life outcomes is to desire higher degrees of positive emotional experiences, which requires you to take action and move toward that goal. This is enthusiasm and assertiveness—extraversion.

If you want to do something enjoyable—let's say play the harmonica—you must decide what experience you need to have so that you may enjoy playing the harmonica. By nature, this indicates that you want to succeed in your quest to play the harmonica at an enjoyable level. Yet, you need reference points to know what constitutes an enjoyable experience of playing the harmonica. If you've never heard one, how can you possibly know what it is to be good at it? Therefore, you look to others who also play the harmonica. More precisely, you look at the broader scope of the collective population of harmonica players from those who are considered masterful to those who are considered terrible harmonica players. The harmonica players who sound painfully awful would be at the low end, and those who can draw you in would be at the very top. Since you want to achieve an enjoyable experience of successful harmonica playing, you have to know how good you are. This puts you in a hierarchy of harmonica players who provide you with a spectrum of reference points to indicate where you are positioned in the hierarchy. You probably want to be better than the worst player, so you practice until you are at least better than that person. This is a hierarchical victory that progresses you closer to the place in the hierarchy you wish to be.

It is hierarchies—and your position in them—that determine whether you have positive emotional experiences or negative emotional experiences. Regarding some desired life outcomes, the bottom of the hierarchy can be quite precarious. One wrong move could be the death of you or, to a less severe degree, the end of a goal. If you are at or near the bottom of the hierarchy, the proper experience of that should be that of negative emotions. You should not feel elated and accomplished down there, for it is the furthest away from the desired life outcomes you have for yourself. Feeling good there would be inappropriate and absurd. You might even face the threat of being hospitalized because you are delusional. The pain and discomfort of being as far away as possible from the life you want for yourself, the bottom of the hierarchy, should be evident to you. Therefore, pain and discomfort are intended to motivate you out of this rather precarious circumstance and further up the hierarchy toward a more harmonic and balanced outcome—no pun intended.

As you experience more hierarchical victories, you become more assured in your abilities, affording you a greater degree of mastery in navigating hierarchies and achieving success. The increasing confidence equips you with more skills—and the mastery of them—to better manage the distractions and objections to your goals. In relationships, attraction is based on, by and large, your capacity to be reliable, trustworthy, competent, industrious, and valuable.

The more confident you are, the more attractive you are. If you spend too much time at the bottom of the hierarchy or consistently struggle to elevate yourself from the bottom, your attractiveness as a partner is severely diminished. This notion suggests that confidence is not only important for success in your own individual desired outcomes but is paramount for success in the agreed-upon outcomes shared by you and your partner based on your respective desires.

Mastering your responses to negative emotional experiences while approaching them with the frame of mind that seeks to receive the gifts they bring allows you to grow in your ability to manage chaos. By positioning yourself to experience an optimal degree of emotional experiences, you will find that you have elevated yourself to a superior version of the one that once held you back. It is a version of you that opens you up to see more promise than threat in the anomalies you encounter with your partner's feminine nature. It is a version that begins to learn the ancient feminine language, which, until now, has appeared as a superficial, unnecessary aspect of chaos—making her seem ungrateful, angry, or closed off—or, rather, the juvenile idea of what you expected a partner to be.

An ancient, more truthful language begins to speak through today's woman as you achieve confidence through hierarchical victories in your relationship. It speaks through her voice, actions, silence, and chaos. We begin to hear the words of the feminine nature once deeply suppressed beneath the rather generic aspects of women—traits that, over many centuries, were made socially desirable by men who were too concerned with orderliness and unwilling to give the effort to achieve balance with the feminine chaos.

These now-prominent generic aspects of women were much easier to bring to order than the more full and true feminine aspects once embraced by the integrated men of old. To learn the ancient feminine language in your quest to conquer the dragon of chaos within your partner, you must prepare yourself for battle. Your preparation requires you to master the four pillars, particularly confidence. In this context, confidence is the awakening of the true masculine within as a result of having mastered the pillars of assertiveness, character, and frame. Even then, awakening the true masculine is predicated on mastering your abilities to achieve life outcomes through hierarchical victories and the acknowledgment of them. This starts with adequately grasping the fundamentals of victories, what they do, and how to achieve them.

Mastery

To strive toward living a remarkable life, we need to position ourselves for success. To do this, there are two factors we must keep in mind: positioning ourselves for victories by capitalizing on opportunities and acknowledging the victories and rewarding ourselves for our achievements—be they big or small—while making the association between the reward and the victory. Positioning ourselves for victories means we learn to recognize opportunities to elevate ourselves to a more magnificent version. We must stop avoiding conflict and begin engaging with it in assertively, transforming it into an opportunity that allow us to showcase our most magnificent selves. It is through this that we set a more steadfast course toward our desired outcomes.

The conflict we face in relationships, particularly the conflict you are facing now, can be intimidating—perhaps even daunting. It is best to take a gradual approach initially, especially if the discord in your relationship is disruptive. The utilization of the first three pillars to achieve hierarchical victories is without parallel. The implications of our success in relationships are beyond measure. The benefits others gain through the increased value we inspire them to bring increases value in return. Consequently, the relationships in our lives become less turbulent, and we can engage with people with more and more confidence.

Victories are not just about alleviating undesirable experiences in life; they are also about producing positive emotional experiences. It is one thing to rise out of the bottom of the hierarchy; it is another thing to reach the top. If we seek to alleviate our negative emotional experiences, we will be the very ones who holds ourselves back from reaching the top. Understanding this will help us achieve victories, which helps shift our eyes toward goals and dreams that allow us to appreciate the present, rather than live our lives looking back over our shoulders.

As we achieve more victories, we realize our capacity to see beyond the pain and discomfort of negative emotional experiences. We open ourselves up to positive emotional experiences, and our interactions with others become more meaningful. This, in part, is because our head is not on a swivel, as it was when we were at the precarious and dangerous bottom. This allows us to accomplish what is important to us and to achieve a more enriched sense of self.

A renewed sense of self can spark a more defined sense of direction, which plays a pivotal role in reaching our goals. Of course, none of this will happen until we take action. When our actions result in desired outcomes, they inspire us to do more. With wholehearted and deliberate attention, we gain a deeper sense of purpose as we do more. That is why it is important to practice confidence.

All the victories in the world won't help us very much if we don't acknowledge them. The best way to encourage behaviors is through positive reinforcement. The brain operates on a reward system. If we do a good job, our brain rewards us with serotonin, a naturally occurring "feel-good" chemical. Serotonin is correlated with confidence. The more well-regulated our serotonin, the more confident we feel. This works by the brain's reward system receiving a message saying that we've done something good or positive. Once the brain's reward system gets the message, it releases serotonin to the body, and we feel outstanding. Our brain's associative machine correlates the good feeling with the good and positive things we did. We like this feeling, and it inspires us to repeat those behaviors. The feeling itself provides a sense of assurance in ourselves. This is confidence. These repeated behaviors result in an improved skill set. This is increased confidence.

Chaos

Recognizing, acknowledging, praising, and celebrating desirable behaviors shapes the direction people are going. Practicing confidence means behaving in ways that are indicative of being the person you want to be or the experience you want to have. Narratives about an individual's path, including subjective experiences of the past and simulations of the future, play a prominent role in developing a secure sense of self.[78] We have an image of the person we see ourselves becoming, and our actions are what get us there. The image is the goal we have for ourselves; our actions are the means to get there. Reinforcing the actions that get us to where we want to go is paramount. Yet, to get somewhere we have never been, we must first go through the unknown world of uncertainty. This is one of the simplest forms of basic human experience. Peering into this most basic experience of navigating the unknown world that lies between the current, known world and the desired place—or outcome—reveals to us an ancient and deeply rooted human process that is universal to all of us.

The orienting reflex—the involuntary gravitational pull toward novelty—lays the groundwork for the emergence of (voluntarily controlled) exploratory behavior.[79] The unknown world is unknown because of the anomalies it presents to us that can only exist in unexplored territory, whether the anomaly is novel in nature or simply within a novel context. That is, exploration of the unknown world presents us with completely new objects and events, or it presents previously known objects and events in new contexts that hold motivational significance never before associated with the object or experience. This is essentially the basic human ability of classification, enabling us to determine whether the encountered anomaly is dangerous (and should be avoided) or a resource (and should be utilized). Of course, it is easy to make these distinctions in hindsight. An explorer can never know what he is exploring until it has been explored.[80]

The experience of encountering anomalies in the unknown world is one that will continue, be it multiple times within a single domain of unexplored territory or a single occurrence in multiple domains of unexplored territory. The successful classification of each anomaly we encounter is stored in the brain. That is, the anomaly either caused us harm, yet we did not die, and it ultimately progressed us further toward our goal, or we correctly evaluated the anomaly at the onset and progressed toward our goal.

The stored information from the prior encounters is recalled as we encounter more anomalies. This recall consists of factoring in all of the occurrences surrounding the previous encounters, whether they were intentionally manifested by us or occurred outside of us, simultaneously. That is, we amalgamate all the things we did that orchestrated the successful navigation of the anomaly and the external environment. We do this to enable ourselves to predict more accurately what to do the next time we encounter similar circumstances to be successful. Essentially, when we try to repeat those things to navigate unanticipated events more precisely, we will encounter in the next attempt to achieve a goal.

The recall of prior navigations forms an identification process—we encountered a new situation, this is what took place, this was the outcome—and these stories are replayed in our unconscious as we navigate new territory. The replaying of these stories requires identifying the behaviors and occurrences associated with our experiences as an efficient way of understanding what we are encountering and what we should do with it. From this identification process, language emerges.

Language is a way to understand the world and others within it, as well as a way for others to understand us and, perhaps, most importantly, a way for us to understand ourselves. Peterson states in *Maps of Meaning*, "Even development of spoken language, the ultimate analytic motor skill, might reasonably be considered an abstract extension of the human ability to take things apart and reassemble them, in an original manner."[81] Language is composed of words, which, as they are strung together in a sequence (as a way to understand our experiences of the unknown territory), form narratives.

Narratives capture the nature of experience. They help us make sense of our experience with anomalies, particularly the occurrences within those experiences we cannot consciously comprehend yet experience nonetheless. From those narratives, stories emerge as a method of conveying the conscious and unconscious representation of ourselves within the context of our environment, especially within unknown territory. This representation, once conveyed, provides an image of ourselves designed to guide us toward successful outcomes. The image we have of ourselves is determined by our experiences and the language we use with ourselves within the context of those experiences. This ancient human process is an ineradicable aspect of hierarchical ascension. That is, the image we create for ourselves is directly correlated with, if not causal to, successful life outcomes. In other words, our behaviors gravitate toward the image we have of ourselves.

Acknowledging our victories with precise language is key to hierarchical success. Such success is only attained by navigating the unexplored territory between you and your goals and desires. As we determine our goals and desired outcomes for ourselves, we must place an appropriate amount of care and attention on the language we use, which creates our self-image. For example, when declaring for themselves who they want to be regarding particular goals, many people will often say, "I want to be someone who does not buckle under pressure." While this is a remarkable goal, the language can backfire. The human information process that has to do with language, image, behaviors, and outcomes is simple and basic. It sees the parts of language that can only produce an image. The words in the phrase "does not" cannot, by nature, produce an image. The words "someone, buckles, under, and pressure" likely produce the image of someone who buckles under pressure. If this is the image we have of ourselves, then it is probable that our behaviors will produce the experience of someone who buckles under pressure. Therefore, using more precise language, such as "I want to be someone who performs exceptionally well under pressure," tends to create an image of who you want to be. This would be the positive opposite of the previous goal, which was worded with negative imagery.

Lastly, the following perspective on the pillar of confidence is vital to establishing a sound and well-rounded comprehension of its significance. Confidence is built through chaos. Such comprehension of confidence is best attained by exploring the role of chaos in building and increasing confidence. Moreover, understanding the implications of either avoiding chaos or engaging with it reveals to us the impact of our character and actions within the context of a given environment. Within the context of a long-term relationship, anomalies are unexpected clashes of the fundamental (usually moral) differences between each person within the relationship. These unexpected clashes are barriers to harmony within the relationship. It is within the clash—the chaos—that the very antidote to the chaos lies. Conflict itself contains the resolution to discord and holds the way to magnificence as a man. The resolution to discord seeks harmonious outcomes when faced with chaos in relationships by putting care and attention into the other person's experience while strongly considering the value of that experience. The way to magnificence as a man is through the act of rising to the occasion, which demands the best from him, allowing him to bring into consciousness important aspects of himself as a man.

For relationship conflict to successfully extract the best from you, you must courageously engage with the chaos of it, which consists of exchanging distressful information and willfully subjecting yourself to the negative emotions of the conflict. This experience often brings to light faults and inadequacies that have only recently became known to you.

For some men, the notion of building confidence through chaos is relatable on a more superficial level, such as being open-minded and willing to modify their behaviors when there is little exploration of themselves required. However, the deeper, more difficult aspects of ourselves hold the truth of what fundamentally needs to be changed. Part of the difficulty with such aspects is that we are unconscious of them. Another reason for its difficulty is the willful denial that there are other things about us that we need to know.

Unconscious Avoidance of Feminine Chaos

All too often, the lack of awareness and denial of these deeper aspects of ourselves, which often hold the very truth we need to become more magnificent versions of ourselves, culminates in self-deceit, whether implicit or explicit. The self-deceiving that occurs regarding these deep and vital aspects of ourselves is directly correlated with the degree to which we deem them too chaotic and painful to explore. That is, some things require efforts too great for our current capacity to explore courageously. It is the set of beliefs we hold about life and ourselves within the context of our relationship (and the conflict within it) that leads to such deceit, whose narratives tell us that the knowledge we currently hold about the issue is all that is necessary to know. This type of thinking produces a false dichotomy that suggests, "either I am wrong, or you are wrong." This only exacerbates the conflict within the relationship and tends to produce ideological identification, which seeks to eliminate the other's presumptions and propositions that deny necessary truths, which reveal exactly what is needed to elevate yourself.

Both destructive and creative, the feminine chaos is a deeply misunderstood force in life. Perhaps, due to its severely difficult, symbolic, and abstract nature, it is all too easy to deceive ourselves into thinking there are no gifts of truth that lie within the feminine chaos—and its role in the integration of a man. Or, in some cases, even though we may be willing to mine the most difficult unexplored territory for its truth courageously, the deeply abstract and obscure nature of the feminine chaos may make it all too difficult to detect the truth that lies within it, making us unaware of the possibility that such a valuable unknown place exists. Yet, what brings us to such an awareness? What has to happen for us to consider the possibility of the unknown and to declare for ourselves that we must look into such a precarious unknown and the potential significance it holds?

To even begin such a treacherous journey, there must be a fundamental belief in the value of exploring the unknown. For most men, this belief either takes form through a slow, cumulative process of their collective experiences, or it emerges from a jarring experience that jolts them into an awareness of a need for such value. As a result, we are not easily enlightened to the most important explorations necessary for becoming the best versions of ourselves. It is as if great struggle is a prerequisite for exploring the deeper aspects of life, and ourselves, for truth, rather than its consequence. The exposure to such unexplored territory, particularly in areas where we only recently believed there was nothing more to discover, generates an experience of skepticism and curiosity.

The phenomenon of becoming aware of something activates the exploratory process of evaluating threat or promise that the newly discovered, unexplored territory holds. Imagine embarking on a journey through the unknown, as you've done numerous times, only to find that this particular unknown world contains a force stranger and more disruptive than anything you have ever encountered.

Encountering the strangest thing you have ever experienced is not only likely to produce fear, but may produce a fear so great that you involuntarily begin to rationalize its occurrence as something more manageable to deal with. You might even manufacture a false reality for yourself in an effort to keep from slipping into a deep neurosis. Even if the false reality is terrible, it is easier than the actual reality that is most difficult. That is, we dissociate from a reality too terrible to bear as a way of keeping our cognitions intact.

Today's man experiences this in his relationship with his feminine partner. The feminine nature can be great and terrible, creative, and destructive. So much so that today's man wants to make her small, although he is unaware that he is doing so. This is not the result of immorality or maliciousness. Rather, it is a basic, involuntary fear response so primal that he does not consciously perceive it as fear. Rather, he places a meaning more easily comprehensible, even if it means placing responsibility on the other person. By the time this experience becomes conscious, he will create an easier yet false reality, seeing his actions as an act of prevention and averting disaster. However, this inadvertently suppresses the feminine nature, causing it to build pressure as it seeks only to express itself.

Responding with confidence to his feminine partner's desires, whether those desires are expressed subtly or violently, creates an environment conducive to harmony and balance. Sometimes it is rather easy to respond to the feminine. Other times it is most difficult and highly chaotic. In these moments of chaos, true confidence is built, and today's man can transform into a more integrated man, one who walks the razor's edge between order and chaos, between masculine and feminine, and apprehends a truth unknown to most.

Successful Implementation

Practicing confidence is just that: practicing. We have probably all heard the saying, "fake it 'til you make it." While there is some debate about the usefulness of this cliché, it is worthwhile to look deeper into its meaning. Perhaps it really means that to become assured in your abilities in something, you must act in ways indicative of the very thing you wish to be good at.

For example, when children want to learn how to tie their shoes, they mimic what they think adults do when they tie theirs. In their mind, they see someone twisting and looping two strings together, and a little bow emerges. Twisting and looping equals tied shoelaces. They don't know about the techniques of manipulating the two strings through various loops, pass-throughs, and twists, all in a particular order. They uncoordinatedly attempt to put the two strings together in a manner that seems like the strings do the work for them. They become frustrated as the two strings fall apart from their original position. Or they might manage to tangle up the two strings in a loosely bound knot. Yet, through practice, the acts indicative of tying shoes help master the task they will eventually take for granted.

Conceptually, this process is the same throughout life. We have a greater goal in mind of mastering something. We then come to realize other things we need to learn to master the greater goal. As we take on these individual tasks of learning to do the things that allow us to achieve our greater goal, we realize there are even more things to learn. This is life. There is so much to learn, so many abilities to master. Therefore, we must act in ways indicative of the mastery we wish to achieve. This requires conscientiousness and creativity.

Confidence is built through chaos. For today's man to arrive at a more integrated version of himself, he must bear the greatest responsibility he can, which can only be done when he gives chaos a chance.

Wrongful Implementation

Rather than seeking to create a life where only order exists, today's man must permit himself to be human and not know how he will arrive at a more complete self. If he does not, he blinds himself to the path that will take him to a more complete self. This willful neglect of chaos causes him to deviate from his path of purpose and meaning. In turn, he will struggle to be confident. He will feign a confidence that will crumble. We can see this occur as overconfidence in people. That is, people who psyche themselves out appear to be channeling true confidence when they are trying to convince themselves of what they are capable of doing, which reveals that they are not yet assured in their abilities.

Psyching ourselves out is a pitfall that many of us fall into. Psyching ourselves out is undermining our own confidence. Although using positive language with ourselves is conducive to changing our lives, we must be mindful of taking things to the extreme. Psyching ourselves out is a pitfall in the sense that we will overestimate our current skill set. When we do this, we fail to recognize important cues that solidify the process of building true confidence.

We cannot speed up the process of mastery, but we can slow it down. Hyping ourselves up without owning our inadequacies can impede the very lessons we need to become confident. Confidence occurs when particular behaviors take place in a particular method. Interfering with this process creates an unreliable foothold as we strive to accomplish our goals and build relationships.

Understanding the difference between confidence and arrogance is vital. On the surface, the two may have some similarities. A person's insecurities will reveal themselves through the veil of arrogance. Yet, genuine confidence will shine through. Never suppress your insecurities. Instead, be open with them through deliberate vulnerability. Typically, it's not the insecurities that we are judged by; rather, we are judged by how well we handle them.

Corrective Actions

As we master life, we often miss the mark. A major part of mastery has to do with how well we learn to adjust to missing the mark—to better our aim. Correcting our mistakes defines our character to a great extent. Make it a habit of asking yourself particular questions that guide you to a more consistent path to confidence. Learn to recognize when you are missing the mark by asking yourself if you are over-hyping yourself or coming across as arrogant. Notice if people are having difficulty warming up to you or struggling to be receptive to you. People do not gravitate toward those whose confidence is feigned or those who seem to spend too much time convincing themselves of their abilities in things.

Seek to be more trustworthy if you've found yourself stumbling into these pitfalls. People love those who are trustworthy. But people also love a good comeback story, so we should strive to correct ourselves. Subjecting yourself to chaos will allow you to master the process of creating order from it.

Keys to Improvement

When we've reached the limits of our abilities and experience, we rely on our conscientiousness and determination. Our ability to do something is determined by our current physical ability and our current knowledge base. We can only perform as well as our physical peak and the information we have. Beyond that is what we have the capacity to do. Once we've reached the limits of our known abilities, we must tap into our capacity, through which growth and expansion occur. This process can be grueling and testing. Here, it is best to muster up all the determination possible to stay on track, and sometimes it is the sheer heroic effort that gets us through to the other side of this process.

Building confidence occurs through this process. Practicing faith in this process positions you to capitalize on opportunities to display genuine confidence and recognize the victories you have achieved. Take solace in your efforts throughout your struggles. Wear it like a badge of honor. There can be great satisfaction in mastering various aspects of our human nature, despite the naysaying messages that often repeat themselves inside our heads. Notice how your experiences shift from surviving situations in which you once found difficult to thrive to flourishing because of them. Praise yourself for the hard work you've put in. Encourage yourself to continue excelling. On days you struggle to feel inspired, return to the most basic notion of change: taking action.

Slaying the Dragon

Rodion's growing confidence has brought him numerous small victories, making him more trustworthy in the eyes of the ancient feminine within Regina. She begins to reveal herself more and more to Rodion, and with each new glimpse into her heart, he confidently steps forward. Though her smiles and laughter are genuine, the dragon of chaos has not lost any skepticism. Too fast, and Rodion's steps toward her will alarm her to retreat back into her fighting stance. Too slow, and his hesitant footsteps will signal impatience in her, and she will lunge forward at him. If he deviates from the path toward her heart, she will unleash a fury fueled not only by her weapons but by his own weapons, which she will have taken to use against him. The direction of Rodion's confidence will determine whether his acquired skills will land him the heart of the feminine or if they will crumble in his hands, leaving him exposed to her fury.

Rodion's confidence is beginning to put to rest much of the outward skepticism the dragon of chaos holds of him. But, at the same time, she readies herself for unleashing her deadliest test. This is where things get interesting. The shield of assertiveness has protected Rodion from the dragon's fiery blaze, incinerating that which is not true, that which is the false and shadowy side of his masculinity. He must learn when to use the shield to protect not just himself but Regina from her own flames, or both he and the ancient, sacred feminine within the dragon will fall. If his confidence is lacking, he will risk mistiming the proper use of his shield by either letting it down too soon—and risk getting engulfed in flames—or hiding behind it too long and preventing himself from seeing the entrance to the heart of the dragon. His timing must be impeccable!

Rodion's character will also live and die by his assurance in himself. The direction of his confidence must be steered by his purpose, to give his gifts from the depths of his being. Here, too, is a delicate balancing act of precision. He must strive to give his all and to do so with the aim of giving the necessary attention to its reception, giving with the hopes of giving his all rather than to have it received. The feminine dragon of chaos will know in her depths if he is driven by his vanity in his attempts to reach her. If she detects this, he will experience the ancient feminine deep within the dragon of chaos pull away from him, and he should expect her flames following her withdrawal, particularly if he continues to press forward without adjusting his character. Yet, if his character is good and true, the dragon will see his commitment to his purpose rather than his potential for meaninglessness.

The dragon of chaos is also reliant upon precise timing. She must know if and when to strike based upon her assessment of his character. If she deems his character untrue too soon, she misses out on his gifts. If she too soon declares his character as good and true, she risks Rodion resting on his unexpected early success, and she will miss out on getting his deepest purpose. If she waits too long to make that assessment, his gifts will deteriorate, and they will be caught in a downward spiral. If his character is not true, and she waits too long, his recklessness will lead to destruction. Here, they both must be skeptical and vulnerable. Rodion must know his true self enough to pass through the Sphinx Gate[82] that only permits he who is true to his courage and purpose.

Rodion's frame has become robust in his quest to become a more magnificent version of himself. He has learned to stand solidly when Regina aggressively tests his character and as she subtly and covertly requests comfort from him. But as he becomes better at responding to her tests, she gets better at testing him. He is stable, committed, and reliable.

His frame has proven that he can be consistent. But the ancient feminine needs to know if he can be flexible enough in his frame to adjust when necessary; he must prove that he can be trusted. He has gained some command over the first three pillars: assertiveness, character, and frame. The feminine dragon of chaos goes into stealth mode, cloaking herself in a shroud of mystery in the sense that Rodion can no longer easily tell if he is moving in the right direction. His shield of assertiveness does not carry enough strength alone to bring him into the dragon's heart. His character has gotten him close, but it is not enough to be invited to come closer. His frame has withstood the volatile storms in her tests of him, proving he is solid as an oak. Yet, the truest confidence is built in the truest chaos. Here, Rodion has no reference points for the direction he must go and the moves he must make. His shield throws him off balance, his helmet blurs his vision, and his heavy armor slows him down. He is exposed and vulnerable and consumed by the murky darkness of his own Shadow.

The thing he needs most is near. It is in this darkest moment that Rodion needs one thing more than anything else. He needs light, for the light shows the Way, the Truth. He settles into his Self and remembers his purpose, which is to conquer, bring order from chaos, and make known the unknown. He finds courage, and it propels him forward. It is as though he senses more than comprehends, intuits more than predicts, and feels more than observes. He has entered into the feminine world and is integrating her nuance into his Self. For the first time, so it seems, Rodion sees the ancient feminine within the dragon of chaos. He understands her now, at least to a degree. Yet, it is enough to elicit the deepest hope within her: to be cut from this belly of this destructive beast so that she may live in purposeful creative expression. His aim is true. He cuts her from the belly of the beast, and she is rescued. Rodion and Regina have been saved by his heroic efforts. But Rodion must elevate the earlier version of not only himself but Regina as well, bringing the ancient feminine within her to a mature feminine. He must transcend himself, for this quest has brought him to the starting point of something greater.

Part 3

Transcendence

Chapter Ten

The Achievement of Compatibility

Today's man must conquer many obstacles if he is to realize his potential and fulfill his purpose. His purpose is contained deep within his unconscious self, and the discovery of it is a wonderful and grueling process. The masculine is consciousness, and for today's man to reach his purpose, he must enter the cave of his unconscious in which it exists, which also contains dark and dangerous encounters with terrible things. However, he must first find the cave. He then has to navigate its numerous passages, which are obscure and confusing. It is easy to get lost in the passageways of this unconscious cave. In truth, it is too complex to navigate alone.

Consciousness and order are the laws of nature for the masculine. The unconscious world within is composed of laws of nature much different from the masculine world of consciousness and order. He needs a guide who was born in that world, one who was molded by it. That guide is the feminine. The masculine's purpose is to bring order from chaos. The feminine's purpose is to create, which requires the destruction of the restrictive, inflexible barriers of the masculine, conscious world, opening him up to her creative, life-giving force. Balance occurs when both the masculine man and feminine woman are subjected to the polarizing effects of the other. Each is the beneficiary of the other's purpose.

If each is the beneficiary of the other's purpose, it could be said that each is the casualty of the other's underdeveloped masculine and feminine, respectively. It is the former that often gives rise to the narrative that masculinity is toxic. Masculinity is not wrong, nor is it useless. What matters is how masculinity is carried out. Be responsible with it, and purposefully do good with it.

Doing good things with your masculinity begins by acknowledging what you understand about it, as well as acknowledging that you have more to learn. Exploring how and why you should manifest your masculinity appropriately can help catapult your relationship into the stratosphere. The key to doing so is to understand what connection, in this context, means. Understanding how it takes place means becoming familiar with the proper ways through which it should occur. Perhaps one must understand why connection is important.

The difficulty with becoming an integrated man in the modern world often lies with the task of connecting this abstract experience of developing masculinity with the observable, surface-level experience of long-term relationships. In other words, today's man experiences cognitive dissonance when he tries to make the association between the irrationality of his woman's behavior and how it is supposed to make him better. The solution is found through the achievement of compatibility with your feminine partner, whom you find irresistible yet irrational.

Achieving compatibility with your partner requires you to practice behaviors that are driven by particular qualities and characteristics. The practice of such behaviors is representative of the explorative process within the unconscious, which is necessary for discovering a sense of purpose. Just as children familiarize themselves with the ways of the world and adulthood through dramatization or symbolic play, today's man discovers his purpose through the dramatization within his relationship with his feminine partner. The conscious engagement with her symbolizes the psychological process that underlies the experience of fulfilling his purpose and realizing his potential. It sets the stage for the integration of the Self. This is also carried out through the act of engaging with others, for it is in his interactions with people that he comes to understand himself, which opens him up to a more defined sense of self.

Therefore, the achievement of compatibility is the medium through which transcending into an integrated version of yourself occurs. It is the passages of that dark cave of the unconscious through which purpose is discovered. It is the feminine guide who leads you through that cave.

Achieving Compatibility

Suppose the achievement of compatibility is the medium through which today's man becomes integrated. In that case, it is the connection with his feminine partner that predicates the activation of the unconscious psychological process of discovering his masculine purpose. Connecting with your partner requires you to gain an understanding of her feminine nature's nuances yet to respond to her feminine nature in a healthy, masculine way. That is, as you get to know her deeper, true nature without sacrificing your masculine purpose, the connection will deepen. To keep from sacrificing your masculine purpose, today's man must stand strong in his magnificence, which is a result of basing his actions on the four pillars of assertiveness, character, frame, and confidence. This is representative of the integrated man, for he is strong and magnificent in action and in spirit. Therefore, implementing such actions is symbolic of the activation of that magnificent spirit.

Many men connect with the symbolism of the oak tree. Responding to her stoically and thoughtfully allows you to be her oak, a symbol of strength, morale, endurance, and knowledge. Under the protection of the oak, your partner is provided safety, security, comfort, and warmth while experiencing excitement and romance. To be an oak is to be unflappable and graceful. As you master assertiveness, character, frame control, and confidence, your roots grow deep and hold you in place as the needs of your partner weigh you down, and her darkest moods crash against you. As you weather the emotional storms of life and of your relationship, you develop a deepened sense of self-worth and a level of responsible leadership that is unparalleled. The experience and wisdom you gain through surviving these storms allow you to stand solidly when your partner tests you, while other men bend and break at the slightest feminine challenge.

Cultivating harmonious connections requires you to be a responsible leader, striving to get what you need while assisting her in getting what she needs. As you master the skills in this book, you will gain a better understanding of your partner's behaviors. You will also learn how to engage with the emotions associated with her behaviors in a masculine way. Masculine and feminine processes are fundamentally different in how we navigate thoughts, emotions, and behavior. When these processes are carried out in accordance with their true nature, both masculine and feminine functions can be sources of freedom. By mastering the skills of assertiveness, character building, frame control, and confidence, you solidify your foothold as you seek to overcome the challenges of connecting to her feminine nature with your masculinity.

Relationships can be difficult to navigate at times due to the fundamental differences between femininity and masculinity. This can be difficult to manage because of some biological factors that show that women have a natural tendency to be skeptical of a man's commitment, which suggests that women often unconsciously gauge a man's capacity to commit to a relationship with them. For the masculine person, this may come across as being tested. How you respond to these tests is crucial, for there are massive implications to our responses to them.

The unconscious thought process of the feminine person interprets that, if he cannot respond well to these simple needs, then he cannot be trusted to manage the deeper, more complex needs, and that is infuriating. These feminine needs are emotional in nature. Therefore, the feminine partner seeks only to experience the emotions of her existence. When that is diminished, she cannot carry out her creative expression, which is necessary for the relationship to evolve.

Support Her Emotional Experiences

People of the opposite gender often conclude that the other gender's traits are flawed. Women may think that a man should be more "in touch with his feelings" when he is operating in his true, masculine nature by trying to be a rational problem solver. Men often experience this as an attack on their manhood, resulting in becoming more aggressive in their masculine stance. By the same token, men are often frustrated when a woman becomes "too emotional" when she is simply processing the gravity of how a given situation is affecting her emotionally, in her own feminine way. A woman will naturally hold her ground to experience her emotions.

Oftentimes, when a woman brings a problem to her man, he defaults to logically solving the problem based on its content. The content of the situation is the observable problem. Addressing the content is not congruent with what the woman needs. Men and women often come to an impasse when men attempt to help by seeking a solution to her problem. It is the focus on the content that creates the impasse; she needs to navigate the emotions of her experience, then processes it logically, if needed.

As your partner comes to you with her emotions, especially her emotional distress, you might attempt to provide reason and logic based on the content she's given you. Thinking logically and rationally is not a flaw; the flaw is failing to engage with—and understand—her emotions within the problem. Feeling her emotions is what she needs to be free to do. Telling her to not worry about something, and offering an immediate solution to the observable problem, is asking her not to feel. You are inadvertently disrupting her way of processing her experience in her own feminine way. Telling your partner not to feel is telling her not to be a woman. Remember, she has her own way of processing her life experiences. Responding with your own emotional distress, and acting irrationally, impedes your partner's healing and growth. Consider what character you need to display in response to her emotional experiences.

Regarding masculinity, it is important to allow your natural process to help you navigate your experiences. This allows you to be emotionally reliable, which provides an optimal environment for your partner to experience her emotions. Instead of becoming frustrated when she becomes "too emotional," be intentional with tending to her needs by responding assertively, confidently, and thoughtfully. As you weather these emotional storms, you create a sense of self-worth and emotional reliability. These are indispensable qualities when it comes to masculinity in relationships. Connecting with your partner requires a balance of meeting her feminine nature with your masculine nature. Today's man often experiences cognitive dissonance in this regard, struggling to grasp how to connect with his partner's feminine side in a way other than becoming too feminine himself. In the way two positive ends of a magnet repel each other, trying to meet her feminine needs with your own feminine behavior will result in repulsion.

Although it is important that you seek to understand the feminine, it is equally important to understand that you only connect with her feminine nature by doing so with your masculine nature—by immersing yourself in her emotional experience. It is the same way electricity works. There is a hot and neutral polarity, and when the two are connected, electric energy happens. When you flip a switch of a lamp to the "on" position, you are completing a circuit, and the light will come on. As you connect to her feminine nature with your masculine nature, there will be a natural flow of energy, and your connection will become more harmonious. In his book, *The Way of the Superior Man*, David Deida says,

---

The best way you can serve your woman is by helping her to surrender, to trust the force of love, so that she can open her heart, be the love that she is, and give this love which naturally overflows from her happiness. This does not involve analyzing the blocks to her loving. Analyzing blocks is a man's way... it's important that you, as a man, don't project your way of doing things onto your woman. Be so full in your loving, so strong and stable in your presence, that she can just let go and surrender the limits she has put on her feelings. Let the emotions of her heart flow unguarded. Let her love be expressed with no limits. Let her go mad with love.[83]

Rodion & Regina XXII

Rodion is learning to connect with Regina by empathizing with her and seeking to understand her emotions, whether it is about the curtains she is considering for the living room or about a coworker's personal tragedy. When she asks Rodion what he thinks of the curtains she wants, a typical response from him in the past might be one of indifference, such as, "I don't care; just get whatever you want." Rodion would mistake indifference for masculinity.

For example, he would talk amongst his friends about not knowing the details of his and Regina's upcoming trip, rationalizing their attitude of indifference as spontaneity and being carefree. Meanwhile, Regina has been spending her emotional labor planning a romantic trip over the past couple of weeks. Indifference is often worse than hatred because there is no emotion or passion. When Regina asks for Rodion's opinion on curtains or some other decor, he could attempt to connect with her by looking for details about the curtains or decor and give her the experience of him being interested in her feminine nature. Perhaps, he would tell her, "I think the blues in the patterns match the couch pillows." Even if Regina disagrees, it is not a problem. She will be excited that he is connecting with her. Whether or not she agrees with his feedback, Rodion's efforts could be enhanced by following up with some emotional reassurance of her feminine nature, saying, "You know, I really like it when you decorate our home. You make it so comfortable. I want you to be able to express yourself when you decorate."

Regina will bring other, more serious forms of emotional distress to Rodion, which may appear to be an invitation for his help to solve an issue she has described to him. Perhaps, one of her employees has experienced the tragic loss of a loved one. As Regina tells him of this tragedy and how she struggles to grasp how she should manage her employee during their crisis, her emotional distress may induce his own distress. Because Rodion loves and cares about her, he does not want to see her experiencing such terrible emotions. He wants her to feel better and be clear-headed to adequately manage her employee without experiencing secondary trauma of the employee's tragedy. With a rigid mindset, resistant to chaos, reminiscent of today's man, Rodion might say, "Well, you have to remember this is about your employee, not you." Although this is true in the sense that the employee is experiencing more suffering than Regina is, his logical approach is dismissing her emotions. As she digs her heels in and reiterates how affected she is, he can either keep up his efforts to analyze and remove the blocks or let her emotions flow and give her limitless expression of them. As an integrated man, Rodion's job is to help Regina surrender to her feminine nature. He can do this by echoing the emotions she is expressing.

Perhaps, he could say, "It must be tricky to navigate being the boss and being understanding of the situation." This shows that he is at least trying to understand what she is experiencing. Once he has shown that he understands the emotions of the situation, he can continue to help her surrender by encouraging her to experience her emotions even more. Perhaps, Rodion should stir the pot and speak about the deeper, more intense emotions than she has articulated by saying, "It must be tough to see your employee hurt so much; you're very empathic." This helps Regina to explore her own feminine experience more fully. Rodion must be cautious not to attempt to express how he feels about the situation—the content. Even if Regina's emotions strongly resonate with Rodion and he wants to share with her that he understands. This will only minimize her emotions, and she will resist him. Today's man must learn to see the emotionality and irrationality of his woman as something beautiful. At the very least, he should find it amusing.

~❖~

As a masculine man, you do love all things feminine. Seeking to find beauty in your partner's chaos is difficult yet paramount. Showing care and attention in this way opens your feminine partner to giving more of her feminine gifts. Showing this kind of care and attention might be difficult for today's man, especially after he has worked diligently on mastering assertiveness by learning how to set boundaries and manage conflict in an unstable relationship, for he had to protect himself while rebuilding himself.

Putting care and attention into connecting with your feminine partner focuses more on positively asserting yourself, rather than using techniques such as negative assertion so often necessary during unstable conflict in relationships. Expressing your affinity with her feminine touch is asserting a positive boundary.

Positive boundaries are not intended to prevent unwanted behavior. Rather, they are designed to allow you and your partner's desires to come to fruition. Praising your partner's feminine qualities excites her feminine nature and encourages her to express herself more fully. Thoughtfully giving your partner compliments and showing admiration for her feminine qualities cultivates them. However, this can be difficult to practice when you feel certain qualities do not exist in her. Hence, you must learn to recognize and acknowledge them. Even when you do not think these qualities are worthy of praise, praise them anyway; it is how you will cultivate them.

People respond best to positive reinforcement. The principle of positive reinforcement aligns with the brain's primary behavioral modification system: the reward center. We can't outrun biology. While assertiveness creates order in relationships, it is the spirit of that order—container for creativity—that helps today's man bring forth his feminine partner's obscured qualities by praising them. He must look for them with a proverbial magnifying glass if he has to. He must water them and tend to them. Praising these unnoticeable qualities will cause them to flourish, and your partner will be free to experience the beauty of her own feminine nature. Additionally, the emergence of those once obscured qualities tends to, by default, push out negative behaviors of hers that would otherwise be detrimental to the relationship.

Responsible Leadership

There are countless quotes on leadership and what it means to be a leader. However, one of the most common themes in such quotes is based on the principle of doing what needs to be done to achieve the greater outcome when two or more people are affected by a situation. Many religions, philosophies, and people have different beliefs about men and their role as leaders in their homes or family. There are a myriad church programs, community initiatives, college courses, mentorship programs, and therapists who have their way of promoting male leadership and "positive masculinity." There are even more definitions of masculinity. Some of these programs have helped encourage men to step up.[84] Many are simply ineffective. Some are detrimental to men.

Regardless of your belief, it is certain that if you assume your partner will lead your relationship, you might be waiting a long time. If you choose to commit to a relationship, assume responsibility for it. No more than you would wait for your colleague to take the initiative on a cooperative project; you should not wait for your partner to take the initiative for the sustainability of your relationship. This does not mean she isn't capable of this; it means you should take the initiative regardless of what you expect her to do.

Do not make the mistake of asking your partner to take sole leadership of the relationship. You may think you are being humble and respecting her capacity to do so, but you are bringing low value to her. You are submitting to defeat and giving up your self-respect. While the feminine brings the masculine to a more complete self in the process of integration, she must find him worthy to receive the gift of her creative spirit. The feminine dragon of chaos must find him to be a formidable counterpart before she will accept him. Bringing low value and sacrificing your self-respect will earn you nothing but rejection as you attempt to connect with her. Falling short of your potential does not bode well for today's man when he is seeking to find his purpose.

Falling short of your potential is inevitable. You are human, and you will fail. What matters is how you respond to your partner's needs and how you respond to your shortcomings. A healthy, directed masculine response is necessary for two reasons: it shows your partner that you have quality character and, most importantly, reinforces who you are as a quality man. Men often complain about their partners when they fall short of their own potential. When they are denied access to their woman's heart, they often imply they should not have to put up with unwanted situations, or they boldly exclaim they don't have to respond in any particular way, and they can do whatever they want. This kind of response is driven by an underdeveloped masculine nature. This is out of frustration or anger. The truth is that you do not have to do any of this; it is your choice. However, you chose to be in a relationship with your partner.

Suppose you want your relationship to be compatible and harmonious. In that case, you must then take responsibility for your decisions, which means effectively responding to your partner in a way that leads you and your partner toward harmony. Remember, you invited her onto your path. Take the necessary actions that steer the relationship toward harmony. If you fall short, take corrective actions from that point on. If done properly, this type of course correction will be an opportunity to showcase qualities that can only be manifested when redeeming oneself. Your partner will admire those qualities in the end.

Responsibility

Responsibility means being accountable for an outcome. It means holding yourself or others accountable. Intimate relationships tend to have a complex set of terms and conditions. These are important, for they pave the way for a relationship's compatibility by allowing the individuals in the relationship to express their needs and desires explicitly.

Each individual has a duty to the other because they have invited the other person to walk with them on their respective paths in life. When we bring someone into our world, we must see to it that they understand what we need and want, and we accept the task of ensuring their needs and wants are also cared for. We must be responsible for showing them how to live in our world without having them sacrifice their self-respect. It is also our responsibility to learn how to live in their world without losing our self-respect. This idea may confuse some. They may think, "If I am responsible for showing my partner how to live in my world, she should be responsible for showing me how to live in hers." This quid pro quo approach is juvenile and irresponsible when utilized as a standalone philosophy. It leads to keeping score in relationships, which results in a transactional connection. This is because the relationship, or its incompatibility, takes on a "me versus you" dynamic. The narrative of this dynamic says,

"Here is why I am right and why I should win." This is the opposite of responsibility in relationships because it dismisses one of the most difficult requirements for achieving compatibility, listening when you don't agree with your partner or hold a different set of values. This is difficult because the "desire for individual self-expression is necessarily limited by the desire for maintenance of the intimate interpersonal relationship."[85] That is, if you want a relationship to work, you must take on the responsibility of making sure you and your partner understand each other.

The clashes in relationships emerge as a result of incompatibility. The failure to resolve these clashes occurs when one partner renders—implicitly or explicitly—the other as inadequate and inferior. This leaves them feeling frustrated, dejected, anxious, and bitter, which only causes the relationship to lose value. In fact, that is not a relationship. While relationship success hinges on the effort and values each person brings, a lack of genuine interest in our partner's well-being will ensure a meaningless connection. We show concern for others when our interactions with them are based on our sense of purpose and giving our gift.

Women tend to experience emotions much more deeply than men and in a more nuanced way.[86] [87] [88] Typically, women navigate relationships well and create positive environments conducive to emotional experiences, for they are well-versed in the nuances of human emotions. They tend to call attention to the softer, more subtle nature of intimacy and connection. We must be mindful of their gifts and, instead of impeding their efforts to share them, we must help create an environment that encourages them to do so. Being a responsible partner means behaving in ways that seek to improve yourself and your partner. Learn to appreciate the gifts your partner has to offer. In your own masculine way, you must allow yourself to experience the emotional nuances she brings. You can experience the emotional awareness she brings without being overwhelmed. As a masculine man, look with curiosity and intrigue at the emotions and other gifts your partner brings to your relationship.

As men, we may value problem-solving strengths and negotiation skills above most other relationship skills. We base the health of a relationship on the value each person brings and the ability to assess conflict from a very logical perspective. We communicate overtly with our thoughts and views. We exhibit stoicism and an unflappable persona. Even if a man is on the high side in the personality trait agreeableness, he will process his compassion-driven experiences with logic and rationale over emotion. He can show stoicism because he can't outrun his biological nature, although it may be obscured by higher levels of neuroticism coupled with ideological thinking. Be they mature or underdeveloped, the masculine tendencies of men are quite evident when we face a crisis.

In your relationship, your partner will often experience emotional distress as well as the occasional emotional crisis. Understand that how we experience emotional distress and crisis is not how women experience them. They are far better equipped for such times than we are. While men view a woman's emotional capacity as weak and fragile, men are the very ones who cannot deal with the depth of emotions that women experience regularly. To tell a woman how to experience her emotions is akin to an Army private coaching a General on how to command the operations in the field. Your partner is the general of her own emotions, but her feminine presence in the relationship cannot actualize to the fullest without a supportive environment. Because the masculine processes emotions in a different way, men tend to look at the emotional experiences of their partner as causing them emotional harm, for he would not function well at all if it were him experiencing the same emotions in the same way. Therefore, he wants to help her by alleviating the emotions of her experience. As it turns out, she is more equipped for them than he is. Today's man must learn to support these emotional experiences so that his feminine partner can heal by creating the container in which her creative achievement will benefit the world.

By now, you are confident and assertive enough to experience your partner's emotional distress without reacting poorly. Your frame is a strong and positive one, which allows you to see your woman's behavior (that you once saw as annoying or vindictive) as something beautiful. Your character is strong and noble. Remember this, for you stand on a solid foundation on which you can present your most magnificent self to your partner and the world.

Although we are responsible for creating an environment conducive to our partner to express her feminine nature, we must not abandon our masculine strengths. We must utilize our masculine values, for we have a duty to defend, support, protect, and provide for our partner. We must be responsible for resolving conflict and removing the barriers that impede intimacy. We must not blame our partner for oversights or errors that we did not help prevent. We simply take ownership of our mistakes and the transgressions against us and seek to correct them.

Leadership

John C. Maxwell stated, "Anyone can steer the ship, but it takes a leader to chart the course."[89] To sustain a harmonious relationship, you need to keep leadership at the forefront of your actions. Leadership is the ability, or gift, to influence others to create processes that ensure positive outcomes.

A leader can create a vision and develop a team mentality that brings that vision into reality. In relationships, you must be reliable and trustworthy for your partner so she can follow your vision for where the relationship is going. In addition, you must be enthusiastic, energetic, and passionate about your vision as well as preoccupied with your sense of purpose, values, and principles.

How you frame relationship conflict is a direct reflection of your leadership skills. Strive to be proactive yet patient. You must progress and evolve; yet, as you transcend the lesser versions of yourself, your partner will need time to adjust to your growth and the changes that come with it. Changes in relationships come with a period of disruption and resistance. Our beliefs, desires, and boundaries are certain to undergo changes, too, as we change. Although it is the result of growth and maturation, it is a change that the other person will have to adjust to. And that can be a lot of work. We must have grace in this process. Homeostasis can have a powerful influence on us, and the adjustments required of us when relationships change require a lot more work than what is expected. You will need the same patience from your partner when she elevates herself, and as her changes naturally disrupt the relationship by shifting the equity of value. Consider her your pace partner. Although you each have your own independent purpose, the paths you walk are merged as one and lead you toward similar goals. As for pace partners, you work to keep pace with one another.

This means, at times, she will be catching up with you, and other times, you will be catching up with her. Having to catch up with your partner does not reflect poor leadership. In truth, it is a sign of leadership in that it reflects your ability to be inspired and to remain teachable. The open-mindedness and willingness you display in these times promote a sense of relatedness with your partner, for she will find that you adhere to the same standards you have of her. Give her this experience, and she will want to match your efforts. This creates harmony in the sense that the interdependence of your relationship is manifested out of desire rather than negotiation or, worse, forced compliance. Rather than eliciting obedience, the integrated man cultivates consensual agreements. And that is difficult! Yet, it is also meaningful.

It is in the best interest of you and your partner to empower each other to be the best versions of yourselves. Your partner is a leader in her own right. Learn to appreciate and honor her leadership. She possesses many gifts, and your work together should incorporate them as an indispensable value. Your cohesive efforts to maximize and reach your individual potential greatly ensure a level of harmony that would otherwise never be realized. Seeking compatibility with the value you both possess creates a more indestructible bond. This kind of bond permeates into connections that you form with others outside of your relationship.

Responsible Leadership

As a man, responsible leadership is characterized by a sense of duty with his relationship obligations and creating an environment in which his partner can fulfill her duty. Responsible leadership is about assuming ownership of the work necessary to sustain a cohesive and harmonious relationship. A responsible leader seeks to make sustainable decisions that take into account the interests of both himself and his partner. He has to be able to ask the right questions and calculate the next step. Responsible leaders take credit and give credit to the people they work with. You have to be vigilant and intentional with your words and actions because your every move is being watched as you attempt to navigate your duty in the relationship. Therefore, live with purpose, and see to it that people leave better than when they came to you.

Let that be your North Star that guides you to meaningful interactions and enriched relationships. Allow it to lead you to redemption when you fail—and you will fail. When you do, get back up and find your guide again, for legacy will be determined more by your redemption than your flawless moments.

Navigating Relationships

A leader emerges in a group of people when the consensus alone is not enough to move the group in any direction. This emergence does not happen without causation. People must assume leadership when a change is not set in motion by normal circumstances or when logic seems to split the pros and cons of choices right down the middle. In other words, some situations are complex, which tend to result in a stalemate or a quagmire. It is in these times that a leader must emerge to influence positive movement. Leadership is a method of influencing another person to enlist collaborative support in working toward a common goal. Leadership translates to a relationship as principally influencing your partner to bring an equitable amount of value in cultivating a harmonious connection in the relationship. In long-term relationships, responsible leadership means taking corrective actions that indicate assertiveness, good character, frame control, and confidence to cultivate a harmonious connection with your partner without compromising your self-respect or hers.

While it certainly takes two willing and capable people to create a successful relationship, one cannot rely on the other to take sole responsibility for the relationship. More importantly, assuming your partner will carry all the weight is a major fallacy in the sense that you might wait indefinitely for your partner to act in such a way. While it would be convenient if the other person would do their job and perform their duties, it is unreasonable to expect and irresponsible to act upon.

Both men and women often fall short of their potential in relationships. This is true in part because human beings tend to take the path of least resistance. In a way, humans are naturally lazy. It should be no surprise that partners will exert low effort in a long-term relationship in which a tremendous amount of work is necessary. This is especially true when there is little to no incentive for the other person to change their behavior.

Two primary factors contribute to this experience. The first is low levels of attraction a woman finds in her man. The other is one person bringing more effort to the relationship—or an aspect of the relationship—than the other person, conditioning the other person to only do the minimal amount of work to get their needs met, while you have to work disproportionately harder to have yours met.

Equitable Value

A responsible leader does not do all the work. He gives effort and brings value, but not more than what is necessary. If he brings too little value, he is, by default, depending on her to do most of the work, which means he is falling short of being his best and curtailing the quality of the relationship. Not to mention, it is simply unattractive. If he brings more effort and value to the relationship than she does, he then removes the incentive for her to bring the necessary value for which she is responsible. A mutually balanced degree of effort from each provides the incentive for his partner to bring equitable value and effort. One should not rely on the other to take sole responsibility for the relationship, for it is irresponsible to assume your partner will fulfill all the duties of the relationship. In fact, acting as though you are responsible for everything in the relationship can be a good place to start. This requires that you take the initiative, which puts you in a position to responsibly influence your partner to support the relationship with equitable value and sustain that support.

Relationships are harmonious when there is an equitable value brought by both partners. This is not about bringing equal amounts. Men and women both have their strengths, and they should both bring forth their best efforts. Partners bringing their best efforts are often more attractive than what their efforts produce. It is the effort itself that is most appreciated. It is healthy for each partner to be able to look at the other and say, "I don't expect you to be perfect, but I expect you to try." Today's man falls short of his partner's expectation of him to try to be perfect. Men tend to hear, "You're not good enough, and I want you to be perfect." Yet, she is really saying, "I want you to be your most magnificent self, and I love you enough to push you toward that." If your partner loves you, then she has standards and expectations for you. She believes you have potential, and it is not in her nature to accept anything short of you living up to your potential. You must understand that she expects you to live up to your potential. It is more than being a good man; it is about being the best man you can be.

When men frame these expectations as unreasonable and irrational, it leads to a skewed view of the function of their partner's behavior. Men might often experience this as skepticism from their partner. It is in her nature to be skeptical of a man's commitment to her and, if she desires you, she will test your character. And she should! She has a duty to ensure she has her needs met; she takes risks when she accepts a man's commitment. The tests your feminine partner gives you may seem amoral, and rightfully so. Many men see this characteristic of women and complain about it, exclaiming that women are too emotional or mean-spirited and only want to cut men down to get what they want. This mindset is a fallacy for men struggling to grasp why they need to improve their assertiveness and how to do it. As a responsible leader, you must be able to assert yourself and set boundaries; you also need to be skillful at reinforcing those boundaries. When your partner tests your character, she is also testing your boundaries. Children test their parents' boundaries to know their limits, and the parents let the child know when he or she has reached them. The parents also reinforce those boundaries when necessary. Your partner is supposed to test your boundaries. It is an effective way of getting to know your weaknesses, what you will settle for, and your potential, which helps determine your capacity to meet her needs. Your partner may experience emotional distress due to a variety of circumstances. If she's invested in you, she will experience emotional distress when you fall short of your potential.

Take action. Being assertive, building character, maintaining frame control, and knowing your worth are imperative to being a responsible leader. Let these four principles drive the other principles you practice in your relationship. They are the foundation on which you will decide what your path is and what is necessary to stay on that path. Bringing someone to walk your path with you comes with great responsibility. You wouldn't bring a puppy home only to become annoyed with it when it whines for food or comfort. You would not expect the puppy to know his boundaries without establishing them. Your partner is more complex than a dog and requires more emotional stability from you as well as other characteristics of someone good at being a man and a responsible leader.

Responsible leadership also means behaving in a manner that shows your partner that she has value and is an asset to the relationship. Showing this to your partner reinforces the positive aspects of her personality, eliciting a desire to contribute and show her value. Showing this to your partner also displays high value in yourself, indicating that you are open to new experiences that promote harmony.

Another quality of responsible leadership is making your path clear to your partner. This requires that you be conscientious with how you and your partner get to know each other and get on the same page. The more conscientious and open to experience you are with this, the more intimacy will be allowed in. This leads to a more harmonious set of agreements between you and her. This kind of intimacy reveals each other's desires. When she is not living up to who she agreed to be, you can then hold her accountable for her own desires. And when you are not living up to who you agreed to be, she will test your character, and you will respond assertively and confidently.

Insecurities, Failures, and Why You Should Voluntarily Enter into Battle

Denial and a lack of initiative are two important hurdles to overcome when improving relationships. The nice guy must accept his insecurities, take responsibility for overcoming his fears and failures, and become a more exciting leader. The former alpha must regain his lost confidence and learn to balance his alpha traits with thoughtfulness. The unprincipled leader must accept his failures and be willing to correct his ways to become a more stable partner who can effectively lead. All these partner types must be willing to take on more than they think they can handle.

Human beings are quite capable of tremendous endeavors, creations, and ideas. We have sent people into space, harnessed radio waves, invented computers, and developed cures for many illnesses. Being intimidated by goals and obstacles is natural. Being intimidated to the point where you are immobilized by the fear and the sheer immensity of the obstacle indicates you doubt your capacity to overcome particular problems. Part of the problem lies in the level of difficulty you assign to it.

People tend to decide that a problem is too great to handle, given their current skill set. This is an indication of their confidence to manage the problem. For instance, if you believe your relationship issues are daunting and impossible to manage, then your confidence in your ability to overcome the challenges of personal relationships might be inadequate. People manage most relationship issues relatively well. However, from the moment they realize a particular issue is too much for their current experience, they begin to question if the relationship is fixable. People will unconsciously manufacture a reality that is more acceptable and easier to deal with. They are contemplating giving up before they have stretched their capacity to overcome such issues.

Although it is important to assess the severity of a problem, what is more important is how well you respond to the problem, regardless of its severity. The focus of your responses is also vital. There was a man seeking coaching regarding his relationship with his live-in girlfriend. He told his coach about an argument between him and his girlfriend. He was proud that he had confronted her by saying, "Do you think this relationship is too far gone?" In other words, he was asking her if the relationship was worth working on. He had worked hard to be able to confront people with confidence and assertiveness. He proactively addressed the elephant in the room, yet he may have chosen an easier problem to address. He was not addressing what could be done to improve the relationship when it is most difficult to do so. With a little coaching, he began to address the problem of improving the relationship when it was most difficult. He and his girlfriend experienced growth because he created an intimate environment in their relationship. His relationship improved as a result of exploring his responsibility as a man, rather than blaming his significant other for the relationship issues. He took responsibility for his own happiness and efforts in the relationship. He became open to looking at the relationship from different perspectives. Was it more work that way? Absolutely! Were the rewards far greater than the alternative? Without a doubt!

If your responses are focused on whether or not you need to drop everything and leave the relationship, then all you will see in your efforts to find a solution are indicators that determine whether or not you need to leave; you will not be looking for indicators that determine what actions are needed to improve the relationship itself. That is differentiation. If you simply defer the fault of your relationship to your partner, you are not seeking a solution. It can be difficult to identify and unlearn these habits and develop healthier habits. Therefore, it is important to have self-talk that supports a strong, positive frame of mind. Such self-talk should indicate finding the right solution for the right problem, not the right solution for the wrong problem.

People naturally choose the path of least resistance. This behavior is part of the human condition. People have many biases that contribute to their perceptions and their behavior. Therefore, it's understandable that one may choose the wrong problem to look at if it is an easier problem to solve. Solving the issue of leaving or staying involves much less conscientious effort than solving the issue of improving yourself and the quality of your relationship. Consciously choosing the harder, more treacherous path, which can result in the most desirable outcomes, requires courage. It requires an element of willingness from your internal motivation. Going down the more difficult path may be an overwhelming task in which you do not believe you are capable of navigating. But you might be surprised. Things are not as bad as people believe.

Take on more than you think you can handle. Human beings' capacity to navigate the most treacherous waters has given the world smartphones and spaceships; with a healthy perspective on your responsibility, you can figure out how to manage the conflict in your relationship.

Insecurities

Insecurities are an emotional SOS that your brain sends out to you about an area in which you lack self-worth. These insecurities and inadequacies are often illuminated in relationships when today's man encounters novel challenges from his feminine partner, or familiar challenges he thought were done away with. The experience of these events is not problematic in and of itself. Rather, the unanticipated exposure to them activates the involuntary reaction stage of the human processing experience. The involuntary reaction stage occurs when we encounter an anomaly and initially recognize similar patterns from previous experiences with which we did not fare well. This recognition induces fear, triggering the fight, flight, or freeze responses. The nature of this problem lies in our resistance to acknowledge and accept our insecurities and inadequacies. Of course, it requires courage to look at the ugliness of our incompetence with things.

However, it first requires that we also act upon our curiosity about the unknown—the potential of the future. This is why we embark on dangerous journeys in life in the first place. Or rather, it is what motivates us to become someone we could be, which means we have an idea of who we are not, and that predicates our movement toward that version of ourselves. We believe we would be better off if we were to somehow become more like that far-off version we envision ourselves becoming and that it would produce a more positive experience of the world. Therefore, we are driven by the desire—the need—to establish ourselves further up the hierarchy of our lives. Yet, this idea of who we could be is quite vague and does not tell us what we must do to become that person. We see the peak of the mountain from the other side of the valley. However, as we descend into the valley, the tree canopies obscure our line of sight of the mountaintop, only giving us glimpses from time to time. Down here, the specific actions and steps we take are very important—every one of them! Here, we have to figure out the implementable actions it takes to bring us toward the mountaintop. As we navigate the valley, we are often left to trust our instincts to guide us. Although the tree canopies give us those occasional glimpses of the mountain, we have to watch every step.

It is in those stretches of the trek that we encounter unexpected resistance, which comes in the form of other people's ambitions, for they too wish to climb the hierarchy of their lives. It so happens that sometimes these hierarchies overlap or that we cross paths with someone in the same hierarchy, and we jockey for position. These encounters require a great deal of skill and fortitude. It is easy for the ambitions of others to overbear us and cause us to doubt ourselves. These encounters are crucial in the sense that how we perceive them can make or break us. If we do not try to understand this phenomenon, we are apt to assume a cynical and even nihilistic view of the world. This is dangerous, for it kills the spirit of curiosity. Life is not a result of evil acts from this person or that person. Instead, it is the result of individual actions of people moving toward their goals, which may happen to knock you down along the way. People are not out to get you, and even when it seems like it, you are just someone in the way. You are not cursed. In that sense, you are not that significant. But it is important to recognize that, despite all that knocks you down, you get up, over and again. Despite the gauntlet of other people's ambitions and nihilism, you rise. That is a miracle and, in that sense, you are significant.

Differentiating what makes us significant improves our outlook. This does not mean the goal is to have a positive outlook on life. Instead, it suggests that to succeed in becoming who we could be requires us to see the benefit of that, to see the promise of being that person. This is quite the aim! To aim is to have a target, and the implications of such a target as the ultimate version of ourselves mean the stakes are high.

The implications of missing the mark could be costly. It is of the utmost importance that we possess the skills necessary to hit the bull's-eye. This means that any deficiencies in our skill sets will be exposed when we shoot our arrows at the target. It is through implementable actions that we true our aim. When encountering unexpected challenges in our relationships sends us into the involuntary reaction stage, the flaws in our intuition and proverbial mechanics are exposed, and we are alarmed. We should be alarmed, because continuing without correcting these inadequacies steers us further from the mountaintop. Regarding your partner's feminine nature, she will not find comfort in your subpar abilities and your faulty ways. In order to pass through the gates of her beauty, you must prove to her you are worthy, which means she is the mirror that shows you your true self. This mirror is not kind. However, it is truthful, and the truth presents the best opportunities for growth and advancement toward who you could become.

You can start improving these insecurities and inadequacies by:

1. *Transform your self-talk and self-image.* Consistently remind yourself of the person you aspire to be by saying, "I want to be someone who ______." This will allow your behaviors to reflect the individual you desire to become. Continuously telling yourself who you want to be will cause your behaviors to follow suit. With time, these behaviors will become habitual, resulting in positive outcomes. You will begin to live life through the lens of the person you strive to be, which will enhance your confidence and transform you into the best version of yourself.

2. *Confront your dark and shadowy aspects.* Don't project insecurities onto your partner. Instead, practice stoicism to regulate emotions and control responses. This acknowledges incompetence and helps sort out insecurities. Remember that stoicism isn't about suppressing emotions but rather regulating them. Using stoicism as a crutch stifles growth and prevents a nuanced understanding of challenges, leading to destructive chaos. Stoicism is a way to become a better version of yourself, not the end goal.

3. There is a useful tool, called a Thought Restructuring Sheet,[90] that aids in regulating our emotions and decreasing our tendency to base our reasoning on our emotions. A version of this sheet can easily be found online.

Invariably, over time, this exercise reshapes our experience of the events that trigger our insecurities and allows us to regain emotional regulation of them, allowing us to effectively address our inadequacies. As we address them, our aim is made truer, and we gain confidence. This confidence gives our partners the assurance they need for us to pass through the gates of their feminine nature.

Rodion & Regina XXIII

Rodion has established a fundamental grasp of the four pillars. This foundation has given him a platform on which he can begin to see the world with which he contends. However, the arrival at the elevated view brings into focus how difficult his journey has been and how daunting it will continue to be. Rodion fights and battles his own messy humanity. Whether he is motivated by fear or reward, he pushes his way through all the shame, insecurities, inadequacies, and weaknesses. He struggles mightily to assert his masculinity in spite of all these forces weighing down on him. And that is courageous. That is heroic. Rodion knows full well the gravity of all that he must contend with. He knows that the limitations placed upon him squeeze him into precise implementable actions, and often painfully so. The barriers of his personality and ideological thinking are the impediments he must face and conquer.

The weight and intimidation that come from the revelatory truths of his insecurities and inadequacies are agonizing. They are the fire in which the feminine dragon of chaos engulfs Rodion, burning away his insecurities and all that is impure. Confronting the agonizing truth of the restrictive impediments of his personality and ideological thinking indicates the psychological process of the unconscious aspects of himself emerging and becoming present in his consciousness. Jung suggested that neurosis occurs when the conscious and unconscious are not aligned.[91] Perhaps, when they are realigned, the initial contact between the conscious and the unconscious is violent. Perhaps, it is akin to the grinding together of tectonic plates or the violent energy of atoms colliding.

As Rodion consciously makes contact with these agonizing truths, as they emerge from his unconscious, they disrupt his very existence. This process is symbolic in nature of his resistance and disruption regarding the difficult and daunting encounters on his journey. Consciously, this process is experienced on a relational level. Here, the activation of Rodion's symbolic, psychological process occurs. The feminine chaos of Regina is representative of the violent conflict between his conscious and unconscious. This level of conflict is made manifest as a result of his engagement with the world, with other personalities. Otherwise, there would be no need to resolve such inner conflict.

Rodion's marriage presents him with the maximal degree of engagement with external forces that bring to light such conflict. The surface-level engagement with Regina provides the dramatization necessary for activating the emergence of unconscious truths that Rodion must accept if he is to fulfill his purpose. This is his story, and it must be played out. Regina has a role to play in it, and Rodion must brave the fierce limitations placed on him by her. Rather than trying to eradicate her chaos, he must subject himself to her fire.

Failures

Have you ever watched a movie or read a story that went perfectly well the whole way through? You probably have not. That is because they do not make them. And if they do, it is probably safe to assume they are unsuccessful. What people want is excitement; they want a journey. A common misconception among men is that if they remain mistake-free, their feminine partner will see them in a more favorable light. The problems with this view are 1) we are human and cannot remain mistake-free; and 2) when we don't openly acknowledge and correct our mistakes, we prevent our partner from having the experience of our redemptive qualities.

You might say that our feminine partner wants all of our qualities, and when we shield her from seeing our mistakes—attempting to give the illusion that we are better than what we are—we then limit the qualities she sees of us. As a result, we inadvertently discard the qualities of redemption, causing her to miss out on them. When we openly and confidently correct our mistakes, our feminine partner gets to experience a broader range of our qualities. She gets to experience the whole story, and she likes that! So, we're going to make mistakes: the key is that, when we do, we correct them, and we give her a story.

To extract the utility from this notion, we must broaden our view of failure by understanding that failure is often predicated on a lack of confidence to deal with the issue at hand forthrightly. Such failures are also exacerbated by misattributing their causes. We not only implement strategies poorly, but we also attempt to use strategies that are less effective. If we recognize how our ability to manage conflict hinges on our confidence, then we are able to modify our behaviors in such a way that ensures elevated levels of confidence. This does not mean we will not get knocked down and suffer hierarchical defeats. But it does mean we stand a chance to get back up and make adjustments with some degree of precision. Suppose we do not recognize that our success—and redemption—depends on our confidence and how we nurture it. In that case, we set ourselves up for one failure after another, making it more difficult to climb back up the hierarchy. Sure, while making mistakes is inevitable, we don't want to be careless and make too many, because we will cross that threshold and find ourselves at the precarious bottom of the hierarchy, and that is not good.

Rodion & Regina XXIV

Once again, Rodion is faced with the call to courage. Though he takes some hits, he persists—ever forward, ever onward. He practices vulnerability in the sense that he is capable of being wounded and attaining the glorious heights of his endeavors. He remains steadfast in the greatest doubt, particularly when that doubt is self-induced by his own mistakes rather than the ambitions of those with whom he encounters. He descends into his cave, retrieves the thing he needs most, and emerges ready to bring salvation through his redemption. And Regina will stand in awe, for he will have surpassed his own abilities right in front of her. All of this is packed into the story contained in each of his failures; it is waiting to be told.

This is his story, and Rodion must give Regina a story, for she longs to experience it, too. As he stands before the chaotic unknown, he must summon the courage to walk through his failures as consciously as possible. Rodion must accept the limitations placed on him by Regina rather than trying to go around her gauntlet. He must accept her fire.

Why You Should Voluntarily Enter Battle

Voluntarily entering into battle means engaging in the war within yourself. The psychological process of engaging with our inner enemy is often activated by the exposure to our insecurities and failures within our relationships. The reasons behind our insecurities and failures contain the answers for their resolution. However, the exploration of these reasons can lead us to some unpleasant truths about ourselves. It is down here where we are often confronted with our dragons, such as trauma, regret, shame, and those suppressed aspects of ourselves that we would rather avoid—this is detrimental to relationships. In fact, it is the Shadow Self within such unpleasant aspects of ourselves that often steers our experiences and leads us to misattribute the cause of our insecurities and failures to manufactured reasons. In the context of relationships, these manufactured reasons are experienced as shortcomings of our partner. In essence, this experiential avoidance of the unpleasant aspects of ourselves becomes a form of deceit. It is an attempt to manipulate reality to achieve a selfish outcome without having to do the dirty work. Little to no meaning can be derived from that.

In a world where everything we do matters, it is imperative that we pursue the truth about ourselves by voluntarily entering battle with those dark and shadowy dragons. And that is not easy. In fact, it is an unpleasant and frightening process. Finding our "true selves" is painful, for it reveals the error of our ways. Perhaps the greatest degree of pain in this process is having our own humanity revealed to us. This is also likely to be more frightening because it shows us how delicate life is. When faced with this truth within ourselves, we see the scale of the mountain we must climb, and the odds are not good. It is here we stand at the edge of the world, and we have every reason not to climb anymore, to give up, to choose a life of cynicism and nihilism. It is here we stand at the edge of the world, where even the light does not promise glory. It is here that our highest redemptive quality is the will to rise.

Entering into battle with ourselves is to live out one of the most universal and deeply human stories—the story of descending into the cave, slaying the dragon, and emerging with the dragon's gold, the thing we need most. In a sense, the experience of navigating the challenges of our partner in the real world also provides the stage for psychological development deep within. The difficulty of relationship challenges can begin to cast a light upon our deeper fears. The odds are that if you can easily name the thing you are most afraid of, then that is not it. Part of what makes the battle within so difficult is that we rarely know what frightens us the most. Suppose, for a moment, that we, in fact, can accept the notion that there is a deep-seated fear and, although we cannot identify it, we know it somehow causes us to stall in life, or worse, causes us to self-sabotage. Where do we look? How do we know when we see it? What will we do when we get there? It is the case that what deters us from entering into battle with ourselves is a failure to understand why it is necessary. With so many questions to answer before we even set foot onto that path, why bother? We find plenty of available reasons to continue with what we have been doing. Yet, if we hit a wall long enough, and we are determined to ascend the hierarchy of our lives, we will admit—if only to ourselves—that we must do something different. "Why bother?" you may ask. We bother with this because it is meaningful. We are faced with the reality of our battle. We have no weapons, no shield, and no friends here. It can be quite disheartening and lonesome. For these reasons, it is understandable why one would return to their familiar world of predictability and certainty. But it is also here that we feel the tug of our soul pull us toward greater heights. It is here that we are faced with the fork in the road that takes us to a life of nihilism or a life of purpose.

The battle within provides us with the platform necessary for broadening our personality and conquering the chaos within and the creative potential it holds. This factors into the achievement of compatibility in your relationship through the ability to bring order from a wide range of chaos and conflict. Voluntarily enter into battle within your relationship. This does not mean you should fight your partner. It means fighting for her regarding her inner conflict by bringing order from her chaos, providing an optimal space for her to experience creative achievement. It is important to remember that the aim is not to remove the battle within her; it is about helping her engage in her own battles and ensuring she emerges victorious in them. This is a crucial distinction to make. To remove the battle within her—well, to attempt to—is to distance her from her humanity, her chance for meaning. What then do we do if we can neither alleviate her battles nor simply comfort her? This puts us in a peculiar situation, for we become very limited in what we can do. This is what those limitations are for. They squeeze us into a narrow path, making us act with precision. If we are to be her man, the one whose masculine order provides the container in which her feminine chaos can attain creative achievement, then we must also be her enemy, so to speak.

Friedrich Nietzsche elaborated on this notion in *Thus Spoke Zarathustra as Zarathustra* said, "Be at least my enemy!" — thus speaks true reverence, which dares not ask for friendship. If one would have a friend, then must one also be willing to wage war for him: and in order to wage war, one must be capable of being an enemy. One ought to honor the enemy in one's friend…In a friend one shall have one's best enemy. You shall be closest to him with your heart when you withstand him."[92] To be her enemy means to go to battle for her in the sense that you are battling her inner conflict with her, which is with her Shadow Self's resistance to the confrontation. Your partner's feminine nature is marked by chaos, both destructive and creative. For her to embody her true nature, there must be room for her to live out the destructive and creative aspects of her feminine chaos. It is difficult to accept that destructive chaos is not inherently negative. It can be directed to destroy outdated beliefs and oppressive behaviors. And that is good because it gives rise to helpful beliefs and behaviors conducive to growth within the relationship.

The ability to be her enemy sets the stage for victory over her inner battles. If you love her, tell her the truth, for it is the ultimate weapon in any battle. Of course, she will not jump for joy when you summon the truth about her own conflict—it is an unpleasant experience to disturb the dragon within. You must show good character and remember that the truth without love is a weapon against the one to whom the truth is delivered. And love, as with truth, must be delivered with the thoughtfulness necessary for its reception by her. To paraphrase the words of Father Gregory Boyle, "If love is the answer, then tenderness is the methodology."[93] To conquer the great schism between friend and enemy, truth and tenderness, destruction and creation, we must master both sides. We master it not for its eradication but rather for its supreme meaning. While we need to be a safe place for her to exist, we must by all means voluntarily enter into battle with her feminine dragon of chaos, for it is in victory that compatibility is achieved. To quote Alain de Botton, in his book, *The Course of Love: A Novel,* "Compatibility is an achievement of love; it shouldn't be its precondition."[94] You and your woman have work to do in this world, and together your lights will shine bright and illuminate the path of humanity for more to see the Way. It is time to put your trust in each other to work and direct it outwardly. The world needs it. Enter into battle, voluntarily, and will the relationship to its potential and beyond, for glory waits. The quest will be steep and jagged. It will be heavy. It will be frightening to her. Yet, you will protect her. You will always protect her. Even when she cannot tell, you will be protecting her.

Rodion & Regina XXV

To voluntarily enter into battle, Rodion must willingly subject himself to the fiery gauntlet of Regina's feminine chaos. The gauntlet, on a practical, real-world level, is comprised of Regina's tests and challenges toward Rodion as well as the confusion caused by the obscure nature of the language and behavior through which tests and challenges are delivered.

The gauntlet symbolizes Rodion's arduous journey through which he encounters dark and shadowy aspects of himself, bringing him face to face with the things he most resists. It is in these encounters that the violent contact between the conscious and unconscious occurs, in the way a meteor begins to burn upon entry into Earth's atmosphere. Making an entry into his unconscious is symbolically represented as the feminine dragon of chaos breathing her fire down onto Rodion. This symbolic representation is manifested relationally as Regina's implicit and explicit emotional and psychological demands of Rodion. Before she accepts him into the sacred and centermost place in her feminine world, he must reveal to her the truth in the form of his masculinity. He must give her his most magnificent self. This storyline occurs at the conscious level: within his marriage.

The character Rodion develops results from the fiery truth burning away his willful blindness, leaving only his gifts to give. Regina's challenges of Rodion strengthen his frame, providing her the assurance that he will not falter. In other words, his determination to improve himself as her partner allows him to master his relationship skills to successfully manage the conflict in a way that progresses his relationship. This, in turn, provides Rodion with more victories, for he becomes better equipped for them. These victories increase his confidence, which paves the way forward in his marriage. All these components make up the story Rodion must act out, for he can only attain glory as a man through battling his own chaos. However, he cannot do this alone. He needs the feminine. And the feminine he will get! In the beginning, Rodion's youthful confidence got him the girl. To get the woman—the full feminine—the quest would be more difficult than he could ever imagine.

His boundaries became blurry; his character would be dissolved, he would falter in his frame, and his confidence placed in the greatest doubt. All the destruction brought about by the feminine chaos is necessary, for Rodion's fate rests in becoming his own hero, Regina's hero. In the words of perhaps the most courageous psychologist who ever lived, "…but you grow if you stand in the greatest doubt, and therefore steadfastness in great doubt is a veritable flower of life."[95] Rodion's heroic transformation can only take place in the dark and chaotic unknown. For glory, he must journey through the feminine world, going first through her fiery blaze, then onto her divine and sacred beauty. Rodion must fall in love with her fire.

Chapter Eleven

Integration

The feminine, capable of destruction and creation, is representative of the adversity and precarious sets of obstacles in life that shape the Self into a more wholesome and complete version. It is through the chaotic push and pull from one extreme to the other that gives rise to the experiences necessary for transformation. These extraordinary and violent fluctuations stretch us beyond our current capacity to comprehend our sense of self. As painful and uncomfortable as it is, this stretching exposes us to new realms of possibility that contain truths that set free particular aspects of the Self.

The unconscious aspects we discover through our interaction with the feminine are necessary for understanding our purpose and the will to carry that out. The challenges presented by the feminine chaos reveal to us the vastness of the world and our existence within it. This process seems to cause cognitive dissonance with today's man, for understanding himself is more attainable within a relatively small, definable corner of the world. There, he can familiarize himself with his environment with the aim of establishing stability and predictability. However, he cannot grow there. The masculine—consciousness and order—cannot fulfill its purpose without having things to bring to order and into consciousness. The masculine seeks to bring order from chaos rather than to find permanence in the orderly world his conquests produce. He lives to conquer! That is his purpose. By nature, the masculine cannot thrive within the confines of his small, familiar, and predictable world. Today's man must venture out into the unknown world if he is to find completeness. Ironically, while in the vast unknown, he is squeezed into a narrow passageway when he encounters the feminine, which is necessary for his integration as a man.

This narrowing forces today's man to shed the useless and outdated skills and beliefs that hinder his progress toward a more integrated Self. That is, he has to shed his old skin before he can grow. This can be a painful and exquisitely tender metamorphosis.

The exposure to such vastness is experienced as disorder and needlessness. The reactions to this, characteristic of today's man, involve a resistance to limitations and restrictions. The vastness of the unknown the feminine brings to our attention is disruptive to our predictable, established corner of the world. Disruption occurs in the balance of chaos and order—when order is disrupted, the solution is not to remove the chaos from order but to bring order from the newly encountered chaos. Our existence, and our understanding of it, are important for navigating the world with precision, which is paramount for discovering a deepened sense of purpose. In long-term relationships, we are often thrust onto the outermost walls of our abilities by the demands of excellence of us from our partner. She needs to know how spacious an environment we can provide for her to express herself as fully as possible. To do this, the feminine has to extract from today's man his hidden ability to do so. The integration of the Self for today's man involves coordinating the different aspects of himself into an effective personality. This process is perhaps most effectively done in the context of relationships. It is in his interactions with the feminine nature of his partner that he is met with the necessary confrontations that lead him to the Self. The feminine interacts with the Self in ways that reestablishes contact with the unconscious,[96] which is a part of the process of the completion of consciousness. That is, the feminine brings today's man to a more magnificent version of himself by confronting him and demanding his best. He is rigorously subjected to myriad trials and tribulations that could bring him to an end or, if he passes, emerge with an expansive knowledge of the borders of his realm and everything in between. To know the limits, we must push them. If today's man is to find completion, he must not only know who he is, but he must also settle into his natural, precise personality. There, his most important aspects can exist and fulfill their purpose.

This rather existential analysis of a man's experience with the feminine nature of his partner speaks to a deeper psychological transformation. On one hand, the interaction today's man has with his woman can culminate in a superficial degree of struggle on a conscious level, which he will take as the only level of experience. On the other hand, today's man rarely becomes aware of what's happening on a deeper, archetypal level, which can be better understood through a story-like narrative. If today's man explores his relationship through the context of a story, he is opened up to a deeper understanding of himself, which will position him to revolutionize his relationship. This can only take place within the proper limitations that force him to be precise with his character in a manner that allows him to live a meaningful existence.

Revolutionizing Personality: Rules about the Rules

Sometimes, your personality will be optimally matched for the current environment. There will also be times when your current environment will be ill-suited for you. Our personality serves to simplify the wildly complex world in a way we can comprehend it. Due to such complexities of the world, there is an infinite pool of personality traits that may be called forth. This results in a particular set of traits becoming crystalized to deal with the complexities of the world based on preferences, interests, and the ease with which he can learn and execute certain skill sets, which are best suited for a small range of problems or environments.

Personality traits are "probabilistic descriptions of relatively stable patterns of emotion, motivation, cognition, and behavior, in response to classes of stimuli that have been present in human cultures over evolutionary time."[97] Based on their personality, people deal better with certain kinds of people or situations than others. The diversity of personalities, in part, explains why people gravitate toward certain environments and toward certain personality types that they prefer in their relationships.

Some situations and personalities are more preferable to others because they can navigate them with optimal efficiency. Even if someone's personality is not preferable, if they are interested enough in the person or situation, they will be more inclined to engage in that particular environment because it optimally matches their interests. This speaks to an idea about our attitudes toward the things that define us, for better or worse. People generally detest being put into a box; their disdain for labels is not hard to notice. This is a valid experience, for it is in our resistance to conformity that we begin to establish ourselves as individuals, particularly in our youth. Nevertheless, this process is the act of breaking away from too much order so that the individual can explore a wider range of identities because the orderly end of the spectrum holds too many restrictions for us to declare for ourselves who we are. The world of infinite possibilities and, ultimately, promise often lies on the other end of the spectrum. However, this infinite world is chaotic, holding not only promise but also threat.

Virtues as Shaped by Personality

It is important to understand the faults and virtues of our personality to broaden ourselves so we can more successfully navigate a wider range of environments and other personalities. Relationships can, to a degree, be defined by the challenges of contending with other personalities. Perhaps, to put it more succinctly, relationships are often a clash of virtues. When our virtues are contradicted by the virtues of another person, we tend to dismiss their virtues as misguided morality at best and, at worst, as evil. In truth, the virtues we cherish will make us too inflexible if we continue to hold those few precious virtues above all others. Such rigidity will inevitably prevent us from broadening ourselves in such a way that improves our relationship.

The world is tremendously complex. As great as the computational power of our brains is, it is no match for the complexity of the world. How then do we attain success in life if this giant world is so insurmountable? It would be easy to go down the rabbit hole here, but for the sake of understanding the nature of how our virtues clash in relationships, let us consider success as the degree to which positive emotional experiences are consistently attained. Therefore, any experience of extracting promise from the world is a positive emotional experience. Despite the world being so complex, we successfully navigate it enough from time to time to achieve some degree of success. The understanding of the ways of the world we develop also shapes how we navigate and meet our needs and, in turn, gives rise to many of our most cherished virtues.

Perhaps, we were born with an inherent disposition for navigating the world in a particular way. Maybe we learn through experience from an early age how to ensure our needs are met. The narrative drive behind the successful navigation of the world determines your actions in the sense of what your virtues produce. For example, Rodion falls on the lower end of the trait agreeableness, and his narrative drive says, "I will look out for myself to get what I need, and you will look out for yourself to get what you need. That way, we all get our needs met, and we can get along." Hence, his virtues indicate that negotiating for one's own needs is important for achieving success. This is no small matter. It could be said that his entire life depends on his ability to negotiate for himself—and that you should also negotiate for yourself. It very well might be the case that harmony is achieved through these virtues. If that's true, his morality hinges on his adherence to such virtues.

Yet, in another part of the world, Regina's personality differs, bringing with it different virtues. Her narrative says something along the lines of "I will look out for your needs, and if you look out for mine, we both will be ensured that our respective needs are met. If we act this way, we will all get along." Therefore, she embodies the virtues of nurturance and caregiving—and their reciprocity—as the most important regarding achieving positive emotional experiences. Well, this is no small matter either. It could just as easily be said that Regina's entire life depends on tending to other people's needs and the notion that you should do that, too. It seems that harmony is also possible through these virtues. Hence, Regina's morality also hinges on her adherence to such virtues. You have probably guessed that this presents a common yet astronomical dilemma—a clash of virtues in relationships.

Left unaddressed, such clashes will result in moral contempt for each other, among other negative thoughts, experiences, and behaviors such as bitterness, resentment, arrogance, deceit, unnecessary suffering, character assassinations, emotional accusations, arbitrary declarations of the other's intentions, and even malice. However, we must consider how the clash occurred in the first place. We have already established that the world is complex and that we develop particular skill sets that afford us some degree of success. We also determined that these skill sets—rather, personality traits—shape our virtues. Perhaps, more than anything else, what makes this world overwhelmingly complex is that we have other personalities to contend with. What happens when Rodion and Regina enter into a long-term relationship when they have such disparity in their virtues? They will clash. Yet, they will not understand why. Assuming both of them are, to any degree, decent people, it is unlikely that immorality is at the root of the negative behaviors toward one another. Yet, this is often the view partners take of the other in relational conflict, especially when the stakes are high and needs aren't being met. People tend to look at the behaviors of others through a moral lens. While morality should shape the outcomes we choose, it distorts our perception of people when we judge their actions in relation to us. Moral views through which we judge others are too often rooted in our own virtues rather than the higher perspective of considering all virtues. In other words, because they don't hold the same virtues we do, and with the same degree of reverence as we do, we cannot even comprehend that they have virtues—or at least that their virtues are worthy. Rather, we assume a position of moral contempt, arbitrarily declaring their virtues as vices and even malicious, and that is dangerous.

It is imperative that we consider how our personality shapes our virtues, especially when there is disparity in personality traits with our significant other.

Having already established how disparity in the trait agreeableness can result in a clash of virtues, it is important to gain an overview of how the other traits of our personality shape our virtues. Regarding the trait conscientiousness, it could be said that those who are low in this trait are able to relax despite the chaos that surrounds them, that they have the proclivity to be unfazed by disorder. While this particular temperament potentially contains the faults of laziness and procrastination, it could also indicate that they know what their priorities are. Being low in conscientiousness might suggest that one would know how to enjoy life without having to overexert oneself. And that is a gift!

Perhaps, the virtuousness of low conscientiousness is that it is useful for appreciating downtime for its restorative purposes—to ensure a present experience of positive emotions. The narrative drive here says, "If we conserve our energy, we will have enough for when it is most important. And if you value that like I do, we will all be on the same page. We can have harmony, and all get along."

On the flip side, a person high in conscientiousness stays on top of things, whether through their industriousness, orderliness, or both. This person puts off rest until it is absolutely necessary and plans ahead to ensure their needs are met—to guarantee positive emotional experiences in the future. This narrative says something along the lines of, "If we all work hard, we will ensure that we have harmony when the work is done, and we will all get along."

The person low in conscientiousness may look at the person high in this trait and believe he takes himself too seriously and does not know how to relax—he sees him as a buzzkill. The person high in conscientiousness looks at the other and thinks they are lazy and do not pull their weight. By understanding the clash of virtues in the trait conscientiousness in our relationship, we begin to see that where we fall in this trait also has its faults. Only then can we begin to appreciate the virtues of the other person's degree of conscientiousness. Furthermore, by broadening ourselves regarding this trait, we can more positively influence the other person to broaden themselves with the same trait, creating compatibility with it.

Extraversion is a particularly unique trait in this context because it is the trait that is directly associated with positive emotional experiences. Those who are higher in extraversion tend to be talkative, spontaneous, and generally fun people. They are most commonly defined as sociable. Many people who are high in extraversion make friends easily and are open with their feelings. They are also those who exhibit a take-charge attitude. Influential leaders tend to be higher in extraversion. They also tend to value the present over the future, often leading to engaging in more risks, for better or worse. The virtues of being higher in extraversion are that it provides us with higher degrees of positive emotions. On the other end of the spectrum, you will find people who have an easier time delaying gratification and spending time in introspection. Perhaps, the virtues of low extraversion allow us to be more calculated in how we navigate the world. Extraverts may find introverts too quiet and aloof, believing their introversion creates a drag on their attempts to generate a socially rewarding experience. Introverts may consider extroverts as too pushy and reckless. Both introverts and extroverts have faults and virtues. Yet, since this is the personality trait directly associated with experiencing positive emotions, it is generally the case that introverts stand more to gain by broadening this trait. However, extroverts could also certainly benefit from learning to be more introspective and delay gratification.

Neuroticism is the experience of negative emotions. More specifically, it is the sensitivity and reactivity to pain and discomfort. It is the only personality trait with which there is an exception to the rule of compatibility. Both people in a relationship being high in neuroticism is much less preferable than any degree of disparity in any other trait. If both people are high in this trait, it is going to be a miserable time together. However, assuming there is disparity in this trait, there are virtues of being lower or higher in neuroticism, albeit surprising to most.

People low in neuroticism have an inherent ability to not allow the occurrence of pain and discomfort—or the potential for it—to influence their emotional experiences. They are able to defend against and deflect the threat of pain and discomfort as a way to successfully navigate the world by seeing there is more to the world than pain and discomfort. Those high in neuroticism can and do more easily detect pain and discomfort—or the prediction of it.

The virtue of this proclivity is that people will see pitfalls that could potentially undermine the relationship. Conflict sourced in disparities in this trait occurs as one person thinking the other is too emotionless and insensitive or too high-strung or, well, neurotic.

Last is the personality trait Openness to Experience, characterized by imagination, curiosity, creativity, intellectual interests, perceived intelligence, artistic and aesthetic interests, and unconventionality.[98]

Disparity with this trait in your relationship is likely to have its most significant impact on your motivations, perceptions, and actions, as well as your understanding of each other in that regard. This will often manifest as conflicts of interest and preferences. Suppose you are higher in Openness to Experience, and your partner is lower in this trait. In that case, you will possibly view her as predictable, conventional, and perhaps, narrow-minded and lacking variety. She will often see you as an overthinker, hard to understand, quirky, unpredictable, and difficult to keep up with—as your perspective evolves more quickly than hers, she will not know your current position on certain topics.

Additionally, people higher in Openness to Experience seem to be more interested in abstract ideas and complex problems—they may even be more concerned with society as a whole. If your partner is lower in Openness to Experience, she might seem a little more interested in concrete ideas and discussion. One area, in particular, can attribute to a commonly experienced conflict in many relationships, which is the type of friends each of you prefer. Preferring different kinds of friends is often mistakenly handled by assuming moral contempt for the other's friends, rather than supporting the compatibility the other finds in his or her own friends.

When partners unfairly judge the other's friends as immoral or toxic, they are, by default, withdrawing their support for the other's individuality, and that is not good. Such behavior indicates a narrowing of the relationship that promotes a dependence solely on you, which leads to enmeshment. Too much enmeshment, and there can be no individual thoughts and experiences conducive to intimacy and harmony.

Clashes of virtues often predicate the painful conflicts in relationships. Yet, observing these clashes with curiosity provides us with useful contrasts that illuminate the beauty of the other's personality, which can afford us the necessary insight for restoring connection. A phenomenal experience occurs as we shift from a contemptuous view—often rooted in our cherished beliefs—to a view that holds gratitude. Hence, we arrive at a monumental realization with ourselves, and that is knowing we have a choice in the direction we go. Perhaps, one of the most undetectable forks in the road is the direction that the smallest, most inconsequential decisions take us. Each action either directs us down a path whose subsequent actions hold meaningful implications or a path whose subsequent actions are, at best, a means to an end or, worse, seen as trivial.

To see the meaningful implications is to make the connections between the smallest implementable actions we take and how they ultimately lead to the highest aim—gratitude, meaning, purpose, in that order. To see our actions only as "one more damn thing I have to do" leads down a path that only gets darker—triviality, cynicism, nihilism, also in that order. Will you succumb to ignorance and inexperience? Or will you transcend your temptation to walk that dark path by practicing the virtues of love and courage? Let yourself be moved by all the stress and heaviness you have been experiencing and do so while trying to remain grateful.

Jordan Peterson states, in Beyond Order (Rule XII Be Grateful in Spite of your Suffering): "It is not as if the suffering and betrayal, the catastrophes, are of insufficient gravity to make bitterness a real option…The temptation to become embittered is great and real." We must consider our own intolerance for willful ignorance and of all the people around us who exhibit it and how all that intolerance makes us bitter and cynical. That is not effective. It is not meaningful. Peterson continues, "Despite the fact that the world is a very dark place…we see in each other a unique blend of actuality and possibility that is a kind of miracle…perhaps it is active love that aims at its betterment."[99] Be grateful in spite of your suffering, and by all means, strive to see the beauty in the one person committed to walking on your path with you.

Nuance in Perceiving and Navigating the World

The world is enormous and complex, and our place in it is infinitesimally small. How then are we able to achieve the great heights of humankind? From the 10,000-foot view, we can see that the odds are not in our favor.

Suppose we descend into the life of a single person, in an environment of innumerable actions and choices. In that case, we are overwhelmed by unlimited freedom to choose a direction at each fork in the road, which accumulates infinite forks in the road. This is where we develop pronounced personality traits.

Personality is our own unique way of perceiving and navigating the world, which is developed on a foundation of an inherent temperament and somewhat shaped over time by early developmental experiences.

Over time, we become more and more nuanced in our own unique ways of understanding the world. As a result, the particulars of our personality become better suited for certain situations and the methods for dealing with them.

The more we practice these methods, the more we prefer the situations best suited for our personality. The same is true for dealing with other people, especially people whose personalities are profoundly different from yours. The markedly different sets of personalities mean each person navigates the world in very specific ways, and these distinctions can be observed as a conflict of interests and preferences.

To effectively manage relationship conflict regarding personality differences, it is paramount that we first understand the nuances of where we fall on each trait. Recalling the previous section in which disparity in personality traits causes clashes of virtues, it is useful to consider the faults and virtues of each trait based on where we fall. Reference your Big Five personality report to enhance your understanding of the basic descriptions of your personality traits. Pay attention to your interactions with others and notice how your personality traits contribute to your behaviors and experiences. This exercise will begin to illuminate the nuances of how you perceive and navigate the world.

Additionally, pay attention to how the effectiveness of your personality contrasts with your own experiences of dealing with different types of personalities. You will see how your personality is more effective in certain situations or personalities than with others. This contrast gives you more insight into the nuances of your own personality, which illuminates the faults and virtues of each of your traits. Nuance in perceiving and navigating the world ensures a viable degree of mastery over our personality in the sense of successfully reaching the highest point in the hierarchy of our lives. The particulars of such mastery ensure our needs and desires are met. That is, until we discover needs that can only be met mutually, and that have to take into account a particular personality that opposes yours. This is the point of contact between two personalities, along with the contact between the masculine and the feminine. It is here we are forced to operate from a place outside of our particular place on the spectrum of any given trait.

Behavioral Activation Beyond Our Personality

We are social creatures. We will contend with other personalities, many of which will result in a clash of virtues, interests, and preferences. Because relationships come with terms and conditions, some of our previously established behaviors will violate those terms and conditions, if carried out.

The problem with this is that the person required to change their behavior is faced with making changes on a deeper level—behaviors serve a purpose, and therefore have a deeper meaning. Where personality comes in is with how it shapes our behaviors and experiences, and this is important to us.

Its importance lies in the nuances of how we perceive and navigate the world. In essence, when we are asked to change our behavior, we are often being asked to abandon the tried-and-true methods we value the most—those that we cherish the most. This is asking a lot of us, and who in their right mind joyfully does that?

So, perhaps we are not too thrilled to change our behaviors and the cherished beliefs behind them. It is very disruptive, after all. It is frustrating, too. Not only must we change some of our behaviors, but we also have to know what behaviors to replace them with. That is even more difficult. The more difficult it is to figure out what behavior we need to replace the old one with, the easier it is to revert to old behaviors. Then, when we thought it could not get any harder, we discover that these newly acquired behaviors are not good enough—because we are not nuanced enough in them. And to top it all off, we have to carry out those new behaviors in slightly different circumstances.

No wonder it is easy to stick to what you know. Yet, as we have seen what the disparity in personality traits can produce, we know it is crucial that we seek to resolve the conflicts they give rise to. We do this by broadening our personality.

We cannot shift our personality in the sense of changing our primary position along the spectrum of each trait. However, we may be able to make minor changes to our traits, although this process requires a change in characteristic adaptations.[100]

Therefore, we can expand the capacity of our personality to become more nuanced with a wider range of behaviors and characteristics that lie outside the particular place we occupy on that spectrum. If we were to use a bell curve to illustrate our place on any given personality trait, and assuming we have not broadened ourselves, we would see a pronounced narrow bell curve with its peak directly over the percentile we fall in regarding that trait. This would indicate a few important details about ourselves, such as the characteristics to which our behaviors and experiences can be attributed to, the ease with which we can learn and implement the skills that coincide with that place on the spectrum, the areas outside our place in which we are not nuanced, and possibly the types of environments most optimally suited for our personality. These details give us a more comprehensive view of our personality.

By understanding the characteristics that correlate with our place on a particular trait, we are provided the contrast necessary for defining where our nuance ends, and the unknown world of that trait begins. This is where we begin to broaden our personality by practicing the behaviors characteristic of those beyond our realm of nuance within each trait. If you are on the low side of the trait agreeableness, and your partner is high in agreeableness, defining where your nuance ends means that you widen the bell curve toward the high side by behaving in ways that indicate compassion, politeness, or both.

In the context of relationships, broadening your trait agreeableness means trying to be more nurturing. If you are low in conscientiousness, practice more routine and work more diligently with your tasks and responsibilities. If it is the case that you are low in extraversion, particularly if you are low in assertiveness, delving into the world of assertiveness

266

skills would help to broaden your extraversion. If you are high in neuroticism, broaden this trait by learning how to reframe your circumstances and the personalities with which you are contending. If you are low in neuroticism, you may come across as cold and calculated when your partner is experiencing emotional distress.

Broadening this trait would involve you becoming more attuned to her pain and discomfort, providing you with an opportunity to tend to her emotional needs and connect with her.

Regardless of where you fall with each personality trait, it is imperative that you broaden them, particularly in the direction of where your partner may fall in her personality traits. This broadening lessens the divide between you and her in ways that resolve the clash of virtues rooted in your personality differences.

As you become more nuanced with the area outside your particular place on the spectrum of each trait, you begin to hear the language of your partner more acutely. As you master this, you will begin to hear the language of the ancient feminine within her—you will begin understanding the language of your partner more fluently. Perhaps more importantly, you will begin speaking the language of the ancient masculine within.

Integration and Mastering Personality

Integration requires an exploration relative to our usual experiences—with the necessary caution to avoid needless chaos, but with enough courage to face the danger that some of our natural characteristics may be invalidated, and with sufficient humility to acknowledge when a current characteristic adaptation is in error.[101] As we become deeply familiar with the nuances of our personality and broaden our capacity to operate in the nuances outside our personality, we begin to master it.

Mastery over our personality means we can channel different aspects of personality to drive our behaviors based on the current environment or the unique personality with whom we are interacting. We know when to be more nurturing or when to stand our ground. We know when to be alarmed by painful emotions or when we should stand back and observe all of our surroundings. We know when it is most important to assert ourselves enthusiastically when social rewards are paramount.

We will also know when to retreat into solitude and contemplate serious abstract issues. Such an ability affords us tremendous adaptability as we move from personality to personality and throughout different circumstances.

The result is enhanced relationships, both in quality and optimal quantity.

In keeping with the notion of paying attention to your interactions and noticing your experiences, we are led to a deeper integration process. As we consider the degree of nuance we possess within and without our personality, deeper aspects of ourselves are revealed to us. These are extraordinarily significant.

These profound aspects indicate a more wholesome and complete Self, in the sense that we have become attuned to who we are and who we could be. This is an experience of tremendous meaning because it places us directly in the path to discovering a deepened sense of purpose—or developing a sense of purpose at all. That is because we are left to shift our perspective from a behavioral point of view to one that is rooted in the world of inner experience—symbolic imagery, intuitive insights, and contact with the unconscious.

How, then, do we tap into this? First, we must know what we are aiming for, and that is purpose, which is the thing we all long for—the thing that is left to discover once we have discovered everything else about ourselves. It is what we all desire to know, whether we are adolescents who have everything to figure out or are in our prime and are well established.

Pay attention to your interactions with people. Only this time, notice if they walk away better than when they came to you. Think about why that is. The nuances of consciously assessing whether or not people walk away better can feel unnatural and immoral, for we must make arbitrary judgments about the nature of people's existence when they walk away from us.

In other words, you have to determine for yourself if they are better off, be it now or later. We don't always get real-time feedback with these sorts of things, either. It would be nice if, in our interactions, the other person would say, "Thank you! I am immediately better off now that we have had a meaningful chat!" You can be certain that this will rarely be the case.

At best, you will have to wait and see if they walked away better than when they came to you, for it is usually the case that the meaning of an experience occurs to them after some time has passed. It takes time for meaning to grow roots. We have just begun this exploration into our purpose, and it is already difficult.

Once we have spent sufficient time with this, we may begin to detect patterns and themes with ourselves regarding what we say and do in those times when we make people better. We are remarkably efficient at developing behavioral patterns because of the constant positive and negative reinforcement we receive.

Part of the effectiveness of this process of discovering purpose lies in our ability to develop habits rather quickly, which proves to be useful when trying to identify the behaviors that occur in those interactions from which people walk away better.

Once we have a pretty good idea of what we say and do in those positive interactions, we then try to replicate them so that we may consistently experience those life-changing interactions with others. However, we might often find ourselves perplexed when we realize that the patterns we were certain of turn out to be hit or miss.

Perhaps, we noted that the interactions in which the person usually walked away better correlated with particular behaviors that were readily apparent to us. Hence, we confidently stuck with them to reproduce the same type of positive interactions we have been experiencing. Why, then, is the result so inconsistent when we replicate them, we might ask ourselves in frustration.

Rodion & Regina XXVI

This is very painstaking for Rodion, and it is easy for him to become discouraged—and even cynical—at this point. But he must press forward, or rather, he must dig deeper. To go to the depths necessary for deepening his sense of purpose, this frustrating turn of events provides a pivotal contrast that shows him the difference between what makes people walk away better and what does not. It is not what he says and does; rather, it is something intangible. It is akin to the distinction between being polite and being sincere. The two are not the same. Being polite may seem sincere, but it could very well come from a place of mere habit instilled in childhood.

By the same token, sincerity may not be polite—although it very well could be. Sincerity is less about the formalities of social interactions with others and more about the passion and intensity behind those interactions. It is the emotion and frame of mind, so to speak, that reflects the purpose deep within—and that is ultimately what helps Rodion make people better.

Once we realize that simply saying and doing the right thing is not what makes others better, we are forced into a more restrictive set of limitations. It is in these limitations that Rodion finds a more defined path to his purpose, for it is through a process of narrow rebirth that we come to see the truth that is a light unto our path.

This narrowing pulls Rodion to a place where he begins to understand what is underneath the surface in those times when people walk away better than when they came to him. He looks at his frame of mind, emotional state, and what feels right when those moments occur—he listens to his soul.

What moves us to give our gifts? Who are we when that happens? Is there a tug that pulls at our heart? Do we feel an indescribable meaning? As we strive to get in touch with those deeper aspects of ourselves, we begin to channel the unconscious aspects in our interactions with others more easily. We become more consistent, and the wake we leave behind creates the waves that help others feel alive.

Perhaps, Rodion notices for the first time that he, too, leaves a wake—an unfamiliar story to him. He sees this, and he feels a deepened sense of purpose. For many, we consciously sense purpose for the first time when we tap into this experience. Rodion is becoming an integrated man. He sees that what he says and how he says it matters, yet he knows he must operate from a place that seeks meaning in his interactions, and this is what it means to live in accordance with his purpose.

It is in transformational paradigm shifts such as this that Rodion finds himself resistant to moving beyond a cherished belief that has been a primary motivator for him. Some of his most cherished beliefs have often served as his will to live at times, or at the very least, inspired him to persevere through some of life's lowest moments.

This strongly held belief has an unintended dark side with potential generational consequences. It is one of the last places he wants to look for growth. This place is the cherished belief that people are his purpose—that Regina is his purpose. It is understandable that we would declare for ourselves that someone is our purpose. Those closest to us, spouses and children, truly inspire us to be our best, and we want to give these people a wonderful life. And there is virtue in that. In fact, it is awfully easy to settle on our wives and children as our purpose, as our reason to live. But there are also pitfalls in this orientation that have potentially devastating effects.

The problem is that there is a high cost for this, and Rodion is not the one who will pay that price—it is Regina! Making her his purpose places undue pressure on her to perform in a manner that is best suited for him, and that does not mean it is best for her. It essentially puts Regina's purpose in jeopardy, for she now lives so that Rodion can have a purpose. What happens if, God forbid, something terrible happens and he loses Regina? Does his purpose die with her? We find the virtue of nobility in this idea of placing our mate as our purpose, for it shows that we love deeply—so it seems.

Here is a thought, albeit a sad and unpleasant one: what would your wife or child say to you if you told them you would live without purpose if they died, that you would live a life with no meaning, and that you would probably die, too? You can be certain that they would not have a pleasant experience of processing the thought of you dying, or worse, living without meaning and purpose. It does not matter to Regina that she would also be dead; she would prefer that Rodion not only live but that he live with tremendous meaning and purpose in spite of the suffering caused by the loss—perhaps, even because of such loss. And she would be right. People are not our purpose, for they have their own to discover, and they will be hard-pressed to find it if they are too busy being yours.

Such a discovery suggests that relationships are a lot more serious than Rodion had imagined. This causes Rodion to stare down the barrel of a task that is exhausting just to think about. It is a disheartening realization to know people are not his purpose—as he has believed all this time—which means he has to dig much deeper than he imagined.

This realization brings him back to square one, so to speak. To find his purpose, he must let go of the idea that people are it, that he has to go discover it for real this time. With great dismay and heaviness, Rodion asks himself, "Where the hell do I find my purpose?" The answer is in his question: Hell—the place he least wants to look. Things are not as easy as he thought. He has to explore the limitlessness of his world for his purpose, and that is in and of itself a heavy burden.

There is so much to sort through. He will be tempted to declare that other aspects of his life can be his purpose, and he would be wrong. Rodion will be especially tempted to imitate others who seem to live purposely, who carry a meaningful burden—their cross.

Just as the imitation of Christ is so often misperceived, so too is our understanding of discovering purpose and finding the heaviest cross to bear. It is incredibly difficult. Imagine that you aim for the highest thing imaginable. Perhaps, something as high as the story of Christ, whose story holds the ultimate cross. So, we set out to find Christ so that we too may write a story that has us carrying that ultimate cross. Perhaps, if your aim is high enough, it could be the most meaningful thing you can do. Perhaps, if you are courageous enough, you will set out to find the heaviest cross you can carry, and you will bear it. Carl Jung deeply contemplated this idea of human nature and developed some profoundly insightful articulations on the matter. In his book, *Modern Man in Search of a Soul*, he stated,

---

"Are we to understand the "imitation of Christ" in the sense that we should copy his life and, if I may use the expression, ape his stigmata; or in the deeper sense that we are to live our own proper lives as truly as he lived his in all its implications? It is no easy matter to live a life that is modeled on Christ's, but it is unspeakably harder to live one's own life as truly as Christ lived his."[102]

Suppose we set out to find and bear the cross. Somewhere on our long and arduous journey, we encounter Jesus. We think to ourselves, "Finally! I found Him and His cross!" In great relief, we express to Christ that we are here to take up His cross so that we may also bear it and have meaning, too. However, Christ would recoil at this idea and say, "This is my cross! Go find your own!" This would undoubtedly come as a surprise to us—as well as a disappointment. Imagine coming all this way only to be denied the cross you seek. How disheartening this would be! Yet, we have come too far and are determined. We look at Jesus again, asking Him, "Well, Christ, since I cannot have your cross, tell me where I will find mine." Again, much to our surprise, Christ does not seem to be very helpful, for He replies, "I have no idea! You have to go find it. I found mine, and I had no one to tell me where it was. I had to fight battles to find my cross, and I am not giving up my cross."

Therefore, the journey truly begins. Yet, there is hope. The fact that we have been searching so diligently, with an unwavering spirit, makes our interactions more impactful. Although we may feel frustrated with our journey to discover purpose, this frustration is an indication that we care and find meaning in carefully and attentively broadening our interactions with others. And people notice that. Therefore, take solace in the thought of your journey as something people experience.

Perhaps, Paulo Coelho put it best in writing his book, *The Alchemist*: "No heart has ever suffered when it goes in search of its dreams, because every second of the search is a second's encounter with God and with eternity." Glory awaits, and as you experience the beauty of the feminine world of your partner, you will find that beauty has been there all along. It was your inner feminine—the anima—that you have been integrating. You will see that the dragon of chaos you have been slaying in your encounters with your partner was, in fact, within yourself.

Rodion & Regina XXVII

Rodion's heroic journey has brought him to a higher level of conscious awareness of the demands placed upon him by his conquest. His transformation thus far has given him a newfound perspective. Where he once came to Regina from a place of weakness, shame, and fear, he now enters her feminine presence from a place of strength, courage, and curiosity. Where he once dreaded the fire of the feminine dragon of chaos within Regina, he voluntarily and heroically enters this exploratory process necessary for developing his masculine.

Rodion has begun to embrace Regina's fire. This is to subject himself to the transformative character of the feminine, which leads him through "suffering and death, sacrifice and annihilation, to renewal, rebirth, and immortality," a transformation that is possible only when he enters wholly into the feminine principle.[103]

He voluntarily enters into battle within himself, yet he quickly realizes the battleground is much more complex and nuanced than anticipated. Although he knows the feminine challenges from Regina are opportunities to activate deeper, unconscious aspects of his masculine, he stumbles into the pitfalls of the vast expanse of the feminine world and the sudden limitations placed upon him.

The limitations experienced by Rodion bring him to an excruciating reality that indicates that every action is a fork in the road. Perhaps, one of the most undetectable forks in the road is the direction that the smallest, most trivial decisions take us. Each action either directs him down a path whose subsequent actions hold meaningful implications or a path whose subsequent actions are, at best, a means to an end or, worse, seen as trivial.

To see the meaningful implications is to make the connections between the smallest implementable actions and how they ultimately lead to the highest aim—gratitude > meaning > purpose. To see his actions only as "one more damn thing I have to do" leads Rodion down a path that only gets darker—triviality > cynicism > nihilism. Will he succumb to ignorance and inexperience? Or will he transcend his temptation to walk that dark path by practicing the virtues of love and courage?

Rodion is weighed down by the heavy burden of having to dig deep for his purpose and the responsibility of acting as consciously as possible with each and every action. Rodion is beginning to see how his quest is much more difficult than he ever imagined. The heights to which he must climb are dauntingly immense. As Rodion looks within to see the peak of the mountain before him, he is at once shaken and afraid, not because of the fear of failure, but of what it will cost him. And that is constant frustration with reaching the limits of his abilities, a lot of work and exhaustion, struggling to balance satisfaction with ambitiousness, great uncertainty, heartache from understanding the world, and from not understanding the world enough. Yet, he knows it is worth it and that if he shies away from his journey, he will not experience fulfillment whatsoever.

To live is to climb the proverbial mountain that is his life. That mountain is made of Rodion's interests, preferences, loves, dreams, meaning, and purpose. To climb is to exert effort in an attempt to reach an aim set above him. The steepness and difficulty of mountains are what challenge him. It is his duty to the world that gives rise to the responsibilities waiting to be assumed on his ascent.

He also has an abundance of incentives to remain comfortable at the base of the mountain. At the very least, he is incentivized to choose small mountains. The risk with this is that he makes comfort the aim. And that is dangerous. Glory is not found in comfort. Meaning cannot be found at the base of the mountain. Rodion must not ask where he can find comfort. Instead, he must ask where glory and meaning are found. If he is honest, he knows the answer. It is the ascent to the summit of his mountain.

This brings him to a question for which most do not want to know the answer— "What awaits us upon its peak?" This bold question is answered by his soul, simply saying, "Death!" If death awaits Rodion at the peak, then what might he attain by staying at the base? It is also death, but a meaningless death. Therefore, the peak is a glorious and meaningful death, signifying a life lived to the fullest based on all the implications of his life. Here's the key: he gets to choose the mountain he climbs. Choose a small mountain, and he dies in vain, either literally or spiritually. Choose the biggest mountain he can find, and he dies with purpose, and his literal death activates his immortal legacy. Rodion must choose boldly! He must be magnificent!

Chapter Twelve

Be Magnificent!

As today's man integrates himself and masters his personality, he is often brought into contact with the most painful depths of his Self. This contact is predicated by a violent and disruptive re-entry into the atmosphere of the world that holds his past. That atmosphere is symbolic of the resistance to the notion that there is good to be mined from his past. This section of his past is often seen as a black mass from which there is no return if he were to cross over into it. He is fortunate if he ever moves past it and finds another life to live. However, attempting to live another life absent of his past is to willfully subdue the healing necessary for transforming his suffering. If he is lucky, he can acknowledge his past and at least not loathe the recurrent memories of it.

However, not hating something and loving something are two different things. How then, he might wonder, with great cognitive dissonance, could he love something so awful and painful? What good could possibly come from such horrible darkness? Why subject himself to the reliving of such a terrible monster? Why would he want to glorify his past? The answer lies in giving meaning to the cross he bears.

To acknowledge our past and not loathe its memories is nothing short of miraculous. To claw our way out of the pits of Hell is quite transformative. Yet, emerging from Hell and ascending toward the glorious heights of heaven are not the same. Perhaps, the greatest burden we all carry is redeeming the sins of our past, to rescue ourselves from the underground of the past. We take our ability not to loathe our past, and we give hope to others so that they too may move on from hatefully recalling the past. It is possible that they too can begin to heal, such as you have. And perhaps it is openly healing in front of those people that gives them the much-needed permission to heal, too.

It is in this experience that we begin to find a little solace that maybe, just maybe, our painful past will not have existed in vain. Perhaps this is how we start to take back a piece of us that was stolen from us by tragedy and misfortune.

This is not the precipice on which the glorious transformation of suffering occurs. No, that place lies beyond the edge of rationalization and acceptance. To give meaning to our great suffering, we must step into the most frightening unknown truth about ourselves: that we must be grateful for all that has molded us into who we are.

Who we are inspires the world to remember, to forgive, to heal, to inspire others, too. This means we face the very things that hurt us. We visit the ruins of the past and rebuild a new life from within. We look around and see the lives saved by our story of openly healing. We become painfully grateful for the tragedy inflicted upon us by the life we love so dearly.

You carry every rejection and disappointment you've ever experienced. You undeniably possess a sense of frustration with all the insecurities and pain you've ever felt. You may be tired and even angry, but most of all, you want to be understood and to feel useful. Perhaps, you hate to admit that you carry bitterness and resentment. Hatred. Hatred toward some aspect of life and the universe when it fails to serve you.

You have dreams and goals, and the more you strive for some of them, the more impossible they seem, and the more you question your own capacity to reach them. It's discouraging and heavy, particularly when burdened with the responsibility of providing for others. The pressure you're under is often immense and suffocating.

Who will rescue you? You've most likely seen yet denied the real answer multiple times when it has been so blatantly presented right in front of you. Yet, the struggles that burden you are the same struggles that got you to the point where you even have a chance to succeed. Those ever-so-difficult challenges made it possible for you to aspire to the magnificence you strive for. It's hard and grueling. At times, you may be confused as to what you should do, and you're torn between swallowing your pride and looking for guidance or falling into a cycle of inefficient effort and a subpar lifestyle. The fault lies in believing those are your only options.

The other option, the only effective option, is rescuing yourself with efficient effort and high-quality actions. Yet, it is hard and grueling. At times, you may feel as if you are about to break. Perhaps, it is only at this point can you begin to accept that the answer, the rescuer, is you!

You are the only one who understands you the way you need to be understood. You are the only one who can reject your sense of self and disappoint you. You are the only one who can address your insecurities and tend to your own pain. You are the only one who can bring the energy you need. You are the only one who can absorb the bitterness and resentment you have projected onto others. You!

You are the only one who makes your dreams impossible. You are the only one who determines your capacity to endure your struggles and reach your goals. All the pressure you feel is up to you to shed as if it were light as a feather. There is no pain too great to bear. There is no boundary you can't establish and enforce. There is no challenge too hard. There is nothing you will ever be too tired to do. Your hard-won experience got you this far, but those times are behind you now. Gather yourself and take responsibility for everything in your life. There is no rational excuse to ever get angry at others. You are the only one who can anger yourself, which is by giving up and falling short of your potential. Your plan should entail being the most magnificent person you are meant to be.

Transcendence

Living magnificently is about living by your deepest purpose. Iain Mc-Gilchrist states, "The kind of attention we bring to bear on the world changes the nature of the world we attend to."[104] Whatever you choose to pay attention to, be intentional with letting it guide you to a sense of purpose. Who you are at your deepest purpose is what most profoundly impacts the world. It is what makes you your most magnificent self and what is best for the world around you.

This notion suggests that we be mindful of the world and our place in it. The more we understand our place in the world, the more in tune with our purpose we become. Becoming the best version of ourselves involves a process of discovering a sense of purpose. Discovery is an action. Therefore, it is only through change that we find purpose.

The process of change and growth is necessary to be our best, which means the harder it is, the better we can be. It is a constant overcoming of rawness and chaos with refinement and order, over and over again.

It seems like a complete and detailed road map of your future would make life better, but part of becoming our best is figuring out the hard way what makes us our best. Slow down, get centered, and be patient with yourself—and others—as you adjust to distressful changes.

These challenges are often excruciating. They push us to our limits as men. Our perseverance and tenacity are stretched beyond our current capacity, and it is in these times that we often fail to understand what more we can do. Our principles and values, combined with our limited realm of experience, leave us with the belief that we are as good as we will ever be. We are frozen. We find ourselves at the apex of our potential and cannot fathom a fear worse than this.

At the precipice, we will transcend. The tipping point is often frightening yet necessary. There, our nobility is exemplary in the sense that we choose courage and bravery over cowardliness and avoidance in the face of fear. The precipice is where we change and transform, yet it is not where the paradigms within us shift, preparing us for something greater; it is not where purpose is born.

Experiencing such tipping points is quite glamorous, for we can display our newfound confidence and exhibit our newly refined skills. Yet, this is not where strength is gained. It is not where raw skills are refined, nor where we are battle-tested.

No, that place is much darker and lonelier. That place is where our entire being approaches life's bottleneck, where we are squeezed so tightly that we must shed every trait and skill that is not absolutely necessary. This is the place where our entire existence hangs in the balance and any hope of a life well-lived hinges on our precise response to each and every obstacle in our path.

`This place does not warn us of its coming. On the contrary, its very purpose is to surprise us, to catch us off guard, unprepared, and minimally equipped for the grueling process of learning life's deepest lessons. Here, we are stretched beyond our limits and our capacity to endure is most tested. These times force us to consciously decide to give our all, for we need to know we can give our all and what we are made of.

How beautiful it is to endure! What splendor we experience when coming out the other side scraped, bruised, torn, scuffed, cracked, broken, healed, mended, polished, clearheaded, and tough as hell. We become untouchable for a moment. But it's only for a moment, for while we are soaking in the victory, life has already formulated its next deep, grueling lesson for us. But we are not ignorant of this. We know, and we crack a smile at it, thinking to ourselves, "Bring it!"

Give your Gifts and Teach

Being genuine and authentic with our stories can enhance our well-being. It also can inspire others to be courageous with their stories, which, in turn, can create enriched relationships. It is paramount that we immerse ourselves in the presence of those who mean the most to us. It is often in their presence that our deepest purpose is reflected back to us, providing an accurate view into what we most need to learn about ourselves.

Therefore, growth involves learning new information about yourself. In relationships, this learning extends out onto the other person. Just as they may have a hard time adjusting to our changes, discovering new aspects of the other person is disruptive to our homeostasis, and we struggle to adjust to this in a positive manner, too.

We are now presented with an opportunity to practice what we preach. We have learned to hold frame while our partner adjusts to our newly expressed desires and boundaries; now, we must extend that same grace to them. And this is not easy. We did a great deal of work to get here, yet, if it were not for all the grace that has been extended to us, we would not be here.

Grace is the time and energy one person invests in another person when there is little to no return on investment for the person extending the grace. It only benefits the recipient of the grace. It is love at its finest, for grace is often given despite the limitations of the recipient. People have invested in us even though they could not predict that it would impact us and that we would thrive as much as we have.

We owe it to those people to ensure the world understands this. We honor them by paying forward the grace they extended to us. To do this, we strive to be our most magnificent selves. We must not subscribe to the narratives of naysayers and shy away from giving our gift to the world because some say we are delusional. Not all will understand your gifts.

On the contrary, if you never appear delusional, either to yourself or to others, then you aren't risking enough or aiming high enough. We are unique individuals. We honor the time and gifts others have given freely to us by celebrating our individuality and uniqueness because it is those gifts that made us much of who we are. Life is hard.

A good life is very hard. It is hard because the quest to be our most magnificent self means we contend with the ambitions and virtues of others. It is the imposing of their most precious virtues onto you—which they declare as universally most important—that threatens your uniqueness. In other words, people lean on their favorite virtues as a crutch yet disguise it as striving for equality. The effectiveness of this disguise lies in the moral contempt they place you in. This inferior position in which they attempt to place you requires you to gain the approval of the masses to become sufficient. We do not need permission to be extraordinary.

Honoring Masculinity

The integrated man has faced a significant number of enormous and daunting challenges. He has overcome each one he encountered and, if not, he has a chance to do so as long as he is alive. Many of these challenges cut him deeply, resulting in painful recoveries. The scars from these injuries are profound and impressive. He must wear them proudly, for they are reminders of his hard-won wisdom and confidence. They are his allies, and they have a purpose. They are not only evidence of his mastery; they are a beacon of hope when he gets lost in his own dark, uncharted waters. Faith and courage are the message his scars express to him. Faith allows him to do the footwork even when he does not know the reason why. Courage allows him to be open to what he is charged to do.

Then, there's honor. Honor allows him to give purpose to his pain and suffering—and the invaluable worldly experiences that caused them. Sharing our hardest thoughts and feelings allows those around us to heal. That is purpose at its finest, and it is in carrying out that purpose that we heal.

He ascends to his greatest heights by embracing his suffering and transcending his capacity for nihilism. And that is miraculous! Therefore, our scars are reminders of the wounds suffering has inflicted upon us—they are also a symbolic representation of what we are capable of.

In the words of Viktor Frankl, "But there was no need to be ashamed of tears, for tears bore witness that a man had the greatest of courage, the courage to suffer."

So, we honor our suffering with courage. We honor the losses, too, for we did not get here alone. We had companions along the way. Their names are Sorrow and Suffering, and while their names often make others tremble in fear, you have befriended them. They taught you what darkness looks and feels like. You know how to react to it and transform it.

To honor your masculinity is to honor not only your light but also your darkness, for it shows you what destruction looks like. And that is of great utility. All of these things thrust you toward the forefront of your life, which "initiates the emergence of consciousness"[105] from the unconsciousness of the world around you.

Live Up to Your Masculine Virtues

Practice your principles and display your value daily. Show integrity, dignity, humor, courage, purpose, clarity, wisdom, warmth, excitement, self-control, strength, morale, endurance, knowledge, and other important virtues that symbolize your own masculine nature. The integrated man has creatively and conscientiously built his character and distinguished himself from other men.

Practicing masculine principles paves the way to an elevated version of yourself, which opens you up for a more harmonious connection with your partner. This allows you to thrive, not despite your partner's fiercest tests, but because you undeniably permeate her emotions with purpose and warmth. This is the active engagement in the process of the feminine bringing you closer to the Self.

Making your virtues evident through your behaviors, clarifying your path to your partner, and taking responsibility for having her on your path indicates a great sense of purpose in you. If your relationship strategies are implemented on the foundation of your masculine virtues, your partner will connect with you more naturally, and the process of integration becomes more effective. If you implement them on a foundation that lacks experience in displaying these virtues, you will be met with more resistance to these strategies.

Nonetheless, implement them anyway. Execute a plan, even if your plan is not the best. Behaving virtuously increases your value. In the beginning, you will be awkward in the implementation of these new strategies. Like all mastery, it will take time to learn all the nuances of each skill and how they produce a positive result. As you use these strategies over long periods of time, you will see how they are all connected.

Embracing Today's Woman

Life and its amazing complexities are beautiful. Perhaps, there is no beauty as complex as the feminine. As conscious beings, we have a tendency to live on the surface, and too much time here results in a too-limited understanding of our unconscious psychological aspects.

We fear what we don't understand, and our inner selves are concealed so as to not alarm others, especially those with whom we wish to develop relationships. So, we put on a mask in order not to be rejected by society. The masks we wear are an integral part of human interactions. The mask is our persona, what we display to others to get what we need from a particular relationship.

On some level, this is manipulation. This doesn't make us evil; it makes us human. To become frustrated with this notion when we experience it is an indication that we have reached the limits of our ability to navigate people's masks. We then become susceptible to morally judging others for not being transparent with their intentions. This is lazy of us and irresponsible.

As men, we become annoyed and frustrated with our partner's behavior when we fail to navigate relational conflict and stretch our capacity to manage the challenges and tension we experience with the feminine.

Embracing today's woman while honoring our masculinity is the key to our success in relationships. An assertive woman who fights to get what she needs is a sign of a healthy woman. By challenging you and desiring the best from you—even demanding it—she ensures you provide the optimal environment for creative achievement and freedom. In a way, she is just doing her job.

Our partners often say and ask things in ways that are open to multiple interpretations. This allows them to choose the interpretation that best suits them at any given moment, especially when they are cornered. It is a beautiful strategy, and we must not become perturbed by this, nor should we succumb to the fallacy of thinking that women are dishonest and liars.

We must embrace their modern femininity. Women have gone through great pains in their fight for survival in their own right. They possess hard-won experiences, and it is through those experiences that they have evolved. Like us, they must honor the work they have done as well as the gifts given to them by their predecessors. Women from all walks of life have a story, and how they respond to life defines their stories. If we dismiss their story, we refuse the very same gift we crave. Failing to embrace today's woman diminishes our masculine values and cuts us off from our masculine purpose.

Understand that this does not mean we water down our masculinity so that our partner can advance. This would be counterproductive to the very reason for embracing her femininity. Instead, we must reveal our masculinity in all its glory; it will free her to express her femininity in all its glory. Her reason for trusting you is to give you her glory as a gift. It is what you seek with her.

Such deep and profound wisdom is difficult to understand. If we happen to catch a glimpse into its meaning, we are often too intimidated to explore it. This is why it is important to utilize the four pillars to develop your own personal set of guiding principles.

This does not suggest that you do not already have intrinsic value and worth, nor does it mean that your experiences up to this point in your life are worthless. In truth, your experiences up to this point in your life are exactly what should inspire you and determine your path.

The problem of being intimidated by the deep and profound wisdom of the feminine lies in what our predecessors did not teach us. In other words, we were not taught about the glorious gifts of the feminine and how to connect with that. We missed out on a wealth of information that would have given us a road map for life. This left us with a severe lack of skills.

This is not an excuse. Nor is this about blaming those people for missing the mark with some things. This acknowledges that our predecessors are human, and if we are to be our best, we must stand in their humanity. We must honor their stories and do our part to illuminate the world with our own magnificent humanity. The message of this book is to do so responsibly and thoughtfully and to start in the most powerful and intimate connections.

By improving ourselves in the context of long-term relationships, we subject our character to the most intense trial-by-fire, which is the sacred place where our masculinity connects with the feminine nature of our partner.

The challenges today's man faces with his feminine partner are due to the feminine drive and desire to experience creative achievement. She wants to harness that creative, regenerative chaos, for there is beauty there—if it can be manifested. She needs a container in which she can actualize her creative potential.

The masculine brings about that container, for his purpose is to provide the orderly and appropriate set of limitations for her creative beauty to be experienced—both by her and the world. Her challenges are often to get you to provide that space. The feminine serves as a barometer that reflects changes within you, especially regarding whether you are moving toward your potential. This can be observed in your partner's actions in relation to you. If you are moving toward your potential, you will experience a certain kind of love and appreciation with her. If you are moving away from your potential, you will experience a certain kind of challenge and tension with her. Neither of these experiences is a bad thing; in fact, they are gifts. The challenges and tension you experience with her when you are moving away from your potential simply mean that she has high standards and expectations for you, which means she believes in you. Your partner should challenge you and do so with absolute zeal. The key to your success in your relationship is to respond to such challenges with your most magnificent self.

The key to her success in your relationship is to value herself enough to not settle for anything less than you giving her your most magnificent self.

Rodion represents the hero within each of us, waiting to be manifested. He represents anyone who has struggled in his relationship with his feminine partner. We are Rodion.

We are the product of youthful confidence beaten down by our own ambitions. We are the result of too much desire for order and an inability to bring chaos into consciousness. Rodion symbolizes a journey that we men have embarked on as we have stumbled into an awakening of our masculine spirit through great struggle. He symbolizes the poetic journey of redemption of today's man who transforms into an integrated version of himself. He signifies the salvation men find through exploring the Hell of his existence and letting it catapult him into the heavens of his purpose.

Rodion is the song of the hero.

When we recognize Rodion within us, we reflect in gratitude to the heroic struggle of finding meaning and purpose in this harsh and brutal world. To recognize the hero within is to acknowledge our willingness to differentiate everything and transcend all ideology as we expand our capacity to find beauty in the world through the pursuit of truth. You are Rodion, for your purpose calls for you to be the hero of your own story—to ask, "Who am I?" to slay your dragons, to transcend your limitations. The glorious answers and treasures are found in the places you fear most.

There is a Latin phrase, *in sterquiliniis invenitur*, that speaks to what many believe to be a universal truth. It means "in filth, it shall be found" or, in other words, the thing we need most is often found in the places we least want to look.

The willful rejection of this reality implicitly causes us to miss out on particular gifts found only in the strangest, most frightening places. This theme is found in allegorical stories throughout history in which the hero goes down into the dungeon to face the dragon—who has been wreaking havoc on the village—and slays it. The hero emerges with a reward—typically "the girl." This story, and its variations, contains allegories that represent the deeply abstract, unconscious experience of human beings since the dawn of time. The story's allegories are a representation of the unconscious experience men have with their journey into the chaotic feminine world of their partner.

Rodion has entered the dungeon of chaos and emerged victoriously. He has cut up the dragon and retrieved the ancient feminine from today's woman. He has become the hero, Regina's hero, his own hero. He sees the many layers of his feminine counterpart, and they are beautiful to him, for his frame is strong. Her distress is his conquest, for she is life in waiting. He awakens her with his masculine spirit. Rodion has transcended into a magnificent version of himself. He has brought to consciousness the unconscious feminine within Regina—order from chaos. Yet, as he brings order from the chaos of Regina's feminine nature, she sees in him a new potential, and her endless thirst for his excellence already hatches her next gauntlet for him. And another dragon is born.

ACKNOWLEDGMENTS

My deepest gratitude lies in the inspiration from my wife, Nikki, who remained unwavering in her support and belief that this was a worthy cause for me. And for giving me the grace to miss the mark and then to true my aim. You make me better.

To my good friend, Ronnie Swain, for being the encouraging friend and my often-needed enemy, but most of all, for being my most faithful companion in the sacred dialogues of our traditional Thursday night meetings. Withstanding your onslaught has made me close to you.

I undoubtedly must thank all the male clients who showed me why this book is essential. I thank you for being another good man in this world.

I would be remiss if I didn't pay special tribute to a particular female client of mine. Her insights into her feminine nature helped contour the rough edges of my direct and often brash delivery. I am indebted to you for bearing your soul in some of the finest and most significant conversations in my life.

To Dr. John Rowe, the man I pay to be my father. Thank you for helping me navigate my soul, both the light and darkness within.

To my daughter, Bella, for teaching me the art of thoughtful consideration with the feminine spirit, for she requires a tenderness that was unnatural for me until she came along. Her sweet and beautiful spirit showed me that how I father her will shape her understanding of men. Thus, I knew my job was to teach her what to expect from a good man. Such a responsibility can propel a man to become his most magnificent self. Thank you, baby. And I say unto you, my child, endure!

WORKS CITED

1   Piaget, J. (1967). *The Psychology of Intelligence.* Routledge & Paul.

2   Bendixen, M. (2014). Evidence of Systematic Bias in Sexual Over- and Underperception of Naturally Occurring Events: A direct Replication of Haselton (2003) in a more Gender-Equal Culture. *Evolutionary Psychology, 12*(5), 1004-1021.

3   Cyrus, K., Schwarz, S., & Hassebrauck, M. (2011). Systematic cognitive biases in courtship context: women's commitment—skepticism as a life-history strategy? *Evolution and Human Behavior*, 13-20.

4   Haselton, M.G., & Buss, D.M. (2000). Error Management Theory: A New Perspective on Biases in Cross-Sex Mind Reading. *Journal of Personality and Social Psychology, 78*(1), 81-91.

5   Henningsen, D.D., & Henningsen, M. L. (2010). Testing Error Management Theory: Exploring the Commitment Skepticism Bias and the Sexual Overperception Bias. *Human Communication Research, 36*(4), 618—634.

6   Koenig, B.L., Kirkpatrick, L.A., & Ketelaar, T. (2007). Misperception of sexual and romantic interests in opposite-sex friendships: Four hypotheses. *Personal Relationships, 14*, 411—429.

7   [3] Cyrus, K. et all (2011)

8   Maslow, A.H. (1943). A Theory of Human Motivation. *Psychological Review, 50*, 370-396.

9   Peterson, J. (1999). *Maps of Meaning.* Routledge.

10 Whittle, S., Yücel, M., Yap, M. B., & Allen, N. B. (2011). Sex differences in the neural correlates of emotion: Evidence from neuroimaging. *Biological Psychology, 87*, 319—333.

11 Engman, O., Linnman, C., Dijk, K.R., & Milad, M.R. (2016). Amygdala subnuclei resting-state functional connectivity sex and estrogen differences. *Psychoneuroendocrinology, 63*, 34—42.

12 Baron-Cohen, S. (2005). The Essential Difference: the Male and Female brain. *Phi Kappa Phi Forum, 85*(1), 23-26.

13 Hirsh, J.B., & Peterson, J.B. (2008). Extraversion, neuroticism, and the prisoner's dilemma. *Personality and Individual Differences, 16*(16).

14 Sinek, S. (2009). Start with Why: How Great Leaders Inspire Everyone to Take Action. Portfolio.

15 [9] Peterson, J. (1999)

16 Bradley, M.M., Codispoti, M., Sabatinelli, D., & Lang, P.J. (2001). Emotion and Motivation II: Sex Differences in Picture Processing. *Emotion, 1*(3), 300—319.

17 Dictionary, O.E. (2021). *curiosity*. Retrieved 2021, from Online Etymology Dictionary: https://www.etymonline.com/word/curiosity

18 Shirer, W.L. (2011). The Rise and Fall of the Third Reich: A History of Nazi Germany (50th Anniversary Edition). Simon & Schuster.

19 McCarten, A. (Writer), & Wright, J. (Director). (2017). *Darkest Hour* [Motion Picture].

20 [8] Maslow A. H. (1943)

21 Schmitt, D.P., Realo, A., Voracek, M., & Allik, J.". (2008). Why Can't a Man Be More Like a Woman? Sex Differences in Big Five Personality Traits Across 55 Cultures. *Journal of Personality and Social Psychology, 94*(1), 168—182.

22 Dolcos, F., Katsumi, Y., Moore, M., Berggren, N., Gelder, B.d., Derakshan, N., Dolcos, S. (2020). Neural correlates of emotion-attention interactions: From perception, learning, and memory to social cognition, individual differences, and training interventions. *Neuroscience and Biobehavioral Reviews, 108*, 559—601.

23 DeYoung, C.G., Quilty, L. C., & Peterson, J. B. (2007). Between Facets and Domains: 10 Aspects of the Big Five. *Journal of Personality and Social Psychology, 93*(5), 880—896.

24 [21] Schmitt, et al. (2008)

25 [22] Dolcos, F., et al. (2020)

26 Reis, H.T., & W. Andrew Collins, E.B. (2000). The Relationship Context of Human Behavior and Development. *Psychological Bulletin, 126*(6), 844-872.

27 [21] Schmitt, et al. (2008

28   DeYoung, C.G. (2014). Cybernetic Big Five Theory. *Journal of Research in Person-ality*, 33-58.

29   DeYoung, C.G., Quilty, L. C., & Peterson, J. B. (2007). Between Facets and Do-mains: 10 Aspects of the Big Five. *Journal of Personality and Social Psychology,* *93*(5), 880—896.

30   Deida, D. (1997). The Way of the Superior Man: A Spiritual Guide to Mastering the Challenges of Women, Work, and Sexual Desire. Plexus.

31   Funder, D., & Ozer, D. (1983). Behavior as a function of the situation. *Journal of* *Personality and Social Psychology, 44*(1), 107-112.

32   [9] Peterson, J. (1999)

33   Kahneman, D. (2013). *Thinking, Fast and Slow.* Farrar, Straus and Giroux.

34   Jung, C. (1959). Collected works. Vol. 9, Pt. II Aion: Researches into the Phenom-onology of the Self. Princeton University Press.

35   Qualls-Corbett, N. (1988). Sacred Prostitute: Eternal Aspect of the Feminine. Inner City Books.

36   [4] Haselton, M.G., et al. (2000)

37   Glover, R.A. (2003). No More Mr Nice Guy: A Proven Plan for Getting What You Want in Love, Sex, and Life. Running Press Adult.

38   Jung, C. (1973). Letter to Kendig B. Cully. In C. Jung, *C.G. Jung Letters* (Vol. 1). Routledge & Kegan Paul., LTD.

39   Jung, C. G. (1928). *Contributions to Analytical Psychology.* Kegan Paul, Trench, Trubner and Co., Ltd.

40   Smith, M.J. (1979). *When I Say No I Feel Guilty.* Bantam Books.

41   Peterson, J. B., Driver-Linnb, E., & DeYoung, C. G. (2002). Self-deception and im-paired categorization of anomaly. *Personality and Individual Differences, 33*, 327-340.

42   Vygotsky, L S. "Mind in Society: The Development of Higher Psychological Pro-cesses." Open Journal of Modern Linguistics 7.4 (1978).

43   Jung, C. (1955). *Modern Man In Search of a Soul.* Harcourt Brace.

44   Andreano, J.M., Dickerson, B.C., & Barrett, L.F. (2013). Sex differences in the persistence of the amygdala response to negative material. *Social Cognitive and* *Affective Neuroscience, 9*, 1388-1394.

45   [41] Peterson, J.B., et al. (2002)

46   [3] Cyrus, K., et al. (2011)

47   [5] Henningsen, D.D., et al. (2010)

48   [2] Bendixen, M. (2014)

49   [3] Cyrus, K., et al. (2011)

50   [4] Haselton, M. G., et al. (2000)

51   Alba, J.W., & Hasher, L. (1983). Is memory schematic? *Psychological Bulletin, 93*(2), 203-231.

52   [26] Reis, H. T., et al. (2000)

53   [30] Deida, D.

54   Geangu, E., Hauf, P., Bhardwaj, R., & Bentz, W. (2011). Infant pupil diameter changes in response to others' positive and negative emotions. *PLoS One, 6*(11).

55   Nichols, S.R., Svetlova, M., & Brownell, C.A. (2014). Toddlers' Responses to Infants' Negative Emotions. *Infancy*, 1-28.

56   Peterson, J. (2021). Beyond Order: 12 More Rules for Life. Penguin.

57   Stephen B. Karpman, M. (2014). A Game Free Life. The definitive book on the Drama Triangle and Compassion Triangle by the originator and author. The new transactional analysis of intimacy, openness, and happiness. Drama Triangle Publications.

58   [11] Engman, O., et al., (2016)

59   Hamann, S. (2005). Sex Differences in the Responses of the Human Amygdala. *The Neuroscientist, 11*(4), 288-93.

60   [1] Piaget, J. (1967)

61   [34] Jung, C. (1959)

62   Peterson, J. (1999). Maps of Meaning. Routledge

63   [35] Qualls-Corbett, N., (1988)

64   [35] Qualls-Corbett, N., (1988)

65   [22] Dolcos, F., et al., (2020)

66   [26] Reis, H.T., et al., (2000)

67   [22] Dolcos, F., et al., (2020)

68 [55] Nichols, S. R., et al., (2014)

69 Phelps, E.A., & LeDoux, J.E. (2005). Contributions of the Amygdala to Review Emotion Processing: From Animal Models to Human Behavior. *Neuron, 48*, 175—187.

70 [22] Dolcos, F., et al., (2020)

71 Hirsh, J.B., Mar, R.A., & Peterson, J.B. (2013). Personal narratives as the highest level of cognitive integration. *Behavioral and Brain Sciences, 36*(3), 36-37.

72 [41] Peterson, J.B., et al. (2002)

73 Nietzsche, F.W. (1990). Beyond Good and Evil: Prelude to a Philosophy of the Future. New York: Penguin Books.

74 Rogers, C. (1961). On Becoming a Person: A Therapist's View of Psychotherapy. Houghton Mifflin Harcourt.

75 Peterson, J. (1999). Maps of Meaning. Routledge

76 Hyde, D., & Raffman, D. (2018). *Sorites Paradox.* Retrieved from Stanford Encyclopedia of Philosophy: https://plato.stanford.edu/cgi-bin/encyclopedia/archinfo.cgi?entry=sorites-paradox

77 Frankl, V. (1946). *Man's Search for Meaning.* Beacon Press.

78 Hirsh, J.B., & Peterson, J. B. (2009). Personality and language use in self-narratives. *Journal of Research in Personality, 43*, 524—527.

79 [9] Peterson, J. (1999)

80 Bateson, G. (1972). Steps to an Ecology of Mind: Collected Essays in Anthropology, Psychiatry, Evolution, and Epistemology. Jason Aronson Inc.

81 [9] Peterson, J. (1999)

82 Petersen, W. (Director). (1983). *The Neverending Story* [Motion Picture].

83 Deida, D. (1997). The Way of the Superior Man: A Spiritual Guide to Mastering the Challenges of Women, Work, and Sexual Desire. Plexus

84 Salter, M. (2019, February 27). The Problem With a Fight Against Toxic Masculinity.

85 [9] Peterson, J. (1999)

86 [22] Dolcos, F., et al., (2020)

87   Kret, M., & Gelder, B.D. (2012). A review on sex differences in processing emotional signals. *Neuropsychologia, 50,* 1211—1221.

88   [10] Whittle, S., et al. (2011)

89   Maxwell, J.C. (2007). The 21 Irrefutable Laws of Leadership: Follow Them and People Will Follow You. New York: HarperCollins Leadership.

90   Nissen, E. (2023). *Thought Restructuring Sheet.* Retrieved from ednissen.com: https://ednissen.com/thought-restructuring-sheet

91   Jung, C. (1963). *Memories, Dreams, Reflections.* Collins and Routledge & Kegan Paul.

92   Nietzsche, F. (2012). *Thus Spoke Zarathustra.* New York: Sterling & Ross.

93   French, A. (2017). *Father Gregory Boyle, author of new book, to Pasadena audience: Consider radical kinship and compassion.* Retrieved from Los Angeles Times: https://www.latimes.com/books/la-et-jc-gregory-boyle-20171213-story.html

94   Botton, A.d. (2017). *The Course of Love.* Simon & Schuster.

95   Jung, C. (2009). *The Red Book.* W. W. Norton & Company.

96   [35] Qualls-Corbett, N., (1988)

97   [28] DeYoung, C.G., (2014)

98   DeYoung, C. G., Grazioplene, R. G., & Peterson, J. B. (2012). From madness to genius: The Openness/Intellect trait domain as a paradoxical simplex. *Journal of Research in Personality, 63—78,* 63—78.

99   [56] Peterson, J., (2021

100 [28] DeYoung, C.G., (2014)

101 [28] DeYoung, C.G., (2014)

102 [43] Jung, C., (1955)

103 Neumann, Erich and Ralph Manheim. The Great Mother: An Analysis of the Archetype. Princeton University Press, 1983. Neumann 2015

104 [35] Qualls-Corbett, N., (1988)

105 McGilchrist, I. (2019). The Master and His Emissary: The Divided Brain and the Making of the Western world. New expanded edition. New Haven, Yale University Press.

106 [35] Qualls-Corbett, N., (1988)

BIOGRAPHY

Ed Nissen is a psychotherapist, coach, and founder of the Institute of Purpose. He is dedicated to helping individuals discover and deepen their purpose. His work draws from influential historical thinkers like Carl Jung, Fyodor Dostoyevsky, Friedrich Nietzsche, and Viktor Frankl, as well as contemporary minds including Jordan Peterson, David Buss, Colin DeYoung, Jonathan Haidt, and Iain McGilchrist. His work primarily encompasses the frameworks of Jungian, personality, evolutionary, existential, and moral psychology, along with the themes of redemption so often found in mythology and religion. His work spans relationship dynamics, male psychological development in the context of relationships, coaching, and aiding people to become their own heroes, and is anchored in his commitment to truth. His roles as a husband and father are what he loves most about life, deriving profound meaning from these roles. Above all else, he hopes to inspire others so that they, too, can experience transcendence.